# THE OTHER ISLAM

ALSO BY STEPHEN SCHWARTZ

*Spanish Marxism vs. Soviet Communism:*
*A History of the P.O.U.M.* (with Victor Alba)

*From West to East: California and the Making of the American Mind*

*Kosovo: Background to a War*

*The Two Faces of Islam*

*Sarajevo Rose*

# THE
# OTHER ISLAM

. . .

*Sufism and the Road to Global Harmony*

STEPHEN SCHWARTZ

DOUBLEDAY

New York   London   Toronto   Sydney   Auckland

DD

**DOUBLEDAY**

Published in the United States by Doubleday, an imprint of The Doubleday
Publishing Group, a division of Random House, Inc., New York.
www.doubleday.com

DOUBLEDAY is a registered trademark and the DD colophon
is a trademark of Random House, Inc.

Permission to reproduce extract of Massignon, Louis, *Hallaj: Mystic and Martyr*,
© 1990 by Princeton University Press, granted by Princeton U.P., 2007.

Permission to reproduce translations of Rumi granted by Nevit O. Ergun, 2007.

Book design by Ellen Cipriano

Library of Congress Cataloging-in-Publication Data
Schwartz, Stephen, 1948–
The other Islam : Sufism and the road to global
harmony / Stephen Schwartz. — 1st ed.
p. cm.
Includes bibliographical references and index.
1. Sufism—History. 2. Religious pluralism—Islam. I. Title.
BP188.5.S34 2008
297.409—dc22
2008007673

ISBN 978-0-385-51819-2

PRINTED IN THE UNITED STATES OF AMERICA

1 3 5 7 9 10 8 6 4 2

First Edition

To all those of all faiths
Who have given over their lives, sometimes unto death,
For the liberation of Muslims from oppression,
And above all
To the families of the martyrs
Luan Haradinaj of the Bektashi Sufis,
Shaykh Myhedin Shehu of the Halveti-Karabashi Sufis,
And Shaykh Zejnelabedin Dervishdana
of the Sa'adi-Jibawi Sufis.
*Fatiha.*

*Im Mohrenland gefangen war*
*Ein mädel hübsch und fein;*
*Sah rot und weiss, war schwarz von Haar,*
*Seufzt' Tag und Nacht und weinte gar,*
*Wollt' gern erlöstet sein.*

*Da kam aus fremden Land daher*
*Ein junger Rittersmann;*
*Den jammerte das Mädchen dehr,*
*Juch! rief er, wag' ich Kopf und Ehr,*
*Wenn ich sie retten kann.*

In Morocco's land a captive lay
A maiden fair and fine.
With blushing skin, and night-black hair,
She sighed all day and night in hope
A rescuer she would find.

There came then from a foreign land
A young and noble knight;
He saw the tears shed in her plight.
"Yes," he pledged, "My honor and head
I'll risk, to her unbind."

—*The Abduction from the Seraglio*;
Music by Mozart,
libretto by Christoph Friedrich Bretzner,
adapted by Gottlieb Stephanie the Younger,
translated by S.A.S.

# CONTENTS

# THE OTHER ISLAM

# INTRODUCTION

## Sufism—Islamic Spirituality in a World of Fear

O N MAY 27, 2007, a huge bomb struck the mosque and shrine of Shaykh Abdul Qadri Jilani in central Baghdad, killing at least twenty-four people and injuring many more. The Jilani shrine is a prominent landmark in the Iraqi capital, and the explosion damaged its dome and minaret.

Shaykh Jilani, who lived from around 1077 to 1166 C.E.,[1] has been described as a "patron saint" of Baghdad, and the celebration of his birthday, a custom known as *mawlid* in Islam, is a favorite festival in the city. His *mawlid* had taken place a month before the May 2007 blast.

Because Shaykh Jilani was a Sunni Muslim, some Westerners immediately assumed that the attack on his shrine was committed by Iraqi Shia Muslims. But they were wrong. The perpetrators of the Jilani bombing were also Sunnis. The difference was that Shaykh Jilani was known as a Sunni Sufi, and the bombers were Wahhabis (alias "Salafis"), probably from Saudi Arabia, who militantly claim the Sunni banner.

If the fighting between Muslims in Iraq pitted Sunnis against Shias, most Americans would ask, why would Sunnis bomb a Sunni shrine? Was this some bizarre provocation aimed at blaming Shias for the crime and rousing the anger of Sunnis? Every Muslim in the world knows the answer to that question: Sunnis attacked Sunnis in the Jilani shrine bombing because Wahhabis, representing the most extreme, violent, exclusionary, rigid, and fundamentalist interpretation in the history of Sunni Islam—fueled by Saudi petrodollars—despise Sufis and their shrines. Wahhabis also hate and kill other non-Wahhabi Sunnis, as well as Shias, Christians, Jews, Hindus, Buddhists, and anybody else with whom they disagree, including each other.

The rise of Al-Qaida and of Islamist terrorism in general originates more in Wahhabism and the divisions it has created within the community of Muslim believers than in a conflict with the West. And the field of deadly Wahhabi action against Sufis and other dissenting Muslims is not limited to Iraq. Less than five months after the Jilani shrine bomb, a blast at the shrine of another of the most famous Sufis, Moinuddin Chishti, in Ajmer, India, killed two people and injured twenty. The crime occurred during evening prayers when the shrine was crowded with hundreds of worshippers.

The conflict between Sufis, both Sunni and Shia, and Islamist fundamentalists or clericalists is widening around the world—in terror attacks striking Iraq as well as in reform efforts in Saudi Arabia, amid intrigues among American Muslims at the same time as Sunni fundamentalists and Sufis confront one another in the Balkans, and in the banning of Sufi books in Malaysia.

In November 2007, foreign press agencies reported on another and equally dramatic aspect of Sufism. In western Iran, many people were injured and more than a hundred were jailed when government security personnel stormed a meeting place for a Sufi group well known in the country, the Gonabadi-Nimatullahi order. An enraged mob of Shia

Muslims attacked the Gonabadis in the town of Borujerd, following accusations that the mystics had desecrated a Shia mosque. Fighting left wounded on both sides, and in a piquant illustration of the ways in which Sufi spiritualists adapt to modernity, twenty-five motorcycles belonging to them were reported destroyed.

The Iranian clerical regime is in crisis, and Sufis are increasingly prominent as representatives of a new political and social alternative to the failed scheme of Ayatollah Ruhollah Khomeini (the story of the Gonabadi Sufis will be told in chapter 5). Similarly, Sufis are in the forefront of demands for political and social reform in Saudi Arabia, where the anti-Sufi Wahhabis comprise the official form of Islam. For many years the outstanding opponent of fundamentalism in Saudi Arabia was a beloved Sufi, Sayyid Muhammad Alawi Al-Maliki (1947–2004). When his funeral was held in Mecca, private jets choked Saudi airports for days.

In the Wahhabi mind, to praise a Sufi saint such as Shaykh Jilani, to observe his birthday, and to honor his shrine, is to deviate from strict monotheism, concentrated on God, and thus to treat a personality such as Jilani or Moinuddin Chishti as a "partner" or "equal" of God. According to the same bizarre logic, Wahhabis condemn *mawlid* birthday events for the Prophet Muhammad himself. The fundamentalists deride such customs as a mimicking of Christianity, claiming that extolling the Prophet's birthday is an unacceptable innovation (*bida*) in religion and that Muslims must not stray from the original expression of their faith. That was the Wahhabi posture from the beginning: that acclaiming the Prophet's birthday, Sufism itself (since it is not mentioned specifically in the *Qur'an*), and honoring Muslim and other saints are all novelties in Islam, to be strictly avoided.

But as Sayyid Al-Maliki and other opponents of Wahhabism have written, in texts appearing since Ottoman times, if Muslims reject all innovations after the era of the Prophet, they must abandon the written *Qur'an* (since Islamic scripture was delivered to Muhammad orally, and at first memorized), the production of books of knowledge, the erection of minarets at mosques, the construction of schools and hospitals, and numerous other modern customs, including use of sophisticated weaponry in war. Even the most extreme Wahhabis cannot claim to live by such a set of prescriptions, although they may impose them on others. Wahhabi fanatics will not watch television and the Saudi kingdom has no movie theaters, since both are recent inventions.

THE FAITH OF ISLAM continues to challenge Americans and other Westerners with many questions, which for most non-Muslims have remained unanswered. Is Islam a religion comparable to Christianity or Judaism, a political movement, or a violent conspiracy? Does it aim to conquer the world? Does it urge its adherents to commit atrocious acts of terror?

And then, what are Muslims? What do they believe about Islam? And how do they look at their Christian, Jewish, and other non-Muslim neighbors—if not on the same street in an American suburb, then at least on the same continent, as in Europe, and on a single planet? The West has many academic experts on the Middle East—the core Muslim area—and many Muslim and Arab advocates. But few have provided answers to the basic concerns of non-Muslims. The same inquiries have gone without adequate reply, or fallen into the void of forgetfulness, occasionally resurfacing and usually failing to stir new explanations.

Academic experts on the Middle East and comparative religion speak in their own vocabulary, based on the particular rules of the disciplines they have embraced. Middle East historians are initiated into the convoluted internal politics of Muslim states over the past 1,400 years, as incomprehensible to the ordinary American as the parallel rivalries and conflicts of medieval Christian rulers or the infighting seen today in other remote Third World countries. Government officials and commentators on present-day events discuss relations between Israelis and Arabs, but few Westerners grasp the peculiar involvement of the Israeli-Arab confrontation with varying forms of Islam. Arabs publicly restate their grievance with Israel, but many Arab protagonists in the West are Christian, although they are interviewed in Western media as experts on Islam, about which they may know little.

Outside university and political circles, hate-mongering self-anointed "experts" on Islam have proliferated, but they are heedless of Islamic, Western, or other history and interested only in selling their shoddy wares by sowing panic. They seek to reinforce suspicion in the Western public that the only trustworthy Muslim is one who has left the religion of Islam or otherwise expressed loathing toward it.

After the atrocities of September 11, 2001, followed by American military action, few Americans comprehended the essence of the situation. Many believed that the Iraq intervention was about fighting terrorism; others thought that, as in the Gulf war of 1991, it was mainly about oil. But then details emerged that had been absent from previous American involvement with the Muslim world. It turned out that Iraq had several differing kinds of Muslims: mostly Arab Shia Muslims, but also Arab and Kurdish Sunni Muslims. Aside from the Kurds, who had been protected by the West in the past and were secure friends of America, both Shias and Arab Sunnis appeared to harbor a homicidal rage against the American presence in the country.

Words such as "Sunni" and "Shia" were novel to most Americans, and almost none of the Westerners who tossed them around in the media had a clear picture of what made them different from one another or why suddenly the Iraq war had turned into what appeared to be a blood feud between them. Even many who knew that neighboring Iran is overwhelmingly Shia could not explain what *that* really meant for the Iraqi Shia majority—more than 60 percent of the population of Mesopotamia. Some assumed that Iran, with a Persian, non-Arab culture, sought to take over the Arab East. Most Westerners already distrusted Iran as a clerical dictatorship and rogue state.

Other new terms appeared in the Western vocabulary, also without sufficient explanation. From Saudi Arabia, the home of Al-Qaida, came a sudden awareness of Wahhabism. But certain Western experts, journalists, and government representatives were quickly convinced that Wahhabism and its followers, known as Wahhabis, did not really exist—rather, that the Saudi-based form of radical Islam should be called "Salafism." Once again, none of the Western public figures who talked about "Salafism" showed any knowledge of the origin of the term, its original meaning, or its use by the Saudi Wahhabis (who really are Wahhabis, not "Salafis," as will be explained further on).

On the edge of this quicksand of misapprehension, disinformation, foreign influence, ignorance, and arrogance there occasionally sprouted, like tiny but fragrant flowers, references to something called Sufism. While Sunni and Shia Islam alike were portrayed by some Westerners as dangerous to the West, and even as Satanic inventions, Sufism was typically mentioned with grudging respect, as a peaceful, spiritual way of Islam based on a journey toward God. But here, too, established expertise and common wisdom weighed heavier than the fragile petals of the Sufi blossom. If knowledge of the Middle East and of comparative religions was locked in a prison of academic attitudes, Sufism seemed to be the property of New Age "shoppers for God." Sufism also had its own vocabulary, one even more incomprehensible (and genuinely esoteric in the metaphysical sense) than those applied elsewhere when discussing the Middle East and its religious distinctions.

Worse, among experts at the U.S. State Department and in academic Middle East Studies, Sufism was often dismissed as "folk Islam," echoing a denigration of it voiced by bigots in the Sunni clerical establishment who have long hated Sufism. The "folk" or "backward" label is paradoxical, for in some regions of the Muslim world Sufis are more often than not extremely cultivated in their reading and worldview. In countries such as Egypt, where a fundamentalist style of Sunni Islam has become ascendant, Sufis may be derided as credulous bumpkins, but in others, such as India, they tend to be viewed as an elite.

Americans do know something about Sufism. But their picture of Sufism appears irretrievably stuck in centuries long past. As with Islam in general, most Americans have felt left out of a conversation they heard faintly and did not understand, a dialogue carried out on the other side of a wall, in which only an occasional word, phrase, or explosion—sometimes killing the listener—could be discerned.

THE FOUNDATION OF ISLAM is rejection of the worship of multiple gods and of idols. Islam, like Judaism, recognizes only one divine being, a sole God alone worthy of worship. But for Wahhabis, to emphasize, praise of Sufi saints such as Shaykh Jilani or Moinuddin Chishti leads Muslims back to polytheism. This negative view of the Sufis was despised through most of the history of Islam but was reinvented by an obscure preacher named Muhammad Ibn Abd Al-Wahhab (1703–1792), who was born in the wilds of east-central Arabia. It is he for whom the Wahhabi movement is named. Though Sufis had previously been opposed, and sometimes killed, by narrow-minded Muslim fundamentalists, unrestrained war against this metaphysical form of Islam did not begin until the emergence of Wahhabism, only 250 years ago.

Shaykh Jilani is known to the Sufis as "the sultan of saints." After Sufi mysticism became institutionalized in Islam, its students were grouped in orders or *tariqas,* which are similar to Christian monastic institutions and to the Jewish schools of traditional Kabbalah and sacred communities of Chasidim. The most famous and distinguished group of Sufis has been the Qadiri order. Traditionally, the Qadiris were said to have been founded by Shaykh Jilani, although more accurately put the order was created in emulation of him rather than by him. The life of Shaykh Jilani exemplifies many of the themes found throughout the literature and study of Sufism. He was born in Persia and migrated to Baghdad, which was then the greatest of the Islamic cities, as a young man. He began by studying *Shariah,* or Islamic law, in its fundamentalist form. But he was drawn to esoteric wisdom, and, rather than becoming an Islamic jurist, he abandoned Baghdad to wander in the Iraqi desert for a quarter-century.

When Shaykh Jilani returned to Baghdad, he began his life as a public preacher. He attracted many students from all over the Muslim world. It has been said of him that "he was born in love, grew in perfection, and met his Lord in the perfection of love." Those words epitomize Sufism: love of God, study of spiritual mysteries, and recognition of God's love.

Such a vocabulary will be familiar to some American readers, who have read, in translation, the poetry of Mevlana Jalal-al-din Rumi. If Americans know anything of Sufism, it involves Rumi and Rumi's devotion to love. As Ezra Pound said, literature is news that stays news; and Rumi has remained news for eight centuries. Rumi's insights attract New Age and other readers seeking verse for meditation, to aid in gaining calm and serenity, thus making his Sufism news you can use. A Google search in mid-2007 turned up four million references to him, and the Amazon bookselling site offered nearly eight thousand items associated with him; even restaurants in North America are named after him.

But "Rumi" was not his name. Rather, it was something like a nickname, indicating that while he was born in today's Afghanistan, he had gone to live in "Rum," or "Rome," the Muslim place name for the lands of Anatolia and the Balkans that, not long before Rumi went there, had belonged to the Byzantine Christians. (Through most of classical Islamic history, the original Rome, in Italy, was considered a minor town compared with Constantinople, Venice, and other cities.) "Rumi" could therefore mean "the Anatolian," but that would be a purely geographical reference. In a larger sense, "Rumi" means a man living in a place still filled with Christian influence, although recently conquered by Muslims, and, finally, an individual turned toward Europe. "Rumi" could even be "the European" or "the Greek"—not by birth, but by temperament. It may not be chance that Rumi and his "love of love" are so attractive to Westerners; he represents a generation of Sufis drawn to Western culture. His title "Mevlana" means "the teacher," and among Muslims that is usually enough to refer to him.

The tomb of Rumi in Konya, the former Iconium, in Turkey, is one of the most famous sites in the Muslim world, as well as the object of innumerable pilgrimages. His greatest work, the *Mesnevi*, is a universe of rhymed metaphysical knowledge. An evocation of its breadth—limitless "even if all the forests were pens and all the seas of ink"—echoes the *Qur'an* as well as Jewish sacred writings, reworked in Sephardic Jewish song lyrics, where one finds the lines, "the sea I'll use as ink, the trees I'll take as my pen, to write down my sorrows." This is but one of many examples in which Islam and Sufism seem to have paralleled the idioms of the other religions.

The followers of Rumi have their own *tariqa* or order, the Mawlawis, named after Mevlana. They are known in the West as the "whirling dervishes"—men in long robes and tall hats who turn continuously on one foot. A dervish is a Sufi who has committed to a life of poverty and denial of the present world, often living on the grounds of a Sufi shrine or related structure. The "whirling" of Rumi and his followers is one of many forms of Sufi meditation known as "remembrance of God" or *dhikrullah*, usually referred to among Sufis only as *dhikr*, pronounced "*zikr*." In their "whirling" the Mawlawis memorialize Rumi for his devotion to that specific practice.

Other Sufi orders have their own distinctive ways of *dhikr*. Some branches of the Rifa'i Sufis, who originated in Iraq, perform a *dhikr* that includes piercing the body (or appearing to do so) with large needles, spikes, or other metal tools, cutting their flesh with blades, swallowing burning coals, and handling poisonous snakes—all without leaving wounds or scars—and as ecstatic affirmations of faith. A company of "whirling dervishes" now travels the world, sponsored by the Turkish government, but in a folkloric rather than a religious or spiritual program. Rifa'is, with their unique and often shocking practices, have also performed in cultural events before the Western public. The Qadiris, Mawlawis, and Rifa'is are among the most influential Sufis in the Muslim world, with branches spread from the Balkans to Indonesia and from the Mediterranean to the southern tip of Africa.

*Dhikr*, the remembrance of God, may involve prayer, chanting, silent meditation, singing, dancing, and other physical exercises, including forms of martial arts, and is supplemented by reading, memorization, seclusion, and lectures and sermons by teachers. Some Sufis share collective meals, and nearly all provide charitable services, usually food and shelter, to the poor. Sufis in Islamic societies are always Muslims by religion, though Western Sufi followers may remain non-Muslim.

At a distance from the Sufi-hating Wahhabis, who in the form of Al-Qaida have evoked horror and repulsion from the great majority of the world's Muslims, some fundamentalist Sunnis accept Sufism if it is strictly compliant with rigid *Shariah*, and aims only at cleansing selfishness and other bad traits from the individual character. Yet the legitimacy of Sufism in its most otherworldly forms is long established in Hanafi *Shariah*, the dominant school of Sunni jurisprudence from the Balkans to eastern Turkestan and down into Pakistan and India. At the same time, some who claim to be Sufi devotees and to reject Islamic fundamentalism demand that Sufism remain "sober" and avoid "intoxication" with either love for God or love bestowed by God.

Both the "Sufi-tolerant" fundamentalists and the *"Shariah*-compliant" or "sober" Sufis appear to keep Islamic metaphysics locked in a framework that excludes the universalist and other aspects of Sufism that make it a potential medium for interreligious conciliation and even global harmony today. Nevertheless, Sufis have long reached out to other faith communities, and Sufism persists as an "Islam of the heart." By contrast with Sunni ambivalence toward it, Shia Muslims have seldom rejected Sufism.

Most but not all Sufis follow teachers, whose positions may be inherited, a practice that is controversial. These mentors are known as shaykhs, *babas*, *pirs*, and mullahs (the latter, meaning "protector," had no pejorative meaning before the Khomeini Revolution in Iran). But many Sufis resist the notion that religious authority should be based on titles and offices, either clerical or spiritual. Rather, the best Sufi teachers gain acceptance and support by their perception and capacity for transmission of enlightenment to their students.

The mode of life pursued by Sufis is varied. Some retire into seclusion, living on the grounds of *tekkes*[2] or lodges, also known as *dergahs* and *ẓawiyas,* where resident dervishes meet weekly, twice weekly, or daily with Sufi disciples. Others, after they give up their worldly possessions, wander as pilgrims. Yet most Sufis in the Muslim world maintain ordinary working lives.

In Muslim countries, little of the inner, mystical doctrine of Sufism may be offered to the broad public; in the West, where Sufism has its New Age milieu of aspirants, much more is propagated through books, magazines, videos, lectures, and other media. Western Sufis tend to be more sophisticated than the ordinary "shopper for God." While Madonna follows a "celebrity Kabbalah" figure and Mel Gibson is so fervent a mystical Catholic that he has gone out of his way to offend Jews, the 2007 Nobel laureate in literature, the novelist Doris Lessing, became a Sufi. Although she is better known as a former Communist and mentor of feminism, Lessing's interest in Sufism made the honor to her seem especially appropriate in the year marking the eight hundredth anniversary of Rumi's birth. Her character is shy of the public, complicated, and sympathetic: she shared in the Secret of Secrets as I have sought to present it in this book.

Sufism has attracted devotees and admirers among Westerners of both Jewish and Christian origin, as well as Zoroastrians, Hindus, and Buddhists in the East. It has produced an extensive, diverse, and distinguished literature. But because of Islamist terrorism, Sufism has also become an appropriate, if underestimated, topic for Western policy analysts. Its teaching is peaceful—peaceful but not always pacifist, to paraphrase the West's preeminent scholar of Islamic history, Bernard Lewis. Still, Sufism offers the clearest Muslim option for reconciliation between the Judeo-Christian and Islamic worlds, as well as fulfillment of the promise that Islam shall be, as is so often repeated, a religion of peace.

When presumed Wahhabis bombed the Jilani shrine in Baghdad, Westerners might have perceived that the intra-Muslim struggle in Iraq involved more than rivalries among Sunnis and Shias. In reality, the Muslim-vs.-Muslim fighting in Iraq was both simpler and more complex than Americans realized. It was more elementary in that the driving force of the "Sunni insurgency" was something better labeled Wahhabi terrorism. It was more complicated because the Wahhabis fighting against Sufis and Shias in Iraq were, in their largest number, interlopers from Saudi Arabia, across Iraq's southern border, summoned to a counterintervention against the Western presence in Iraq. But it took the Western media four years, from 2003 to 2007, to begin to report adequately on Saudi involvement in this grim situation. That was because the Wahhabi-dominated Saudi kingdom was valued as an ally of the United States, although the status of most of its state clerics was that of an enemy of the United States, if not the world.

Wahhabis claim their eyes are watching God alone, through strict observance and totalitarian control by clerics, but the Sufis have their own way of getting closer to God. The Sufi aim at purification of the self, or *tasawwuf,* was anticipated in the *Qur'an* and the *hadith,* or oral sayings of the Prophet Muhammad, and developed in Islamic metaphysics—called *marifah* in Arabic. Through this refinement of the personality, the individual is prepared to approach the Creator. Shia Islam tends to emphasize a more intuitive form of knowledge, *irfan,* which one may achieve independently of Sufi activity, through philosophy. *Irfan* is based on a hidden, theosophical side of Islam rather than external practice.

The basic truth of Sufism, developed and reaffirmed over the centuries, is that God and all of creation are one—"unity of being," or *wahdat ul-wujud.* The *Qur'an,* which Muslims consider a discourse by God, is cited by Sufis to illustrate the divine nature of this principle. Among the best-known verses in the Islamic sacred text we find the following: *"To God belongs the east and the west. Whichever way you turn there is the face of God. He is omnipresent and all-knowing."*[3] Sufis point to one of the most famous of the Prophet's *hadith,* which says of God: *"I was a hidden treasure, and I desired to be known, and I created the World that I might be known."* Muhammad described this as an answer by God to a question by the Jewish ruler and poet David, who asked why the world was brought into existence.

MODERATE ISLAM, OR ISLAMIC pluralism, of which Sufism is the most significant example, is not a new idea dreamed up in the West and offered as a cure for Muslim rage. Islam has always encompassed a diversity of religious interpretations. If at one end of the Sunni continuum we find the fanatical creed of Wahhabism, brutal and arbitrary, more an Arab-supremacist state ideology than a religious phenomenon, at the other we find the enlightened habits of Sufism. These stress dialogue between Muslims, separation of spiritual from clerical authority, and teaching in the daily languages of the believers (first Persian rather than Arabic, then Turkish and the Balkan languages; Urdu, which is the main language of Muslims in the Indian subcontinent, and Bengali; Saharan and West African languages; then Malay). But Sufism further embodies respect for all believers, whether Muslim or not.

Sufis seek mutual civility, interaction, and cooperation between every human being. While Sufis trace the origin of their beliefs to the *Qur'an* and the *hadith,* Sufism in history reflects the encounter of Islam with the metaphysical wisdom found in other religions. The growth of

Sufism accompanied Islam's expansion across the globe; Sufism did not emerge from Islam alone. During the great age of Muslim conquests, over a thousand years beginning in the seventh century, Sufis drank from the mysticism of those the Muslims sometimes succeeded, and sometimes failed, in subduing. They received as much from the Christians, whom they could not, in their majority, overcome, as from the Zoroastrians, whom they overwhelmed.

Sufis provided great service to Muslim rulers as agents of goodwill between Islam in power and the religions of the ruled, and have been reproached for this tranquilizing role. Sufi teachings do not conflict with those of the other believers: extreme humility in the presence of divine love, dedication to spiritual harmony in contemplation of the divine, and understanding of other and earlier devotional habits. But Sufism was much greater as a means for Islam to assimilate spiritual doctrines new to the expanding religious community that had emerged on an isolated strip of productive soil along the eastern shore of the Red Sea.

The revelation delivered to Muhammad in the little-known town of Mecca was carried to many of the great cities of the known world, and Muslims had no choice but to account for the religious culture of those they met along the way, from the Prophet's early battles in Arabia, to Spain in the west, China and Indonesia in the east, and black Africa to the south. Contrary to the claims of Islam-haters, the great Muslim armies did not force the peoples they conquered to accept the faith of Muhammad or be killed; rather, Muslim rulers preferred to levy a tax on non-Muslims and then investigate what could be learned from them. Classical Islam prized such knowledge; another famous *hadith* of Muhammad says, *"For wisdom, go all the way to China."*

In a decadent Egypt, as well as in Syria and other Eastern Christian lands, the Muslims found the record of Greek philosophy and science, which Western Christians had rejected as pagan poison—the works of Aristotle and Plato, to name only the most important examples, had become lost to Europe. From Persia, the Muslims received illumination preserved through many changing epochs of political and social governance. Some Persian metaphysics was drawn from the indigenous religions of the Iranian empires, Zoroastrianism and its offshoot, Manichaeism. This last was a faith that viewed light and darkness as equal opposites in power; Manichaeism once dominated central Asia and even penetrated China. But the Sufis also learned spiritual lessons from Hinduism and Buddhism, the shamans of the steppes, and the great teachers of China.

Sufism has passed through three phases in its organizational evolution. The Sufism of individual saints reached its height in the thirteenth century, when the most prolific and permanently influential Sufis flourished, and knew one another, on the Muslim borderlands with the Christian world. The first and most brilliant of these was Ibn Arabi, known as *Muhyid'din* or the reviver of religion, considered by many as supreme among the Muslim metaphysicians and as *shaykh ul-akbar*, the greatest Sufi master. His work has stimulated classic commentaries in every Muslim culture. Ibn Arabi was born, the son of a government clerk, in the southern Spanish town of Murcia, capital of a rich Muslim agricultural territory then on the frontier of the Christian campaign of reconquest. The second was Rumi, whom we have briefly discussed. The third was Hajji Bektash.

The spiritual purification of *tasawwuf* then became systematized in the great Sufi orders, marking off a second, separate epoch. Ibn Arabi has no *tariqa* or order associated with him—his followers are individuals, though they may call themselves Akbarian Sufis in honor of his high standing. But Rumi's followers gathered in the Mawlawi order, and those of Hajji Bektash eventually formed another of the great *tariqas*, the Bektashis. A third stage in the history of Sufism is that of its spread through Muslim societies where rather than being organized in orders, a broad Sufi mentality saturated the Islam of the ordinary believers. Today, although individual Sufi saints are alive and recognized, they are mainly members of orders; the solitary saint has become rare, and the second (organized) and third (generalized) phases dominate Sufi life.

In the countries where organized Sufism is prevalent, Islamic metaphysics is imparted by formal instruction. These include the Arab lands, but also places as disparate as French West Africa, Kosovo, and Malaysia, all known for their elaborate networks of Sufi orders. Elsewhere, from Bosnia-Herzegovina through Turkey and central Asia to the Indian subcontinent and Indonesia, we see a broad "Sufi Islam," penetrating the religious consciousness of the Muslim majority, with the diffusion of the Sufi sensibility at all levels of society. A Pakistani diplomat, Husain Haqqani, has estimated that half of the world's Muslims may be Sufis in this wider sense. But everywhere in the Muslim world—even in Wahhabi-dominated Saudi Arabia—Sufism may be found.

At the same time, three great cultural rather than structural periods are visible in the history of Sufism, and each may be identified with one of the three outstanding Muslim saints of the thirteenth century. The first, and still the most influential in the global Islamic community, is Arabic—both Sunni and Shia—and was refined and brought to its most exalted heights in Muslim Spain. It may be symbolized by Ibn Arabi. The Spanish Arab Muslims produced the first truly European style of Islam, deeply affected by trade and other relations with their Christian neighbors and subjects, and with the Jewish communities that prospered among them. Arab Sunni Sufism is also marked by the cultural heritage of the Abbasid caliphate in Baghdad, ending in the thirteenth century, and by modern developments. Later influences on the Arab Sufis include defense of Islamic lands (notably Algeria) against Western imperialism, as well as the current drama of social transformation in Saudi Arabia.

The second major variant is the Persian Sufism of Rumi and numerous others, and according to many observers, it exceeded Arab Sufism in its intellectual achievements. The Sufism of Ibn Arabi is more difficult to study and comprehend than that of the direct and concise Rumi. These issues may be debated, but one thing is certain: Sufism is central to contemporary Iranian culture. Shia Sufism, which has both Iranian and Arab forms, is distinguished by devotion to classical Greek philosophy as well as to Eastern wisdom. The third major form of Sufism, little known in the West but most successfully merged with the Islam of the ordinary believers, is Turkish and Balkan, and its outstanding representative is Hajji Bektash.

Balkan Islam became the second paradigm for an authentically European Islam, after the Spanish Arabic period. The Balkan and Turkic Sufis represent, with the modern Iranian Sufis, the most vigorous forms today, although lacking the wider influence of Arab and classical Persian Sufism. Balkan Sufism is the only indigenous form of Islamic mysticism in Europe, and it is the most accessible form of genuine Sufism for non-Muslims in the West to encounter.

Regarding less prominent Sufi legacies, which are also vital and active, Moroccan and French-speaking West African Sufism has transmuted the Spanish Islam of the past and merged it with local spirituality, even while opposing paganism in black Africa. Sufism in the Indian subcontinent fused with elements of Hinduism, and it is often repeated that Islam came to the subcontinent through the teaching of Sufis, not by the sword. But the same may be said of Islam and Sufism among the Turkish peoples, who were never conquered, and in Indonesia and the other Southeast Asian Muslim lands. In Southeast Asia, Islam had new encounters with Hinduism, Buddhism, and the Chinese traditions, as well as with local animism and other forms of spirituality.

THE CLASSICAL ISLAMIC HISTORIAN Ibn Khaldun (d. 1406) foresaw that the original Arab embodiment of Islam would become urbanized and rich, losing its initiative, and that "new Islams" would succeed it. His comprehension of the rise and fall of cultures explains the diversity of Islam as it proceeded through the eastern and southern world; one great Islamic society followed another. Saudi fundamentalists want to Arabize all Muslims, uniting them in a single, closely controlled *umma*, or religious community, that would adopt the Arabic language in daily speech, Arabic styles of dress, and Arabic customs. But the majority of the world's Muslims are not Arabs, and although accepting Islam, they have generally held tight to their own idioms and identities.

It may be argued that there is not only one Islam but seven Islamic identities:

- MIDEAST ARAB SUNNI ISLAM, from Syria through the Arabian Peninsula and from Egypt to western Iraq, has developed in societies where Islam has long been the dominant faith, religious life is dominated by clerics and "official" theologians, and the Sufis have come under the most sustained assault. All of Sunni Islam is traditionally conformist in its view of rulers, be they just or unjust, but Mideast Arab Sunnis are by far the most passive and least interested in investigating their past. Sufis in this region tend to be the most *Shariah*-centered.
- SHIA ISLAM differs from Sunnism in its rejection of political conformity and support for radical protest, as well as in its

dedication to Muslim theological debate and the study of philosophy. The Sunni-Shia split is embodied in the drama that took place at Karbala in Iraq in 680, when those who would become Sunnis had submitted to tyrannical rule by a dynasty, the Umayyads, that claimed succession to Muhammad but had no family relation with him. The grandson of Muhammad, Imam Husayn, rebelled in the name of justice and was killed by the Umayyads. Shia Islam is paradoxical in supporting the individual power of a cleric such as Ayatollah Khomeini while still encouraging internal diversity of opinion. Unknown to Westerners, Khomeini gained support in Iran because he was independent of the established clerics instead of serving as their representative.

- NORTH AFRICAN (THAT IS, MAGHREBI, OR MOROCCAN, ALGERIAN, LIBYAN, AND TUNISIAN) AND FRENCH-SPEAKING WEST AFRICAN SUNNI ISLAM. Islam in northwest Africa draws on the wealth and power of the Moroccan rulers, who saw themselves as continuing the glories of Islamic Spain and also as nearly independent from the core Arabs. West Africa is home to a highly developed and widespread Sufi order, the Tijanis. This region has also proven important in recent times as a source of new Sufi orders and interpretations, such as Idrisi Sufism, which challenged the Wahhabis. Northwest African Sufis have produced some of the most beautiful Sufi music, which stimulates a deep feeling of religiosity in its hearers.

- BALKAN AND TURKIC ISLAM, both Sunni and Shia, extending as far as China, cannot be separated from the background of Turkish culture. The Turks were free, steppe peoples—as wide-hearted as the blue sky, which they worshipped as their god before the coming of Islam. Their sultans conquered Constantinople, rescued the Spanish and Portuguese Jews from the Inquisition, and fostered trade with Venice and other Christian cities and states. Turkey and the Balkans have sheltered the most unorthodox forms of Islam: the Alevi community in Turkey and Kurdistan, which fuses Sufism, Shia Islam, and ancient Turkish culture, and the Bektashi Sufis of Albania, Kosovo, and neighboring areas. The Alevis and Bektashis both emphasize female equality with men, secular government, and popular education. They are an important force for progress in Islam, although generally are overlooked by "experts" and are genocidally hated by Islamist ideologues.

- INDO-PAKISTANI-BANGLADESHI ISLAM, also both Sunni and Shia, developed in an ancient, traditional, and metaphysical environment, and long existed in harmony with Hinduism and other local faiths. But like everything else in the region, which is overcrowded and volatile, subcontinental Islam is contradictory. Its saints and orders are often seen as colossal in the subcontinent but are little known in the wider Islamic world. Subcontinental Sunnism produced the Taliban regime in Afghanistan, which governed according to Saudi-Wahhabi principles but claimed an affinity with some aspects of Sufism. The future of subcontinental Islam is unpredictable.

- SOUTHEAST ASIAN ISLAM, almost entirely Sunni but with Shia influences, is the form that aside from Balkan and Turkish Islam shows the greatest respect for other faiths, obviously because of the extraordinary cultural diversity of the region. It has produced Sufi-based mass movements such as Nahdatul Ulama in Indonesia, with 40 million members, which operates schools, hospitals, and similar institutions for the benefit of the whole society. The inspiration for Nahdatul Ulama is Islamic but not "Islamist," that is, religious but not ideological or political. Given that Indonesia, with 235 million people, is the largest Muslim country in the world, and that Malaysia is rich enough from its energy resources to have become one of the "Asian tigers," Southeast Asian Islam could represent the dominant Islam of the future—once the Saudi-Wahhabi influence in global Sunnism is broken.

• Finally, we see a developing EURO-AMERICAN ISLAM, based in converts or "new Muslims" and immigrant communities that have yet to become rooted in their new homes. Both groups are vulnerable to the money and manipulation of the Wahhabis and other seekers of hegemony over Muslims. Although there are many self-styled and unarguably sincere Sufis in Europe and North America, they play almost no role in Muslim public interactions with Western society, which are dominated by Saudi-financed and Wahhabi-directed organizations, which I have called "the Wahhabi lobby." Given the hostility of the Western public to Islam after 9/11, it is impossible to say how a substantial Islamic religious presence will survive in the Euro-American area, and with it, an authentic Islamic Sufism.

Each of these regional Islamic identities has generated a different style in Sufism. Though the leading Sufi orders have branches all over the Muslim world, the life of an Albanian Sufi in Kosovo striving for a European Islam, of a Moroccan Sufi performing music inspired by heaven in the High Atlas Mountains, and of an Indonesian Sufi administering social services may be very different.

Sufi spirituality remains a vibrant, public reality in the world of Islam. Sufi doctrines are comparable to—because they are a source for—Catholic mysticism and traditional Jewish Kabbalah. Yet while traditional Kabbalah suffuses Jewish observance today so that religious Jews participate in its continuity, it is seldom visible to the non-Jewish intellect. Christian metaphysics, except among certain small Catholic and Orthodox communities, has fallen into neglect.

More important, Sufism has always been deeply and beneficially marked by its contacts with Christianity. This view of the historical relations between Islam and the West based on dialogue rather than a permanent jihadist or crusading spirit may appear counterintuitive after 9/11, but it is not original to me and is not novel. I have been mainly influenced by the works of four predecessors: the Spanish Catholic scholar Miguel Asín Palacios (1871–1944), the English traveler and writer Frederick William Hasluck (1878–1920), the French Orientalist Louis Massignon (1883–1962), and a Palestinian Kabbalist, Rabbi Ariel Bension (1880–1932).

All four scholars represent a time when Western intellectual attitudes toward the Muslim world were founded on curiosity rather than anxiety. Aside from that of Massignon, a target of the Arab-chauvinist literary critic Edward Said, who invented the "sin" of "Orientalism" to attack such investigators, these names remain little known, and their writings constitute a secret history of the interreligious linkage of Europe and Asia in the past thousand years. Most of Asín Palacios's work, although it made a great impression in his lifetime, has never been translated from Spanish. Hasluck was long forgotten, and his work is today printed only in Turkey (in English). My discovery of Rabbi Bension was entirely unpredictable, even though his work is acknowledged by the great Jewish historian of Kabbalah, Gershom Scholem—and reading Bension changed my life. A descendant of Jews who had lived in Catalonia and Morocco, Bension was born in Jerusalem and was the first Sephardic Jew from the Holy Land to study at the European universities. He also served as a rabbi in the Balkan town of Manastir, a spiritual center where Muslim Sufis and Jewish Kabbalists studied together, and his knowledge of Islamic and Christian, as well as Jewish, mysticism was authoritative. Like Hasluck, he died young.

ASÍN PALACIOS IDENTIFIED SUFISM as "Christianized Islam" and was an outstanding interpreter of how the Muslim-Christian relationship in Spain was manifested in the life and writings of Ibn Arabi. For Asín Palacios, as well as Hasluck and Massignon, the main notable aspect of Sufism is its reconciliation of Islam and Christianity through the identification of Jesus, named *Isa* in Islam, as a messenger of divine love. Muslims have always honored Jesus as a prophet. But in a reflection of a common Christian attitude, Asín Palacios argued that Sufism brought together Christianity and Islam, the great global rivals, by introducing the benevolence of Jesus into a vision of Muhammad and his life in which the Spanish Catholic writer perceived militant and aggressive elements. Reinforcing Jesus in Islamic thought, according to Asín Palacios, diluted the harshness of Muhammad.

From an Islamic perspective, however, the Sufi adoption of Jesus as the herald of love reconciled Islam and Christianity in an entirely different way. An Islamic Sufi approach to the two main monotheistic religions had nothing to do with differences in the lives of the prophets, since the Jewish prophets, who are equally honored in Islam, were also often military men and severe judges. Rather, Islam cannot accept the proposal that Jesus was the son of God, or that God had any offspring or other "partners." But Jesus as the emissary of divine love was an acceptable Muslim interpretation; and so praise of Jesus was a prominent element of classical Islam. Love for Jesus and honor to Christian saints remained significant in Islam until the rise of Wahhabism, which execrates any and all parallels between Jesus and Muhammad as a Muslim imitation of the Christians and an alleged lapse from monotheism.

Their hatred for comparisons between Jesus and Muhammad encouraged the Wahhabis to ban *mawlid,* or birthday celebrations for Muhammad. In a *fatwa*[4] defending observance of the Prophet's *mawlid,* the anti-Wahhabi Sufi Sayyid Al-Maliki wrote, "It is permissible to celebrate the birth of the Prophet and it is permissible to congregate to listen to the sacred biography of the Prophet and to seek the blessings of God for him, to listen to the poems praising him and to hold feasts—all of which will bring happiness and contentment in the hearts of fellow Muslims . . . Those who achieve nothing for their religion from such celebrations are indeed losers." Sayyid Al-Maliki pointed out that Muhammad celebrated his own birthday.

Westerners can hardly understand how liberating this preaching of Sayyid Al-Maliki was and is in the stifling environment of Saudi Wahhabism. To Christians and Jews, devoted to Jesus and to Moses before him, it is perverse to imagine that Muslims could be forbidden from praising and expressing love for Muhammad, their prophet. But such is the "reforming" radicalism of the Wahhabis and their fundamentalist companions and fellow travelers among the world's Sunnis that in the Saudi kingdom the Prophet's *mawlid* was only permitted in the last decade, and then exclusively behind the walls of private homes. Sayyid Al-Maliki also referred positively to a traditional link between Muslims honoring Muhammad and Christian devotion to Jesus, pointing out that in narratives of the Night Journey of Muhammad to the heavens it is said that when the Prophet of Islam, accompanied by the archangels Michael and Gabriel (Jibril), passed over the town of Bethlehem, he prostrated twice in prayer.

If Sufism may be interpreted as "Christianized Islam," what may be said about Western, or New Age Sufism? One must believe, as a Sufi, that a merciful and compassionate God hears all prayers sincerely addressed to the divine presence. But the Sufi rose gardens in the shadows of minarets, where the sound of the Islamic call to prayer is heard, draping a human voice across a town like a gossamer, almost invisible garment, are very distant from "shopping for God" or "hitchhiker" Sufism. The latter is found in writings by Westerners seeking to make Sufism an exotic self-help program. Sufism is not for sale, spiritually or politically, just as moderate Islam and Islamic pluralism are not Western export commodities. If Rumi is the best-selling poet in America today, in most English-language editions of his writings, Islam and metaphysics have been extracted like internal organs from his verse, and it falls to the idiom of the gift card.

Could Sufism nourish a wider hope and help all individuals and nations find peace in a world of fear? Could Westerners gain personal serenity through Sufism while remaining non-Muslim, or is a call to Islam implicit in genuine Sufism? The Western reader, or seeker, may find spiritual tranquility and psychological stability amid global chaos through Sufism. One way—the best way—is to study with a community of Muslim Sufis, although that should inevitably imply acceptance of Islam. Another way is to embrace some basic Sufi practices, such as concentration on God and the reading of inspired texts, to calm the self when faced with the menace of modern life. Many believing Jews and Catholics without knowing it partake in Sufi principles and may benefit from a higher awareness of Sufism while remaining faithful to their own religions.

A Jew or Christian who desires to attain the peace of the Sufis without entering into Islam will probably not gain much by attempting a Sufism lite, which is comparable to celebrity Kabbalah, any more than one would a tourist pilgrimage through Catholic cathedrals. Still, for discerning Jewish and Christian seekers, to know something of the wisdom of Sufism may lead to greater conviction in the religious tradition of one's birth. It is no paradox that the methods of Islamic spirituality can strengthen the belief of non-Muslims as well as Muslims, as shown by Sufi aspects of Kabbalah and Catholic spirituality. Yet spiritual balance still requires belief, prayer, commitment, work, and attachment to metaphysics. Sufi Islam may be more animated, in the present world, than traditional Kabbalah or Franciscan commitment, but its tasks and responsibilities are no less profound, and, often, are even more difficult, especially with the faith of Muhammad facing increasing distrust in the West, the Far East, and Africa.

A present-day central Asian Sufi, Saparbai Kushkarov, has written, *"Being a Sufi means to be in the world, but not of the world."* But there are exceptions—and they could, if encouraged, occupy a major place in the daily affairs of a world fearful of terror by fundamentalist Muslims. As 2004 came to a close, in a central Asian residence, Shaykh Muhammad Sadiq Muhammad Yusuf, then fifty-two years old and former chief Muslim cleric for the region, commented in a manner seldom heard from Islamic community leaders in the West. He began by declaring that Muslims worldwide need to study and take responsibility for the problem of Islamist extremism. He also spoke appreciatively of visiting Washington, D.C.

He then remarked on how U.S. leaders should formulate a global strategy: *"Sufism, our Muslim spiritual tradition, enjoys support from the American authorities."* This belief, which seems naive at best, is easy to understand, given that certain influential Westerners have advocated such an approach. Bernard Lewis was asked in the same year, 2004, how America might improve relations with Muslims, and he suggested the country's leaders converse with a Sufi. In a study prepared during the first administration of George W. Bush, the Defense Department official Stephen Lambert, a U.S. Air Force officer, recommended that one of seven major strategic goals for Western success in the Muslim world consist of backing Sufis as an alternative to radical Islam. A more public expression of the same opinion came in 2007 when the RAND Corporation issued a major report, *Building Moderate Muslim Networks,* emphasizing outreach to Sufis as a potential Western policy.

As America wrestles with its unexpected leadership in fighting Islamist ideology, Sufism could prove important as a source of Muslim allies against extremism. But while Westerners concerned to understand Islam—including, presumably, many political and other figures with high responsibilities and authority—should most definitely acquaint themselves with Sufism, we cannot imagine Sufism as a mere tool of Western functionaries. To be true to the hearts of its initiates, Sufism must remain independent of political dictation; its insistence on spiritual autonomy makes it a model for pluralist Islam, not simply its "peaceful" counterposition to the violence of the radicals. In the Ottoman Empire and elsewhere, attempts to foster "state Sufism" failed or were discredited by their inveiglement with power. Further, it would be a mistake to portray Sufis or their supporters as perfected beings or as impeccable Muslim friends of the West. There are many charlatans among Sufi teachers; corrupt *pir-sahibs* are common, for example, among South Asian Muslims in Britain. To emphasize the argument of Bernard Lewis, Sufis are peaceful but not pacifist, and there are jihadist Sufis. In this book, I have most often tried to let the Sufis speak for themselves rather than filtering their voices through secondary, even scholarly, sources. While guided and inspired, as noted, by Asín Palacios, Hasluck, Massignon, and Bension, I have not restated their opinions; I have followed my own path and reached my own conclusions. If there is a fault in this work, it is that I have been incomplete and have passed over some eminent Sufi personalities.

As the confrontation between fundamentalist and spiritual Muslims broadens, how will Westerners and Sufis help each other win their common battle against Islamist radicalism? Westerners should first abandon dismissive insults about "folk Islam" and end the monopoly on high-level access to Western authorities that has been granted to the established Islamic clerical class and its supporters. Westerners should put behind them the belief that Sunni or Shia clericalism are the only mainstream forms of Islam and that any relations with the community of Muhammad can only be handled through such intermediaries. The task of the Westerner genuinely eager to help the Sufis on the road to global harmony is to observe and comprehend the internal conflict in Islam. A more advanced strategy would give support to the genuinely enlightening, progressive, and even libertarian[5] Sufi elements advancing in contemporary Islam, without attempting to buy off or manipulate them.

Western diplomats in Muslim countries should visit and consult with Sufis (such as Shaykh Muhammad Sadiq Muhammad Yusuf in his quiet house near Tashkent), and such foreign officials, along with human rights monitors, should offer protection to the Sufis against radical assault as well as against authoritarian governments. This is no less true in the Balkans than in Iraq. But any relationship between foreign or local governments and Sufis must be based on respect rather than recruitment, with a goal of helping, not hiring, the mystics.

In the "crisis states" of Islam—Saudi Arabia, Iran, Iraq, and even Israel through its internal Arab community—Sufism is a factor in the evolution of civil society that must not be compromised for short-term political advantages. The threat of Islamist extremism, however, may be resolved peacefully through change in the Saudi kingdom and Iran, two countries where Sufis are significant factors in opposition to tyranny and clerical rule. This book will detail how Sufism functions in each of these societies—beyond such leading examples as the bombing of the Jilani shrine in Baghdad or the teaching of Sayyid Al-Maliki in Saudi Arabia. Sufism is, finally, an indispensable element in any real solution to conflict between Islam and the West.

ALONG WITH FEAR of radical Islam, the political influence of Christian fundamentalists in the United States has spurred a contingent of new, militant atheists to assail all religion as an antihuman psychosis. Aggressive irreligion has suddenly been revived, to immense popularity in the West, by God-haters who distinguish themselves first by their refusal to take religion seriously. Atheist inquisitors such as Richard Dawkins, a scientific professional, and the journalistic entertainer Christopher Hitchens have challenged religious believers with the oldest and least original demand: that matters of faith should be judged according to practical, scientific criteria. But if scientific knowledge, as they would argue, owes nothing to the rules of faith, the same may be said of religion—there is no justification for matters of the spirit to be subject to the rules of science. Mutual noninterference between scientific knowledge and spiritual insight has long been a principle among monotheists—first Jewish and Muslim, then Christian.

Love between human beings, aside from parental relations with children, is not subordinated to scientific rules. Nobody can demonstrate his or her love for another by conducting an experimental test, and nobody can adequately explain why people fall in love by compelling them to answer neutral inquiries. There is no "clinical psychology of love." Nor is the love of human beings for nature subject to such a proof. The idiom of human love is poetic and irrational, neither technological nor logical. Poems are not written according to mathematical axioms, although mathematics and physics may owe a great deal to poetry and, whether Dawkins and Hitchens like it or not, to religion. The *effect* of nature on a human being—the *sight* of lightning, the *impact* of thunder, the *appearance* of a rainbow, the *experience* of an earthquake, the *grandeur* of high mountains, rivers in their natural course, the ocean, the *beauty* of human individuals or of trees in spring—cannot be fully or in some cases even minimally explained by science, even if each phenomenon, from lightning to the growth of an apple, may be analyzed and classified according to rational categories.

Why, then, would love between human beings and God be submitted to similar judgment? If I believe beyond reason in the beauty of another human being, based on inexpressible sensations and inexplicable events, why should I not also believe in the perfect character of divine creation? If I see the universe in the eye of my human loved one, why should I not also see the presence of God, my ultimate bestower of love and receiver of my love, in the universe? Atheists preach that religion is a fetter upon the mind and a prison cell for thought, but in so doing they ignore the religious imagination and the undeniable contributions of religion to human culture. Dawkins, Hitchens, and others compose their propagandistic rants in an English idiom born in the pages of the King James Version of the Bible. Hitchens, one of the most strident of the religion-haters, frequently compares himself with George Orwell, whose work was profoundly influenced by British religiosity.

The school of Dawkins and Hitchens, emerging from Judeo-

Christian society, cannot seriously grasp the ecstatic transcendence of the Jewish *Zohar*, the classic of traditional Kabbalah; or the affirmation of faith by the Judeo-Arabic philosopher Maimonides; the eloquence of the Catholic writers from Saint Bernard of Clairvaux to Gerard Manley Hopkins; or the mystical inspiration of William Blake. Who can call himself or herself a "bright" English reader and claim to ignore Blake's "New Jerusalem"? It is a poem of equal greatness for a Jewish, Christian, Muslim, or pantheistic believer; an Iranian colleague of mine calls Blake "one of the greatest Sufis." What can the God-haters say about the sublime seventeenth-century English poet Thomas Traherne, who wrote, "The world is a mirror of Infinite Beauty, yet no man sees it. It is a Temple of Majesty, yet no man regards it. It is a region of Light and Peace, did not men disquiet it. It is the Paradise of God. It is more to man since he is fallen than it was before. It is the place of Angels and the Gate of Heaven." And what have the atheist commandos to say of classical Hindu, Buddhist, and Chinese religious wisdom? Nothing worthy of notice.

The "leap of faith" required of believers is liberating, not oppressive. We will journey, in this narrative, on the Sufi roads—through the works of the great Sufis, but also along the byways of this world. While the Sufi *path* to God is open only to those who choose discipline and introspection, the *roads* of Sufism, from the Balkans to the great cities of central Asia, from Jerusalem to Singapore, and in hundreds of thousands of communities in between, may be traveled by anyone, except where those routes are enclosed by oppressive regimes. There will always be Sufism in the history of Islam and of Western metaphysics, but more significantly there will always be a way to God. In following the Sufi roads, this book will seek to offer a new perspective on the struggle within Islam, while also dealing with the transcendent—with the yearning for intimacy with God.

The Sufi road to God may seem shortened, but in the enigmatic words of a wise twentieth-century artist, Roland Penrose, a surrealist companion of Picasso and traveler in the Balkans, it may prove wider than long. That is a parable more than a puzzling image, and it befits a book on Sufism. For the road is not linear, in this narrative as well as in life, but elliptical; it requires digressions and other unexpected turns. In Sufism, as in other metaphysical traditions, the beginning of the journey is its end . . .

# 1

## The Great Age of Early Sufism

THE SUFI SEARCH FOR closeness to God began early in Islamic history. For a long time, it was pursued by individuals who had retired from worldly life. Among several interpretations of the word *Sufi*, the most convincing derives it from the Arabic word for wool (*suf*), referring to rough clothing worn by self-denying mystics.

While all Sufis find the origins of their collective vocation in the *Qur'an* and *hadith*, the most basic Islamic religious sources, the later, organized Sufi orders, or *tariqas*, draw their heritages from one teacher to another until the present day in a *silsila*, or chain of transmission through the lives of Muslim saints. The scholar Itzchak Weismann has pointed out a detail obvious to any observer of Sufism: the *silsilas* of Sufi orders are invented and reinvented by latter-day teachers to conform to their own interpretations, and are idealized legacies based on admiration rather than historical or religious documentation.

The *silsilas* of all Sufis begin with two of the outstanding companions of the Prophet Muhammad: Abubakr and Ali Ibn Abi Talib. Both were among the four original successors to Muhammad, or caliphs, in governing the Muslim community. Abubakr is also considered the progenitor of Sunni Islam, and Ali that of the Shia tradition. The great majority of Sufis, however, claim authority from Imam Ali alone. In this way, the Sufis assert their theological legitimacy as well as their continuity in history. While Sufis may formally be either Sunni or Shia, some claim to have transcended the difference, and many Sunni Sufis honor Imam Ali, the hero of the Shias, as their prime forerunner.

The first Muslim to speak eloquently of divine love, the supreme aspect of Sufi metaphysics, was a woman, Rabiya Al-Adawiyya. Rabiya died some 170 years after the life of Muhammad, in 801. She was preceded in Arab Sufism, which was then centered in Iraq, by a series of individuals described in a biographical dictionary of Sufis, the *Memorials of Saints* by the twelfth-century Persian writer Farid'ud'din Attar. Attar may have been the mentor of Rumi, the best-known Sufi among Westerners today.

Before Rabiya, Hasan Al-Basri, a goldsmith from the southern Iraqi city of Basra, then a great center of Mesopotamian commerce, is said to have lived in the time of Muhammad himself and to have been taught metaphysics by Imam Ali. But it is also related that Hasan Al-Basri mentored Rabiya more than a century later, in one of many examples of Sufi inspiration and companionship said to leap across time, beyond a normal life span. Hasan Al-Basri made one of the most cogent comments on religion and metaphysics known to the Sufis: When asked, "What is Islam and who is a Muslim?" he answered, "Islam is in books and the Muslim rests in a tomb."

Once, Hasan Al-Basri was walking along a river and observed a man sitting with a woman and a bottle of wine. He thought the man was hopelessly depraved and prayed that the man follow a righteous path such as the Sufi himself had chosen. But a passing boat began to sink, and the man Hasan Al-Basri had seen and lamented about leapt into the water and saved six people from drowning. The man then looked at Hasan Al-Basri and said, "If you are above me in the sight of God, at least save the seventh. But you will still have saved only one, while I have saved six." The Sufi failed to help the seventh victim and fell to the ground, crying out to the man, "You saved six people—please rescue me from drowning in the depths of my pride and vanity." Later, Hasan Al-Basri described himself as one whose ship had broken up in the sea and who then floated, barely keeping his head above the waters.

A true Sufi would hope never to be left in the condition of Hasan Al-Basri but would strive always to assist those that others have failed to protect, without judging their presumed sins and shortcomings in the observance of religion. At the same time as Hasan Al-Basri, another early Sufi, Malik Ibn Dinar, appealed for personal humility among believers, remarking, "When I came to know the injustice of the world, I ceased to care about what people said regarding me and my deeds." A Sufi acquaintance of Hasan Al-Basri, Habib Ajmi, mispronounced a word during prayer, which caused Hasan Al-Basri to move away from him and pray separately. But in a dream that night—and all Sufis believe dreams are sources of guidance—God told Hasan Al-Basri, "Your prayer would have earned divine approval, and that single prayer would have equaled all the prayers you have said in your life, if you had remained in prayer with Habib Ajmi. You were disapproving of his pronunciation but ignored the purity of his heart. A contrite heart is more valuable than exact pronunciation." Hasan Al-Basri then asked Habib Ajmi how the latter had achieved his high spiritual rank, and Habib Ajmi replied, "Brightening the heart through prayer is better than darkening paper with writing." Such insights are essential elements of Sufi teaching.

In the metaphysical journey of Rabiya Al-Adawiyya, Hasan Al-Basri was said to be grateful to Rabiya for the blessing that she had conferred on *him* by seeking his guidance, which led *him* to mystical ecstasy. Rabiya was born and studied religion in Basra, in one of the finest Islamic schools of the period. The Indian Muslim author and father of the idea of the nation of Pakistan, Muhammad Iqbal, referred to Basra in that era as "the play-ground of various forces—Greek philosophy, skepticism, Christianity, Buddhist ideas, Manichaeism."

The course of study in Basra at the time of Rabiya encompassed the Arabic language, literary style, and "theological rational grammar." The *Qur'an* was taught in Basra by recitation aloud. Rabiya committed herself to spiritual devotion, declaring that we are compelled to love God as the Creator. The passion of Rabiya for God was profound and fecund. She produced poetry in which she celebrated her love for the Lord of the Universe as well as her gratitude to God for permitting her love to exist.

Rabiya wrote, "I have never worshipped God so that I would be rewarded; nor have I prayed to be saved. If I did I should be an ordinary servant. I pray only because I love God with all my soul. To weep and cry out for God's mercy would be for nothing; for all I want is to approach God and dissolve my inner self in Him." These lines could stand as a summary of all *tasawwuf,* or Islamic spiritual purification, as well as of the main themes in Jewish and Christian mysticism. The writings of Rabiya and many who came after her resemble parts of the *Song of Songs* ascribed to Solomon and beloved by the traditional Jewish Kabbalists.

As a female Muslim saint, Rabiya is a challenging figure, for Westerners as well as for Islamic fundamentalists. Although Westerners presume that Islam completely suppresses women, Rabiya inaugurated a great Islamic tradition. Yet a modern publisher of Farid'ud'din At-tar's work, Bankey Behari, has commented that in the decades before her, "Arabian and Persian women saints especially . . . shed tears of blood in pangs of separation [from] the Lord and kept night-long vigils" in prayer and meditation. In addition, Westerners believe prayer and fear of God are the exclusive bases of Islam. But Rabiya introduced passion into the Islamic idiom. She was said to have walked through the streets of Basra with a torch and pail of water, declaring that her love for God would burn down heaven and drown hellfire.

The simplicity of Rumi has made him popular with Western readers. The verses of Rabiya similarly have a directness that can attract contemporary seekers of Judeo-Christian no less than Islamic metaphysics. Charles Upton is an American author whose literary career began with the help of the beat poet Lew Welch, who in turn was a friend and companion of the Zen Buddhist poets Gary Snyder and Philip Whalen, as well as of Jack Kerouac and Allen Ginsberg. Upton has published sensitive versions of Rabiya, such as the following:

*The source of my grief and loneliness is deep in my breast.*
*This is a disease no doctor can cure.*
*Only Union with the Friend [God] can cure it.*
*I was not born to the Grief of God—*
*I only grieve to be like those*
*Who are pierced with the love of God—*
*I would be ashamed for my love*
*To appear less than the grief of others:*
*Therefore I grieve.*

Many miracles are ascribed to Rabiya. A Muslim pilgrim, Ibrahim Adham, made the *hajj* pilgrimage to Mecca with such dedication to faith that he completed the basic Islamic prayer at each step. His trip to the holy city took fourteen years, but when he arrived he found that the *Ka'bah,* the temple of One God to which all Muslims turn in prayer, had vanished. Then a voice told him, "The *Ka'bah* has gone to meet Rabiya." The *Ka'bah* returned to Mecca and Rabiya was seen approaching the town, slowed down by age. Ibrahim Adham reproached her for "strange behavior that provokes outcry everywhere." She replied, "I do no such thing, while you spent fourteen years traveling to Mecca, for the sake of renown. Your path was covered by prayer, but mine was followed in the way of subordination and humility."

In the age of Rabiya, Islamic metaphysics sank deep roots among ordinary believers. The Islamic author Khalid Durán equated the rise of Sufism with protests against the corruptions of wealth, but also argued that a fracture runs through Islamic history between the "legalists," who are hunters of heresy and haters, and the mystics, who are pluralists and lovers.

The tomb of Rabiya is located near the Mount of Olives in Jerusalem and was often visited by non-Muslims as well as Muslims. The outstanding Muslim thinker Abu Hamid Al-Ghazali (1058–1111), traditionally considered the most important theologian of the religion after Muhammad, described Rabiya's vision by writing of two loves, "first to thank God for his attention shown to her; and [second] her attraction [to] his sight and divinity. The latter is the more attractive and advanced kind of love, because such love was attested by the Prophet, who said in a *hadith, 'I have prepared for my servants eyes and ears which no others possess. They would take pleasure in things that others cannot.' "

THE MOST IMPORTANT ARAB SUFI after the Basra school is known as Dhu'l-Nun (died ca. 859). He was the founder of Muslim mysticism in Egypt, and his tomb is a prominent monument near Cairo. Attar described him as "a spiritual king" but reported that the Egyptians accused him of heresy and harassed him throughout his life. He was denounced to the caliph in Baghdad but released when the ruler observed his piety; he was also imprisoned, then freed, in Mecca. He welcomed his sufferings as God's gift, which produced mystical ecstasy in him. Miracles and lessons associated with him are reminiscent of the Christian practice of mortification of the flesh, or self-inflicted pain, which had considerable influence in Islamized Egypt.

Attar wrote that Dhu'l-Nun came into metaphysical study after hearing of a saint who suspended himself upside down from a tree; the hanged man spoke to himself, saying, "My body, if you will not obey the commands of my spirit, I will task you unto death." When Dhu'l-Nun asked why the saint denied himself, the latter replied, "My body fails to remain alert and permanently in worship of God, and so I punish it." Dhu'l-Nun remarked, "I thought you had been sentenced for murder or some other major crime." The hanged man responded, "There is no greater crime than dependence upon this world, and all that is evil comes from such dependence."

Dhu'l-Nun remarked on the saintly nature of the hanged man, who pointed out another living on a nearby hill. The second had severed his own foot to prevent himself from lustful wandering. That ascetic told Dhu'l-Nun of another, further on, who lived only on honey because he would not beg food from another human being; and yet the bees had followed God's command to feed the saint. As he was returning to his home, Dhu'l-Nun saw a blind bird in a tree and wondered how it fed. He watched as the bird pierced the ground with its beak and found a golden bowl of water and a pile of corn. Dhu'l-Nun was then convinced that all who trusted first in God and were dedicated to metaphysical devotion and meditation would be sustained. He left the affairs of the world behind him and committed himself to repetition of God's names.

The life of Dhu'l-Nun also includes mysterious parables, such as that of the grand palace on the bank of a canal, with a balcony on which a beautiful woman sat. As he approached the structure, he washed himself in the water of the canal for prayer. The woman said to him, "You are neither mad, nor learned in religion, nor enlightened, for a madman would not clean himself for religious observance, a scholar of faith would not have looked upon me, and a mystic would think only of God." The palace and the woman disappeared, and Dhu'l-Nun took this as a divine message to him. Dhu'l-Nun taught that metaphysical Muslims could never think of money and must attach themselves to poverty and solitude. He further described spiritual music, or *sama'*, as a "cure for all desires." He insisted, "Those who claim to have seen God do not know the Creator; those who see God remain silent." He defined remembrance of God (*dhikrullah*), the foundation of Sufism, as "making the most of the present moment."

At his death, Dhu'l-Nun pronounced these words:

*Fear of God made me fall ill;*
*Yearning for God consumed me;*
*Love has brought me to death;*
*But my life belongs to God.*

It is said the funeral of Dhu'l-Nun was protected by birds that massed in the sky and covered the procession with outspread wings. Attar commented, "After he died those who called him a heretic recognized him as a great saint." Dhu'l-Nun was described as a "brilliant" preacher by the great twentieth-century Sufi teacher Baba Rexheb Beqiri[1] (1901–1995), a leader of the Bektashi order, who introduced authentic Sufism in America. Baba Rexheb notes that Dhu'l-Nun distinguished between the forgiveness granted to ordinary folk and that bestowed upon the powerful; the latter are "dazed" by the experience. Dhu'l-Nun further established a hierarchy of knowledge that would be supported throughout the history of Sufism: at the lowest level, the knowledge of normal people; then, the understanding of religious scholars and philosophers, based on study; and in the highest place, direct understanding of the divine, which may be attained only through inspiration. Dhu'l-Nun affirmed, "I have known my God with the help of God within me. If God were not within me, I would never have known God, ever."

Rabiya and Dhu'l-Nun were ecstatic in their love of God. Not long after them, another Arab, Abu'l-Qasim al-Junayd ibn Muhammad of Baghdad, who died in 910, came forward with a metaphysical turn from the loving affirmation of the ecstatics toward "sober" Sufism. This distinction would prove enduring through the rest of the history of Islamic mysticism. Junayd Al-Baghdadi was said to have experienced pride in his observance of religious ritual but was warned by a divine voice that his ego remained strong and he was therefore flawed in his belief. He then dedicated himself to extreme asceticism, and in an expression of Sufi sincerity, he once bowed to the corpse of a thief who was hanged, saying, "He was faithful to the path he followed, and gave his life for it."

Junayd Al-Baghdadi expressed such "sober" sentiments as "One who fears God never smiles," along with the contradictory advice "A good-natured sensual being is superior to a bad-tempered Sufi." "Sober" Sufism, although powerful within Islam, is wracked by these paradoxes. The reputation of Junayd and the "sober" Sufis is further stained by the acquiescence by Junayd to the execution, allegedly for heresy, of his disciple Husayn bin Mansur Hallaj (858–922). As the inspirer of the "sober" school, Junayd Al-Baghdadi is also contrasted in Sufi teaching with a Persian, his "intoxicated" predecessor Bayazet Al-Bastami (804–874).

Al-Bastami introduced the concept of "annihilation of the self in the divine," which he defined as a drunken state. According to Attar, as a small child Al-Bastami asked his mother to commit him to the service of God alone, and she did so. His concentration on the Creator was so intense that he always kept his gaze lowered and never noticed the furnishings in the room of his mentor, Ja'afar Al-Sidiq, the Sixth Imam of Shia Islam and the most important Shia legal authority.

Al-Bastami had once fallen in the street and cried out to passersby, "I am God; why do you not worship me?" He was believed insane, and his disciples left him. But Al-Bastami was happy with silence and solitude. His humility was so profound that he wept whenever he entered a mosque, in fear that his imperfections would pollute the holy place.

Al-Bastami's speech was often enigmatic and, in Attar's words, even "erotic"; he could not be understood at all, and like other Sufis he was accused of heresy. He once commanded, equating himself with God, "Look upon my majesty and purity." He then came to his senses and his students asked him why he had allowed himself such a blasphemous statement. "I do not know what I said," Al-Bastami told them, "and if I say it again, kill me with a sword." He returned to an exalted state and repeated the phrase, whereupon his followers rushed at him with weapons, but hundreds of Al-Bastamis appeared and none could be harmed. He later resumed his normal form and told his disciples that neither the speaker of intoxicated words nor the images were the real Al-Bastami.

In one of Al-Bastami's most profound utterances, he said, "For thirty years I sought God, until I recognized that God was the seeker and I the one sought." He counseled his followers that the subject of their meditations should be God alone and not their own spiritual effort. He also said, "Love of God makes one forget this world and the next world alike." In an encounter reminiscent of the pre-Socratic

Greek philosopher Heraclitus, who said that one never steps in the same river twice, Al-Bastami was criticized for remaining too long in his customary posture of stillness. The critic said, "You stay uninterrupted in one place—do you not know that water, if it stands, becomes brackish and dark?" Al-Bastami replied, "Then make yourself into a river." Another man once came to his house and said he was looking for Al-Bastami. The Sufi answered, "I have spent thirty years searching for Al-Bastami and have yet to find him."

An imam asked Al-Bastami, after prayers, how he managed to earn a living. The Sufi replied, "If you do not understand that God alone is the bestower of food to all, you should not lead prayer." One of his disciples wondered why Al-Bastami did not pray more regularly, given his devotion to God, and Al-Bastami asked in wonder how anyone who attained knowledge of God and abandoned the self to ecstasy could concentrate enough for prayer. Al-Bastami described himself as so lost in remembrance of God that he would ignore the passage of day into night. He taught that God had received enough in the form of individual and collective prayer but desired from the faithful "meekness, helplessness, humility, and agony." He also said, "Those favored by God are rewarded with suffering." When he was requested to pray on behalf of another Muslim, Al-Bastami answered, "God knows your wishes; who am I to interfere between you and the Creator?" He also taught, "Power over the whole world would not equal the single sigh I uttered last night, recognizing my separation from God."

Asked to define Sufi metaphysics, Al-Bastami answered, "Give up all comfort and concentrate on work. This is purification of the soul." Al-Bastami composed a prayer: *"O Allah, remove the veil belonging to me and the veil that is yours, so that my existence may become one with your essence. O Allah, poverty and fasting have brought me close to you, and I see you only in your grace."*

Attar writes that a pious Muslim sought to bring a Zoroastrian into Islam. The Zoroastrian answered, "I lack the courage to pursue Islam in the way of Al-Bastami, and if Islam is what you represent, I cannot believe in it."

A DEATH IN BAGHDAD almost eleven centuries ago hovers over Sufism. A shadow falls across time: that of Husayn bin Mansur Hallaj, the disciple of the "sober" Junayd but an ecstatic even more remarkable than Al-Bastami and also charged with heresy—but executed. Hallaj symbolizes unrestrained love of God, an Islamic identification with Jesus,[2] freedom of conscience, and martyrdom for truth. He is relevant to believers in all faiths, in all times and places. Hallaj is most exalted among the intoxicated Sufis, in desiring a total integration with God and loss of ego. He wrote several volumes with such alluring titles as *The Book of Invented and Eternal Letters, The Book of Roots and Branches,* and *The Book of Justice and Unity.* He said, "I am both the lover and the beloved," that is, both God and the worshipper. He was persecuted for declaring, "*Ana ul-haqq,*" or, "I am truth as a manifestation of God."

A *fatwa* was issued calling for his arrest and imprisonment. After an escape and capture, he was jailed for eight years in Baghdad before he was killed. The Muslim scholars of his time were split over this terrible deed. His opponents called him an unbeliever and atheist.

The biography of Hallaj is found in many volumes. One of the most important sources is an essay by his son Hamd ibn Husayn ibn Mansur. It is a shocking document because it enumerates the tortures to which the dissenter was subjected by the cruel authorities during his execution in Baghdad. But it also describes the great Sufi in his cell the night before the sentence was carried out, repeating to himself, "Illusion . . . illusion," as if evaluating the features and glories of the world, then turning silent, and finally crying out, "Truth . . . truth!"

Attar recounts miracles just before Hallaj was killed. On the third night prior to his death, his followers came to his cell but found it empty. On the second night, they found him present but the walls of the cell absent. And on the night before he was executed, he sat in his cell awaiting his fate. When his disciples asked for an explanation of these happenings, he said that the first time, he had been with God; the second, God had come to the cell; and at the end, "I am here to confirm the holy teaching, which says that no man may put himself alongside God without suffering the ultimate punishment."

The more intimate portrait of Hallaj offered by his son is that of a restless personality of great imagination, and a religious thinker of striking versatility. Like other Muslim intellectuals of the classic period, as well as Christian mystics, Hallaj was reputed to be an alchemist. But it seems that much of the alchemical tradition was based on an analogy: the transformation of base metals into gold symbolized the human attainment of spiritual treasure.

Hallaj was also a traveler and missionary for Islam, going to Turkestan, known as "the land of thousands of saints." The local Turkic population there, called Uighurs, are today a badly oppressed minority in China. They were then ruled by Manichaeans, but the Uighurs also included Eastern Christians,[3] Zoroastrians, and Buddhists. Like other Turkic peoples, the Uighurs came into Islam voluntarily rather than by conquest. Attar tells us that Hallaj journeyed as far as China, via India. The eccentric but able French scholar of Hallaj, Louis Massignon, argued that the ecstatic Sufi's journey to Turkestan set in motion the Islamization of the Turks that culminated in the taking of Constantinople by Sultan Mehmet the Conqueror in 1453. And finally, Hallaj had the internal turbulence characteristic of poets: he turned away from Sufism and frequented the powerful of Baghdad before coming back to metaphysics.

His eventual persecution and execution may have had more to do with public affairs than with alleged heretical speech. A prominent Islamic jurist of the time protected him, finding that metaphysics was outside the strictures of *Shariah* and therefore exempt from legal judgment, and while Hallaj was deprived of liberty during his long trial he was allowed a cell of his own in the palace, where he composed his last works and taught those who came to him, including many politically powerful acolytes. Massignon identifies Hallaj with the threat of an Islamic social revolution; in Massignon's account, which may be skewed by the French scholar's own anti-Jewish prejudice, the intoxicated metaphysics involved in Hallaj's purported heresy fades into the background in a Muslim Baghdad in which public corruption was ubiquitous and supposedly complicated by the role of Jewish bankers. But Sufis claim Hallaj was killed for disclosing state secrets to the people. One of the disciples of Hallaj, Ahmad Al-Amuli, told the court official Hamid bin Abbas that Hallaj's alleged transgressions in religion were nothing compared with the acts of theft and cruelty committed by the rulers; Al-Amuli was then tortured but, like his mentor, refused to submit.

Khalid Durán viewed Hallaj as a saint of the poor, and one Sufi source describes him as the patron of outlaws. Some have taken him as a model of subversive and libertarian⁴ conduct. Hallaj was, however, also a topic of verses by no less than Ayatollah Ruhollah Khomeini, who wrote, *"I forget my own existence and proclaim, 'I am the truth' and like Mansur Hallaj I volunteer myself for hanging."* Khomeini's identification with Hallaj embodies the revolutionary aspect of the dour Iranian cleric's personality but also might indicate Khomeini's view of himself as a martyr to oppression.

The late Edward Said, an academic warrior against "Orientalism," preferred to see in Massignon's work nothing more than a promotion of Hallaj as a Christ figure, to the detriment of Islam. It is true that Massignon himself appears somewhat intoxicated in his reading of Hallaj's Jesus-like martyrdom, but neither Massignon nor Said, both of them Christians, may have possessed a clear understanding of Hallaj, which seems reserved to his Islamic defenders.

The son of Hallaj related that the martyr for liberty recited the following verses, an epitome (in an epiphany) of his thought, while talking on the eve of his execution:

> *I cry to You for the Souls whose witness [the mystic himself] now*
> *goes beyond the "where" to meet the Witness of Eternity;*
> *I cry to You for hearts so long refreshed—in vain—by clouds of*
> *revelation, hearts once filled with seas of wisdom;*
> *I cry to You for the Word of God, which since it perished, has*
> *faded to nothing in our memory;*
> *I cry to You for Your [inspired] discourse before which ceases all*
> *speaking by the wise and eloquent orator;*
> *I cry to You for Signs that have been gathered by intellects—*
> *nothing in books remains of them but dust;*
> *I cry to You, I swear it by your Love—for the Virtues of those*
> *people whose only recourse was to keep silent;*
> *All have crossed the desert, leaving neither a well nor tracks*
> *behind—vanished like the people of 'Ad and their lost city,*
> *Irem;*
> *And after them the abandoned crowd mingles in confusion on*
> *their trails—blinder than beasts, blinder even than she-camels.*[5]

Hallaj was finally taken to a prominent place in Baghdad and was subjected to between three hundred and five hundred lashes. His hands and feet were amputated and he was exposed on a gallows for a day. A crowd of many thousands gathered to see him in his agony. A Sufi came to him then and asked, "What is purification of the soul?" Hallaj answered, "What you see here is its beginning." The mob began stoning him, and the Sufi who had questioned him struck Hallaj with a rose. The martyr did not react to the stoning but shrieked at the touch of the flower, crying out, "The others are ignorant, but this one knows everything happening here."

The next morning he was beheaded by decree of the caliph, and his body was wrapped in a mat and burned. The ashes were scattered—a particular punishment in Islam, which teaches that on the Last Day the dead will be raised in the form in which they perished. But it is said the ashes also recited, "I am the truth," and when they fell into the water, they formed an inscription with the same words and the river began to rise, threatening Baghdad with flood. Even today, the specter of Hallaj floats on the great sea of Islamic devotion, as Hasan Al-Basri before him swam in mystical wisdom to keep alive, and in some Muslim lands, Sufi metaphysics threatens to submerge the palaces of the unjust.


HAVING EXAMINED THE LIFE of Hallaj, let us see how his spirit lives today. We should look first to a numerous and nonconformist Muslim community little known to Westerners, the Alevis. They are often Western European by citizenship and, increasingly, by birth. They are Turkish and Kurdish in origin. When the Alevis assemble to celebrate their belief and their identity, they chorus the phrase of Hallaj: "I am the truth" (in Arabized Turkish, *enel hakk*) to which they add, "My *Ka'bah* is a human being" (*Benim Kâbem insandir*). That is, they pray "toward" the human person rather than a physical structure. They are lovers of Imam Ali and Ali's son Imam Husayn, and are therefore Shia

Muslims. They are also Sufis, and have preserved elements of pre-Islamic Turkish shamanic religion. In Turkey they have been oppressed for generations.

Alevis, although criticized by Turkish Sunnis for their attitudes and practices, reject any attempt to exclude them from the Islamic global community, or *umma*. The traditions and outlook of the Alevis demonstrate the spiritual pluralism within Islam. While reference volumes, including *The CIA World Fact Book*, routinely cite the official Turkish claim that 99.8 percent of Turks are "mostly Sunnis," Alevis do not follow the established precepts of Sunni Islam. Alevis worship "truth" as the representation of the divine Creator.

A young German Alevi writer, Ali Sirin, summarizes the life of his people as follows:

> Alevism is an independent faith community of Muslims characterized by syncretism, or the fusion of many spiritual influences. They number up to 20 million in Turkey itself, or a quarter of the population, and make up some 600,000 out of the 3–4 million Muslims in Germany. Their tradition emphasizes freedom of conscience and the right of dissent, and their religious life is inspired by principles of love, tolerance and humanism, drawing on all the Abrahamic religions—Judaism, Christianity, Islam. For the Alevis, the human personality is at the forefront of devotion, and there is little concern for religious dogmas.
>
> One source of the Alevis' humanistic attitude is their pantheistic perception of the world. The divine presence is universal and resides in the hearts of all humans. Love for God comes first. Alevi openness and inclusion permit no discrimination against anybody, including women.

In the Alevi community, women do not accept so-called Islamic covering in the form of veils, head scarves, or long garments, and polygamy is banned. Alevi men and women share an exalted moral goal, and are not segregated in the development of their personalities. Individual responsibility and autonomy are major principles, and the equality of men and women is protected.

The greatest responsibility for both is to show tolerance, moderation, and respect for others. Alevi parents provide daughters with the same opportunities for education as sons. Based on their humanistic philosophy and open-minded attitudes, Alevis living in non-Muslim countries like Germany and Britain present no barriers to integration into the communities where they live.

Recent efforts by radical Sunnis to define the Alevis as heretics or non-Muslims have been homicidal. Alevis remember, with a profound sense of mourning, an atrocity in the eastern Turkish city of Sivas on July 2, 1993. In that incident, a hotel that rented space for an Alevi cultural conference was burned by rioting Sunni fanatics, and thirty-seven people died. The pretext for Sunni terrorism was the presence at the conference of Aziz Nesin, a popular writer. Nesin was known for his progressive views, including his insistence on freedom to criticize, without limitations, the faith of Islam. This issue has gained universal importance with the challenge of radical Islam to the whole planet, as well as controversies over the Danish media caricatures of the Prophet Muhammad and commentaries on Islam by Pope Benedict XVI. Years before, Nesin had called for the publication of Salman Rushdie's *Satanic Verses* in Turkey.

Similarly, two prominent Alevi representatives I met in Germany in 2006 defended the right of the Berlin Opera to present any work of art it chose, without worrying about "insulting" fundamentalist Muslims. The opera company had just undergone a meaningless controversy over a modernist version of Mozart's *Idomeneo* in which the head of Muhammad was displayed along with those of other religious figures (such stage directions had never previously appeared in Mozart's opera). Ismail Kaplan, an Alevi community leader and writer, commented to me, "It is absolutely unacceptable that art should be repressed on the pretext of religion. Freedom of the imagination must not be surrendered after so many centuries of struggle and development."

His colleague Necat Sahin is an artist and leading Alevi intellectual whose work includes a message to God calling for greater friendship between God and the human community, inscribed on the ceiling of an Alevi meeting hall. Sahin added: "As an Alevi I find such conflicts [over freedom of expression] especially absurd." Meanwhile, the governing AK or "white" (i.e., "conservative" and "clean") Justice and Development Party in Turkey, an Islamist movement headed by the prime minister, Recep Tayyip Erdoğan, includes no Alevis in its leadership, and Alevis believe that Turkish Islamist politicians intend to definitively exclude them from recognition as Muslims.

In the Sivas affair, with its thirty-seven martyrs, a crowd of enraged fundamentalist Sunnis besieged the Madimak Hotel for several hours. They shouted demands for *Shariah* as the sole law in the country while denouncing Nesin and others at the conference as "unbelievers," then set fire to the structure. By the time firefighters arrived, flames had consumed much of the building. Nesin escaped with some others. (He died in 1995.)

For the Alevis, Sivas represents the permanent battle for the soul of Islam—a conflict in which the bigoted Muslim enemies of the West, of Jews, and of Christians are also murderous in their actions against Muslims of whom they disapprove. One should not have to point out that the same hatred that burned people to death in Sivas in 1993 incited radical Sunnis against Sufis and Shias in Iraq. Shias say that the event that symbolizes the beginning of their tradition—the martyrdom of Imam Husayn at Karbala in 680—is a permanent spiritual reality and that Karbala is repeated every day. So do Alevis declare that Sivas occurs every day. For the ecstatic, intoxicated Sufi, loving God and creation above all, and typically called a heretic by narrow-minded Muslims, injustice never ends. Every day is the day of Hallaj's execution. And every day, in a world of intolerance and brutality, Hallaj embodies the insecurity of life—including the life of you, the reader of this book.

Western critics protested radical Muslim rhetoric against Rushdie, but they seldom if ever mention the martyrs of Sivas. Sivas was followed by other atrocities against Alevis in Turkey. In 1995 a machine gun was fired at a teahouse in Istanbul where Alevis gathered. Two men, one of them an Alevi *dede,* or elder, were killed. Police were lazy in their response, and four days of protests in the city produced fifteen more dead, all unarmed and most of them Alevis.

Today the West faces a great challenge: to understand and help those who embody Islamic pluralism, including the Alevi factory worker in the Ruhr Valley of Germany and in Turkey; the Albanian dervish; the Sufi teacher in Saudi Arabia; the spiritual nonconformist in Iran; the Shia Muslim in Iraq or Pakistan. All have seen their peers murdered and their holy places desecrated, most often by violent Islamists. These misunderstood legions are typically ordinary working people and peasants. They have few globally known cultural figures who speak for them. Yet if treated with respect they may be irreplaceable in defending the world against terrorism. They are the voiceless, the humiliated, the poor, and those nourished only by metaphysics: they are the people of Hallaj.

AFTER THE PERSECUTION of Sufis such as Hallaj, Islam produced a vindication of pure religious feeling along with protection for intellectual inquiry. Among the voices of renewed Muslim faith and legitimacy for Sufism would come Abu Hamid Al-Ghazali, known as "the proof of Islam," some 150 years after the death of Hallaj.

Al-Ghazali was born an inquisitive soul. He recalled in his quasi-autobiographical work *Deliverance from Error,* "From my childhood I was inclined to think things out for myself. The result of this attitude was that I revolted against authority; and all the beliefs that had fixed themselves in my mind from childhood lost their original importance. I thought that such beliefs based on mere authority were equally entertained by Jews, Christians, and followers of other religions. Real knowledge must eradicate all doubt."

He expanded,

The different religious observances and religious communities of the human race and likewise the different theological systems of the religious leaders, with all the multiplicity of sects and variety of practices, constitute ocean depths in which the majority drown and only a minority reach safety . . . since I attained the age of puberty before I was twenty, until the present time when I am over fifty, I have ever reckless launched out into the midst of these ocean depths, I have ever bravely embarked on this open sea, throwing aside all craven caution; I have poked into every dark recess, I have made an assault on every problem, I have plunged into every abyss, I have scrutinized the creed of every sect, I have tried to lay bare the inmost doctrines of every community. All this have I done that I might distinguish between true and false, between sound tradition and heretical innovation . . . I said to myself: "To begin with, what I am looking for is knowledge of what things really are, so I must undoubtedly find out what knowledge really is."

As Muhammad Iqbal wrote, Al-Ghazali "examined afterwards all the various claimants of 'Certain Knowledge' and finally found it in Sufism." A Persian who lived in Baghdad between journeys as a wandering ascetic, Al-Ghazali represents the period in which Islamic mysticism extended its intellectual influence through a rebirth of Iranian civilization; Iqbal invoked the Persianization of the Muslim intellect as one of the key interactions of Eastern and Western thought.

Al-Ghazali had no lasting relationship with a Sufi shaykh, although he studied with a number of them, including one Yusuf an-Nassaj. Whereas Hallaj was an exemplar of ecstasy as a means to experience divine love, Al-Ghazali is identified with a systematic quest for spiritual union with God. Al-Ghazali became an eloquent proponent of the religion of the heart over that of formalized, external observance, and he revived the Islamic concept of the soul, which was, as explained by Iqbal, lost in prior controversies among Muslim philosophers. Al-Ghazali's theology incarnates the mainstream tradition in Sunni Islam until the rise of Arab radicalism in the eighteenth and nineteenth centuries, and it is largely because of his heritage that Sufism is a pervasive element in contemporary Muslim societies.

Al-Ghazali demonstrated a literary talent beginning in his youth. He wrote a massive work in Arabic, *The Revival of the Religious Sciences*, that was widely read by Jews as well as Muslims. The book was rendered into Persian by its author under the title *Alchemy of Happi-*

*ness.* Al-Ghazali is presumed to have influenced Bahya ibn Pakuda, author of *Duties of the Heart,* a classic of Jewish mysticism. Al-Ghazali was and remains a valuable example for those Muslims today defending the Islam of the heart against the Saudi-backed Wahhabis and other fundamentalists, who insist on a rigid, externally observant, narrow interpretation of Islam. For Al-Ghazali affirmed a basic Islamic principle: that intentions are superior to outward behavior and only God can judge intentions, and therefore the judgment of one's belief belongs only to the Creator.

The effect of Al-Ghazali's teaching was to alleviate conflict between the Sufis and their enemies. Baba Rexheb Beqiri commented on Al-Ghazali that his greatness as an upholder of religious law gave him the charisma to support the Muslim mystics previously reviled as atheistic adversaries of Islam. Al-Ghazali taught the ordinary believers that metaphysics was an alternative means to gain knowledge of God and comprehension of truth and justice, the essentials of faith. He had also thoroughly analyzed the classical non-Muslim and Muslim philosophers, whose works had been widely debated in Islam, and his commitment to Sufism was made, as Baba Rexheb further indicates, "at the height of his intellectual maturity."

Al-Ghazali's approach to philosophy led him to rejection of earlier Islamic theological commentators. Theology, he said, had offered nothing but a set of disconnected, unsustainable answers to the opinions of the classical philosophers; further, he argued that examination of the philosophers should be based on their own arguments rather than on theological polemics against them. As also pointed out by Baba Rexheb, Al-Ghazali viewed theologians as seeking nothing more than to protect the faithful from heresy, to which end theology offered "arbitrary and confusing" religious edicts. (The same unfortunate situation prevails in Islam today.) Such attitudes reflected limited imagination, according to Al-Ghazali, and would undermine belief, since they were insufficient in answering the views of the classical philosophers. There was even further danger for believers when the theologians were faced with philosophers who rejected the truths of religion but contributed greatly to mathematics and the physical sciences. Al-Ghazali believed that Islam could not fail to account for the facts of the natural world.

His polemics included a work titled *The Incoherence of the Philosophers,* but he is best known in English for *Deliverance from Error,* his account of his spiritual journey, and his *Beginning of Guidance.* He placed the scholars of religion in four classes: the general theologians, the keepers of "authoritative instruction" or infallible guidance (the unquestioning followers of both Sunni imams and Shia clerics), the philosophers or logicians, and the Sufis.

The theologians, in his view, made the mistake of unsystematically studying nature, whereas the proponents of "authority" too often based their beliefs on their own views. According to him the philosophers had all embraced forms of unbelief, but Al-Ghazali recognized the problem presented to the Muslims by the incompetent translation of Greek philosophical works from their original language into Arabic. Still, Al-Ghazali was a counsel of moderation. He condemned as "corrupt" those who would "hastily pronounce a man an unbeliever if he deviate[d] from their own system of doctrine." This wise judgment is another with great meaning today, as Wahhabi terrorists in Iraq and elsewhere shed the blood of Sufi, Shia, and other Muslims they have declared "unbelievers" in fulfillment of the practice known as *takfir,* or excommunication.

Al-Ghazali assailed the thinkers who used scraps of religious teaching to justify the political decisions of rulers, and he further advocated respect toward non-Muslims. He wrote that while a Christian could be described as a disbeliever in Islam, Christians could not be described as unbelievers in the principles of their own religion, which he declared to be "true in themselves." He quoted Imam Ali, who said, *"Do not take as truth what men say, but know the truth, and then judge men by what they say about it. Then you will know who is truthful."*

Al-Ghazali correctly stated that a false doctrine could not be refuted without examining it accurately. The same problem exists today in the study by most Westerners of Islamist extremism: to know what is wrong in the ranks of Islam one must first know Islam, and nobody can know Islam the way a Muslim does. To know Islam most completely, Al-Ghazali inevitably turned to the Sufis.

HE BEGAN BY ADMITTING that for him the intellectual side of Sufism was easier than the self-cleansing demanded in its practical side. But he discovered that metaphysics could not be apprehended exclusively by reading and meditating: mysticism, ecstasy, and personal transformation must be tasted. And what Al-Ghazali wrote nine hundred years ago is no less true today. The abstainer, if he has never been drunk, cannot understand the intoxicated individual. A physician when ill may know his ailment but be unable to cure it. Of course, one could add to these observations that those who have not experienced human love cannot imagine it simply by hearing or reading of it; those who have never fought in a battle for freedom cannot envision such exhilaration and heartbreak; and those who have not surrendered to belief in God cannot conceive it, much less the Sufi goal of proximity to the divine. In a definition of metaphysics, Al-Ghazali wrote, "I apprehended clearly that the mystics were men who had real experiences, not men of words, and that I had already progressed as far as was possible by way of intellect . . . What remained for me was not to be attained by oral instruction and study but only by immediate experience and by walking in the mystical path."

Analyzing the ecstatic mental state, Al-Ghazali wrote, "There begin revelations and visions . . . angels and the spirits of prophets . . . Later, a higher state is reached; instead of beholding forms and figures, come stages in the 'way' which it is hard to describe in language; if one attempts to express these, one's words inevitably include obvious mistakes."

In his *Revival of the Religious Sciences,* Al-Ghazali proclaimed that understanding of God must lead to personal contentment; that comprehension of the human heart is itself a harbinger of, if not a manifestation of, paradise; and that the most plentiful reward in the hereafter would belong to those who had accumulated the most extensive and profound knowledge. Above all, for Al-Ghazali, perception of God and divine creation are means to human happiness. Awareness is the source of joy. The believer who has achieved the greatest insights into creation will find that all obstacles on earth and in the skies vanish before him or her. The individual's heart will become pure and free of earthly temptation. In this, Al-Ghazali challenges those fundamentalist, extremist Muslims who declaim that attachment to this life is worthless when compared with the bounties of heaven and who therefore incite the young and other vulnerable individuals to acts of suicidal terror.

Echoing Dhu'l-Nun, Al-Ghazali also argued that faith exists in three human varieties: that of the ordinary believers, that of the educated, and that of the initiated. The mass of religious folk believe what they are taught and what they observe; the educated demand evidence for the claims of religion; and the initiated seek intimacy with the divine. The majority accept God's dominion over the world; the educated study holy texts to find proof of the Creator's will; but the initiates meet God directly. The initiated therefore attain ultimate truth.

For Al-Ghazali, the simple as well as the educated Muslims encounter barriers to such transcendence in that they must first repudiate daily life and its deceptions and assume total submission to God, acquiring the God-given revelations that the mystics themselves cannot explain. He taught that given the pleasure the human eye and ear derive from beautiful objects and sounds, the pleasures obtained by way of the heart must be ever greater; in view of the satisfaction individuals receive from their relations with powerful rulers and other distinguished people, close relations with the Master of the Day of Judgment must be ever more glorious. And knowledge of God, said Al-Ghazali, comes by "the eyes of the heart," before death, persisting through wakefulness and sleep, and encompassing all the secrets of creation.

In his *Beginning of Guidance,* a short handbook for the spiritual seeker, Al-Ghazali sets out the ways in which believers may assess the state of their souls. He begins,

> With eager desire you are setting out to acquire knowledge, my friend; of yourself you are making clear how genuine is your longing and how passionate your thirst for it. Be sure that, if in your quest for knowledge your aim is to gain something for yourself and to surpass your peers, to attract attention to yourself and to amass the vanities of this world, you are on the way to bring your religion to nothing and to destroy yourself . . . On the other hand, if in seeking knowledge your intention and purpose between God most high and yourself is to receive guidance and not merely to acquire information, then rejoice. The angels will spread out their wings for you

when you walk . . . above all, you must realize that the guidance which is the fruit of knowledge has a beginning and an ending, an outward aspect and an inward. Nobody can reach the end without completing the beginning; nobody can discover the inward without mastering the outward.

Al-Ghazali then delineates the practices needed to test the soul. One should wake before dawn, uttering praise of God; the physical needs and ablutions that come with the beginning of the day should be accompanied by prayers against defilement; one should go calmly to the mosque for daily worship and observe the ritual faithfully, adding such supplications[6] as the following: *"O God, grant me light in my heart and light in my tomb, light in my hearing and light in my seeing, light in my hair and light in my skin, light in my flesh and light in my blood and light in my bones, light before me, light behind me, light to the right of me, light to the left of me, light above me, light beneath me, O God, increase my light and give me the greatest light of all, the light of your mercy, grant me light, most merciful God."*[7]

He counsels that given free time, one should acquire "really useful knowledge," in the phrase adopted by Al-Ghazali's English translator, W. Montgomery Watt, a half-century ago. "Really useful knowledge" contributes to the fear of God, consciousness of one's own shortcomings and errors, and the capacity to serve God. In recommending this course, Al-Ghazali cites Saint Matthew, author of one of the four Christian Gospels, who recounted that the teachers of righteousness would be "called great in the kingdom of Heaven." Those who do not pursue "really useful knowledge" should occupy their time with meditation, *Qur'an* reading, and prayer; if not that, then with good works among their fellow Muslims; and if not that, then by honestly and ethically providing for their family. In other aspects of daily life, one should follow religious law, but the Muslim should also try to fast at times other than the prescribed Islamic month of Ramadan, since fasting "is the foundation of devotional practices and the key to good works."

It was natural that the deep personality and wide perceptions of Abu Hamid Al-Ghazali should have so affected the world in which he lived. A great nineteenth-century Jewish Orientalist, Ignaz Goldziher, was among the scholars who saw the influence of Al-Ghazali on Bahya ibn Pakuda, who lived a generation after the Persian sage. Ibn Pakuda offered an Arabic-language portrait of the pious Jew that includes a striking reference to Islamic metaphysics: "Never does he avenge himself, never does he persevere in his anger. He is a companion to those who practice *dhikr* [the Islamic remembrance of God] and a friend to the poor." In this reference I perceive a hint of a stunning and seldom-mentioned fact: Jews living among Muslims in the past habitually joined their Muhammadan neighbors in Sufi devotions.

A CENTURY AFTER AL-GHAZALI'S death, the most celebrated Sufi shaykhs appeared, including Ibn Arabi (1165–1240), whose Spanish Sufism inaugurated a truly European Islam, providing a model for moderate Muslims living in Christian Europe in the twenty-first century. The glory of Muslim Spain, so often praised for its civility between the three religions, might better be honored for the finest product of that civility—a highly sophisticated, multidimensional Islam.

A Jewish strain linked to Muslim Sufism was long visible in Spain. The Islamic impact on Spanish Jewish spirituality was not limited to the borderlands; it also came to the Jews of Christian Spain from the distant Muslim East. The twentieth-century Jewish genius in religious studies, Gershom Scholem, who pioneered the historical analysis of

Kabbalah, wrote that the mystical impulse toward "a more intimate communion with God and for a religious life connected with this" appeared in medieval Judaism "from fusion of internal [Jewish] drives with the external influence of the religious movements present in the non-Jewish environment. Since their proponents did not find the answer to all their needs in the Talmudic [and other Jewish] sources which purported to bind man closer to God . . . they also drew extensively on the literature of the Sufis." Moshe Idel, the leading present-day historian of Kabbalah, describes "an unbroken chain of [Jewish] authors . . . who developed a mystical trend under Sufic inspiration." This tendency was "transmitted" from East to West in "a fascinating 'migration' of Kabbalistic theory." Idel concludes, "Palestine made a great contribution to [Kabbalah]. This contribution, ironically, was nurtured by Muslim mysticism."

There was also a distinct phenomenon known as "Jewish Sufism." One of the most prominent commentators on "Jewish Sufism," Paul B. Fenton of the University of Strasbourg in France, describes a group of Jews, the offspring and descendants of the great twelfth-century Jewish jurist Maimonides, among whom "there arose a pietistic elite whose search for mystical fulfillment led them to introduce into the framework of traditional Judaism a creative change that drew its inspiration from the nearest spiritual model—Islamic Sufism." These Jewish figures wrote in Arabic, and, according to Fenton, "had historical circumstances been less unfavorable and had their writings been translated into Hebrew . . . the pietist movement could have profoundly and permanently transformed the face of Judaism."

Scholem had also noted that the mystical aspect of works by Abraham Maimonides, a son of Maimonides, "is entirely based on Sufi sources and bears no evidence of any similar Jewish tradition known to the author." Abraham Maimonides (1186–1237) became the leading figure in "Jewish Sufism." Abraham Maimonides went so far as to praise the Muslim Sufis as the spiritual heirs of the ancient Hebrew prophets, expressing his disappointment that his fellow Jews did not emulate the Islamic mystics. He was, according to Fenton, eager to found a Jewish *tariqa*, or Sufi order. He adopted many Islamic practices, including forms of prayer, and took on the woollen garment, or *suf*. The spiritual disciplines he embraced were carried forward and defended by the family of Abraham Maimonides, including his grandson David Maimonides (1222–1300) and the last member of the "Maimonidean dynasty," David ben Joshua Maimonides (1334–1415). Fenton even asserts that had the influence of the Maimonidean *silsila* prevailed, "the face of subsequent Judaism would have strangely resembled that of Sufism."

The impact of Muslim mysticism on Spanish and Italian Christian thought was also extremely strong, especially in the literature of love, both spiritual and profane. An unsurpassable Spanish Christian mystical text, *The Book of the Lover and the Beloved*, bears a title reminiscent of Hallaj, but it was written by the thirteenth-century Catalan Franciscan and classic author Raimón Llull. It includes an explicit reference explaining its composition by Blanquerna, Llull's imaginary philosophical hero: "A Saracen [i.e., Arab] once told him that the Muslims have various holy men. The most esteemed among these or any others are some people called Sufis. They offer words of love and brief examples that inspire a person to great devotion. Their words require exposition, and thanks to the exposition the Intellect rises higher, which develops it and spurs the Will to devotion. After considering this, Blanquerna proposed to make a book in this manner."

The master of all shaykhs, Muhyid'din Ibn Arabi, remains the most sublime representative of European Islam in its Spanish form. Like so many Sufis, he began experiencing transcendent visions as a young man, but he possessed insights so exceptional that he is not only the most admired figure among spiritual Muslims but has also touched thousands of Westerners interested in his message today.

For the Sufis of Ibn Arabi's time, controversies over Al-Ghazali were particularly troubling. Ibn Arabi recalled that one spiritual seeker, Abu Abd Allah bin Zain of Évora, in the Alentejo region of south-central Portugal, soon to be taken back from Muslim rule, was struck blind while reading a polemic against Al-Ghazali composed by a judge from Córdoba, Ibn Hamdin (died 1127). Bin Zain of Évora prayed and pledged he would no longer touch the book, and his sight returned. Ibn Hamdin, according to Ibn Arabi, had ordered the burning of Al-Ghazali's works and once had a dream in which he saw Al-Ghazali dragging a pig—a most repugnant animal to Muslims, as to religious Jews—on an iron chain. Ibn Hamdin asked about the pig and was told that it was Ibn Hamdin himself, who would so remain in the power of Al-Ghazali until he could adequately account for his hostility toward him.

Ibn Arabi frequented the leading Sufis of Muslim Spain and Morocco, whose lives he collected in biographical notes, similar to the Sufi dictionary of Attar, and which have been published in English as *Sufis of Andalusia*. These sketches provide a unique panorama of Spanish Islamic culture and are full of illumination. Many of the Spanish and Moroccan Sufis earned their sustenance by hard work, in the main cities of Sevilla and Fez as well as in smaller Spanish towns such as Ronda and Jérez. Ibn Arabi encountered Abd Allah Ibn Jadun Al-Hinnawi, "the henna sifter," on a visit to Fez. When he came to the fabled and mystical Moroccan town, Ibn Arabi learned that many people wanted to visit him, but he took refuge in the main mosque used for the Friday Muslim collective prayer. Those who inquired of him if Ibn

Arabi was present he told to keep looking for him, echoing the advice of Al-Bastami in similar circumstances.

Meeting Al-Hinnawi, Ibn Arabi recognized the humble dealer in hair dye, who was always poorly dressed and covered with dust from his work, as one of the four "poles of existence" whose presence is deemed necessary by God for the continuation of the world. But Al-Hinnawi "had asked God to remove his good repute from the hearts of people in the world. When he was absent he wasn't missed and when he was present nobody asked his advice; when he came to a town he received no welcome and when people spoke together they overlooked or ignored him." Al-Hinnawi had a severe speech impediment and could enunciate clearly only when reciting the *Qur'an*. Ibn Arabi notes how Al-Hinnawi used this handicap to his advantage: "If he spoke he appeared foolish, when he sat with others they got up and left, and his presence was found tiresome in a group. This situation was pleasing to him"—that is, it provided him with the solitude needed to pursue metaphysics. He was not the only henna sifter among the Andalusian Sufis; others were employed in such demanding, unscholarly trades as tailoring, pottery, ship-caulking, shoemaking, or tannery work. The last was (and is) extremely unpleasant because of the smell left on the human body by the odor of hides, but it comprised a key element in the economies of Muslim Spain and Morocco, "Morocco leather" remaining a prized commodity through the centuries. Of a Sufi called Abu Ali Hasan, "the Tanner," Ibn Arabi commented, "He never uttered the word 'I.' "

Given the tumult in the Iberian Peninsula during the centuries of the Christian Reconquest, it is unsurprising to find that many of the Sufis that Ibn Arabi memorialized had undergone remarkable adventures. Abu Jafar Al-Uryani of Loule, in the Portuguese Algarve south of Alentejo, had been captured by Christians, even though his mystical power allowed him to warn other members of a caravan he traveled with of an imminent Christian raid. He paid a ransom and returned to Muslim territory, which then included Sevilla.

IBN ARABI BEGAN TRAVELING through North Africa and the East after he reached age thirty. He performed the *hajj* to Mecca and journeyed to Mosul in Kurdistan. In the following years he circulated among the main cities of the eastern Mediterranean, Arabia, and Iraq but came to reside permanently in Damascus, where his tomb is a frequent destination for Sufi pilgrims.

He wrote hundreds of works, many of which have survived. These include the widely studied *Fusus al-Hikam* (*Seals of Wisdom*), in which the author summarized the metaphysics of monotheism from Adam (considered a prophet in Islam) to Muhammad. The *Fusus,* as it is known among Sufis, includes most of the Jewish prophets and three pre-Muslim Arab prophets, Hud, Salih, and Shuayb, along with John the Baptist and Jesus, plus an Arab man of wisdom, Luqman, and another Muslim figure, Khalid. It has generated at least a hundred major works of commentary in the literatures of Muslim countries and inspired the scholarship of two of the best twentieth-century Western commentators on Islamic philosophy, Henry Corbin and William C. Chittick.

A larger and more difficult work for the admirers of Ibn Arabi is *Al-Futuhat Al-Makkiya* (*Meccan Openings*), an encyclopedic compendium of Islamic metaphysics. Ibn Arabi developed many principles that have attained universal standing in Sufism, including that of *al-insan al-kamil* (the perfected human) and the conception of God as *wujud* (being). *Wujud* had earlier meant, in Sufism, "mystical comprehension," but in the work of Ibn Arabi it came to be equated with the totality of God and Creation.

The most impressive achievement of Ibn Arabi for newcomers to Sufism, especially those of a literary nature, is his collection of metaphysical love poems, *Tarjuman al-Ashwaq*, or *The Interpreter of Desires*, known to some authorities as *Stars and Sparks of Mystical Love Revealed*. This extraordinary poetical compilation influenced Jews and Christians as well as Muslims. The great twentieth-century Jerusalem-born Kabbalistic rabbi Ariel Bension—the only modern Jewish Sufi of significance—identified Ibn Arabi as a Muslim author of visions of paradise. Bension wrote of Ibn Arabi's "crucible of . . . poetic imagination," in which he "re-created" and evoked "an artistic description" of the world to come, "far superior and far more beautiful than anything that had been conceived up to his time." Bension equated the work of Ibn Arabi with the *Zohar* (*Splendor*), the great imaginative classic of Kabbalah, which was also produced in Spain.

But *The Interpreter of Desires*, overflowing with passionate images, is truly a Muslim equivalent of the Jewish *Song of Songs*. The work of Ibn Arabi seems to fully embody the "dance of the camps" under the starry desert night evoked in the verses of Solomon. The classic edition of Ibn Arabi's odes also includes the poet's commentaries on them. The author himself identified the images in the verses with specific spiritual lessons, and his own prefaces explained the circumstances under which the poems were composed.

*The Interpreter of Desires* emerged from Ibn Arabi's first pilgrimage to Mecca, where he encountered mystics from Iran. His host in the city had an adolescent daughter, Nizam, who was "exceedingly beautiful," in the poet's words, and "renowned for her asceticism and eloquent preaching." Ibn Arabi added in one version that he would say more about her physical and moral perfection but was deterred by the temptation of sin. Nevertheless, he poured into his verses a desire of such intensity that it seems a force of nature, and of such inspiration it could transform the whole of Creation. He wrote:

*When she walks on the glass pavement*[8] *you see a sun on a*
    *celestial sphere . . .*
*When she kills with her glances, her speech restores to life, as if*
    *she, as a giver of life, were Jesus.*
*The smoothness of her legs is like the brightness of the Torah, and*
    *I follow it and walk in its steps as if I were Moses.*
*She is a female bishop, a daughter of Rome, unadorned, with a*
    *radiant goodness.*
*Wild is she, none can make her his friend; in her solitary chamber*
    *she has a tomb for remembrance;*
*She has baffled every learned scholar in our religion, every*
    *student of the Psalms of David, every Jewish doctor, and every*
    *Christian priest.*

The poet's commentary explains each startling image in his text as a reference to mystical study. She, who is wisdom, walks arrogantly, proud of her power over the heart. Death by the glance of the beautiful woman symbolizes complete loss of the self in contemplation of God. The text also shows the extent and force of Ibn Arabi's belief in the unity of monotheism. *Torah* has four faces, our Muslim believer writes with devotion: these are the *Pentateuch*, the *Psalms*, the *Gospels*, and the *Qur'an*. Later in the work appears his most famous statement:

*My heart is a pasture for gazelles and a convent of Christian*
    *monks,*
*A temple for idols and the Ka'bah of pilgrims,*

*The Tablets of the Law in* Torah *and the Book of* Qur'an.
*I follow the religion of Love, wherever Love takes me,*
*There is my religion and my faith.*

Ibn Arabi also composed a major work, the *Kitab 'Anqa Mughrib* or *Book of the Fabulous Gryphon,* that exalts the second coming of Jesus. Ibn Arabi's view of the unity of monotheism reflects *wahdat ul-wujud,* or unity of all things. Baba Rexheb wrote of *wahdat ul-wujud,* "The theory provoked the established Muslim clergy and turned the scholars into fierce opponents of one another. The theory postulates that each essence is nothing more than the essence of the Creator . . . Everything in this world must be created and remains created by the Creator, Almighty God . . . *Wahdat ul-wujud* sees only *one* essence existing in the world."

An outstanding Christian historian of Spanish Islam, the Catholic priest Miguel Asín Palacios, studied the work of Ibn Arabi in depth, describing it as "Christianized Islam." Asín Palacios further demonstrated that the metaphysics of Saint John of the Cross (1542–1591), the supreme Spanish Christian versifier, paralleled that of the Shazali order of Sufis, which to the present day is widely present in North Africa, Syria, and Arabia. Saint John of the Cross would be named, with his elder contemporary Saint Teresa of Ávila (1515–1582), as one of the thirty-three Catholic Doctors of the Church. (She too knew the work of the Sufis.) The most famous conception of Saint John of the Cross, that of a sublime "dark night of the soul," is redolent of Sufism and Judaism alike. The *Qur'an* praises spiritual Jews for their habit of nocturnal prayer, enthusiastically taken up by Sufis, since prayer at night is undisturbed by the demands of life in daytime.

Asín Palacios also found a powerful Sufi influence in the work of Dante, who is often called the preeminent Christian poet. Nevertheless, his lovely collection of poems along with commentaries, *La Vita Nuova* (*The New Life*), greatly resembles Ibn Arabi's *Interpreter of Desires,* and the structured descent into hell in the *Divine Comedy* reproduces, in an opposite direction, the Night Journey of Muhammad to heaven. Asín Palacios believed he had proven that similarities between the works of Dante and Ibn Arabi identified Dante as an imitator of the Sufi.

Thus it was that in Arab Spain Islamic metaphysics flourished, then suffused and transformed the other religious traditions. Sufism made possible cultural and spiritual glory among all believers, and even pointed the way to the Renaissance. Let us imagine that on the global scale the same kind of fruitful exchange, notwithstanding the prevalence of fear and terror, can be realized today in the hearts of people like you who read this book—and not merely the volume you hold in your hand but a continuous, living book of metaphysics that unites many pages, and many individuals, as one, and with God.

# 2

## Turkish Sufism and Interfaith Coexistence

THE GREAT RUMI WROTE in Persian but among Muslims has equal standing in Turkish translations, reflecting his impact on both cultures and his life journey. He was born on the eastern border of Persian influence, at Balkh in today's Afghanistan, but migrated to new lands taken by the Muslims in his era from the Christians in Asia Minor. Rumi participated in one of the most important aspects of Sufism, least understood by Westerners: the movement of central Asian Muslim mystics toward Europe, along with the Turkish advance heralded by the missionary work of Hallaj centuries before. Like his friend and teacher Ibn Arabi, as well as his acquaintance Hajji Bektash (1209–1271), Rumi may represent "Christianized Islam."

The year 2007 marked Rumi's eight hundredth birthday and was declared "The Year of Rumi" by international cultural organizations. An apostle of love, Rumi taught an Islam of the kind praised, also in 2007, by a special study of the RAND Corporation, *Building Moderate Muslim Networks*. The RAND document proposed a global alliance between the democracies and moderate Muslims, comparable to the cold war effort by Western governments that supported anti-Communist liberals and social democrats who undermined Soviet rule. Anti-extremist Muslims from the Balkans through central Asia to Southeast Asia could encircle and challenge radical Islam based in the core Arab countries and Iran.

Rumi easily symbolizes a meeting of Western aspirations and Eastern metaphysics. He represented the generation after the Spanish Muslim Ibn Arabi, and as Jalal-al-din from central Asia became Rumi or "European," and "the guide," or Mevlana, so Islam turned its face from east to west and Sufism consolidated its organized aspect. Rumi's life (1207–1273) paralleled those of a distinguished Catalan Jewish Kabbalist, Moshe ben Nahman or Nahmanides (1194–1270), and the Catalan Franciscan Raimón Llull (1235–1315). We cannot establish how much any of these three knew of each other, but their coincidence in time may embody a single wave, at the crest of a spiritual revolution in both Christian and Muslim lands. The Christian spiritual orders dedicated to self-denial, such as the Franciscans, had earlier emerged simultaneously with similar Sufi groups, and historians speculate on how much they knew of one another. Institutionalization of mystic study occurred in the thirteenth century in all three religions. Mevlana and Hajji Bektash differed from the preceding Islamic figures, Hallaj, Al-Ghazali, and Ibn Arabi, in that Rumi and Hajji Bektash are identified as mentors of outstanding Sufi *tariqas*.

Yet like the eminent Sufis who came before him, Rumi showed an aptitude for mysticism in childhood, and he was given the title Mevlana while quite young, when he had already begun teaching. He was influenced by his father, Baha al-din Walad, to mature early and shun childish games for study and self-discipline. Rumi gained considerable wisdom from the saints of central Asia. But his father came into conflict with the local ruler in Balkh. With the threat of Mongol invasion also rising, Mevlana's father took the family to Syria, not a moment too soon, for their homeland was almost immediately devastated by the armies of Chinggis Khan.

The family traveled to Damascus by way of Baghdad and Mecca, and Rumi spent time with Ibn Arabi and Attar. Mystic study was, for Mevlana, the whole of life; he once commented, "My life is no more than these three phrases: I was raw, I was cooked, I was burned." He moved to Konya in Anatolia, and there he is said to have met a famous dervish, Shemsud'din or Shems of Tabriz, whose insight would impel Rumi to mystical ecstasy. Encountering Rumi in the marketplace at a stall of candy makers, Shems demanded that Mevlana answer whether Muhammad the Prophet or Al-Bastami the intoxicated Sufi was greater. Rumi explained that the Prophet was greater because while Al-Bastami found enough in a sip of knowledge, the Prophet's thirst for understanding constantly grew and he came closer to God in that way.

Shems joined Mevlana but abandoned him after less than a year and a half, out of irritation at the jealousy of Rumi's other disciples. Shems returned a little more than a year later and found Mevlana in a sublime state, performing his circular *dhikr* on one foot while composing verses, in the practice known as *sama'* or spiritual music. Unfortunately, the attitudes among those who studied under Rumi had not changed, and within only eight months Shems vanished, apparently dead. At first Mevlana refused to accept that Shems was gone. But a biography of Rumi published by the Diyanet, the official Islamic religious authority in Turkey, says that after searching for Shems, Rumi was content to keep him alive in his heart. In a literary touch that seems almost postmodern, Rumi called part of his own writings "The Works of Shems of Tabriz."

Mevlana often describes Shems in terms of intense physical affection, yet the possibility of such an attraction being anything but spiritual appears unlikely given the advanced age of Shems when he encountered

Rumi. In the best translation of Mevlana into English (slightly adapted here), by the Turkish expert Nevit O. Ergin, Rumi recalls,

> *I saw an old man, his eyes were red.*
> *His hair and beard were white as milk.*
>
> *I saw a gazelle immediately run toward him.*
> *Skies split, it was such a trick.*
> *The bowl of the sun and moon were broken*
> *Because of the rising uproar,*
> *Because the jugs of the drunks were completely full.*
>
> *I asked the auspicious Soul,*
> *"What is happening?"*
> *He answered, "I am not my self, I don't know myself.*
> *All this must be*
> *At that mischievous old man's instigation."*

The text ends,

> *O Shems of Tabriz,*
> *You know the situation of drunks.*
> *O my Master, if I made a mistake, forgive me.*
> *I have no heart, no hand.*

Mevlana repeatedly refers to Shems as elderly; Shems himself knew another important Sufi, Shihab ad-Din Suhrawardi (1153–1191), who died almost twenty years before Rumi's birth. Born in Iran, Suhrawardi was executed at the instance of fundamentalists. Author of *The Science of Illumination*, Suhrawardi dedicated his extensive writings to a merging of the Zoroastrian thought that had so long ruled his native land with Platonic philosophy and Islam. Shems had also, like Mevlana, conversed with Ibn Arabi.

Rumi insistently evoked Shems in a language of passion, for example:

*The shape of Shemsud'din of Tabriz,*
*His face, his eyes are the soul to the Soul of Love.*
*This has been written in the book of love*
*From the beginning of the beginning.*

Or this:

*Shems of Tabriz's drunken narcissus eyes*
*Are so much like the gazelle's eyes*
*That this gazelle hunts the lions.*

In one of his most rhapsodic texts, Mevlana wrote,

*O morning breeze,*
*Bring a smell from Shemsud'din's face to us . . .*
*What is the head if it is sacrificed to Shemsud'din?*
*I will be scattered under his feet.*
*Mention the name of Shemsud'din*
*And I will give my life.*

*My heart has been dressed auspiciously*
*By his love.*
*My outer clothing is the beauty of Shemsud'din,*
*My underclothing is his love.*

We are drunk from the smell of Shemsud'din.
We are drunk from Shemsud'din's glass.
Give us the wine, cup-bearer.

Our nose is full of Shemsud'din's smell . . .
Shemsud'din stays in the heart.
Shemsud'din talks with the Soul.
Shemsud'din is a peerless pearl.
Shemsud'din is a coin in the hand.

I am not alone in crying,
"Shemsud'din, Shemsud'din."
The nightingales in the garden
And the partridge on the mountain
Are looking for him.

The beauty of beauties is Shemsud'din.
The garden of heaven is Shemsud'din.
The apple of the human eye is Shemsud'din.
The praise of great men is also Shemsud'din.

Bright day is Shemsud'din.
Shining moon is Shemsud'din.
The pearl in the shell is Shemsud'din.
Day and night are Shemsud'din.

The glass of King Jamshid[1] is Shemsud'din.
The endless ocean is Shemsud'din.
The breath of Jesus is Shemsud'din.
The face of Joseph[2] is Shemsud'din.

*I pray to God wholeheartedly,*
*To enter the Kingdom with him.*
*The Soul will stand between us,*
*With Shemsud'din in our arms.*

*Shemsud'din is more beautiful than the Soul . . .*
*Wine and drunkenness is Shemsud'din.*
*Fire and light is Shemsud'din.*

*This is not the drunkenness*
*Which brings trouble, sorrow and regret.*
*Drunkenness coming from Shemsud'din*
*Adds pride to the pride of man.*

*O guide of lovers, O Prophet of lovers*
*O Shems of Tabriz, come,*
*Never pull your hand away from us.*

Rumi writes elsewhere,

*Shems of Tabriz has a seat at the throne,*
*Like the Sultan.*
*My poems are like the best of slaves*
*Standing in rows in front of him.*

Given the personal associations of Mevlana and Shems with Ibn Arabi, a Sufi might argue that Ibn Arabi transmitted the beauty of his own personality, by way of the aged Shems, to Rumi. Ibn Arabi is believed by Sufis to embody "the light of Muhammad" and to introduce himself long after his physical death into the dream life of privileged mystics as a bright presence. Sufis trust in guidance by the souls of dead teachers; this is one explanation for the presence in the Muslim world of Sufis who have no known shaykh or master. Baba Rexheb Beqiri derived the concept of "Muhammadan light" from Hallaj and traced it through Ibn Arabi to the Bektashi Sufis of today.

The *Qur'an* and the *Mesnevi* of Mevlana—Rumi's encyclopedic collection of Sufi parables and stories rendered as verse—are the only two books placed in all Turkish Sunni mosques. Rumi, translated from Persian into Turkish, is not the only Sufi to transcend his mother tongue, for although Ibn Arabi wrote in Arabic and Al-Ghazali in Persian, they and many others became classics in many languages spoken and written by Muslims. While Christian thought was locked up in Latin—by then a dead language—and Greek, and Jewish religious thought was restricted to Hebrew and Aramaic, neither of the latter two widely spoken in medieval times, the Sufis produced truly cosmopolitan religious writings. Mevlana has inspired many more poets in other languages.

FOR THE TURKS, SUFFERING in the thirteenth century from political conflicts, Rumi came as a consolation as well as an inspiration. Other Muslims in difficult circumstances have turned to Mevlana in the same spirit, but some have been disappointed. Recent examples come to us from the Balkans, formerly the westernmost outpost of the Turkish Empire. The Bosnian scholar Rešid Hafizović, a professor at the Faculty of Islamic Studies in Sarajevo, is one of the world's great authorities on Sufism. He has warned, in recalling the Balkan torment of the 1990s,

> In the West, Rumi's poetry and prose work miracles, creating extraordinary, positive vibrations among people. The only

place where the profuse seeds of his Sufi philosophy have failed to fall on fertile ground is the Balkans. The aggression against Bosnia-Herzegovina, the bloodbath in which tens of thousands of Bosnian Muslims (Bosniaks) died, the ethnic cleansing and seizure by the Serbs of the homes in which Bosniaks had lived for centuries: all these constitute compelling evidence that the universal, completely human ideas of Rumi were far from the ears and minds of the Balkan peoples—and this despite the fact that not only in Bosnia-Herzegovina, but also in Croatia and Serbia, Macedonia and Bulgaria, there were many dervish houses (*tekkes, tekijas,* or *teqes*), and many of them belonged to Rumi's Mawlawi *tariqa,* or order.

Nor did it help that major works from Rumi's Sufi opus had already been translated into the languages of the Balkan peoples, and extensive commentaries written on them in those same languages, with particular reference to Rumi's ideas and ideal universal religion of Love, which sees in every one of us the supreme Divine creation, and the most exalted evidence of the Divine Spirit taking up its eternal abode within us. National myths, nationalized spirituality, national exclusivity and total spiritual blindness, particularly among the peoples of the Eastern Balkans (Serbia, Bulgaria, Macedonia), left no space for the values of Rumi's Sufi, universal religion of Love.

According to Hafizović, had the legacy of Rumi prevailed, "the Balkans would by now be a spiritual oasis, a breeding ground and source of the fecund Sufi metaphysics of the kind that Rumi's universal religion of Love has already generated in many other parts of the world."

As a contribution to "The Year of Rumi," a celebration was held in Sarajevo, capital of Bosnia-Herzegovina, at the end of March 2007. Balkan Muslim cultures are among those most deeply marked by Sufism, and were singled out in the 2007 RAND report as a base for partnership with the democratic powers in the strengthening of moderate Islam. But at the same time, events in the Balkans showed a growing parallel with Iraq in that Wahhabi missionaries, terror recruiters and financiers, and other malefactors had begun a new offensive in that distressed region.

From exquisitely decorated mosques in the Albanian-speaking lands to Bosnia itself, Wahhabi men in distinctive untrimmed beards and short Arab-style breeches (worn in supposed emulation of Muhammad), accompanied by women in face veils and full body coverings, appeared, distributing the money and literature of reactionary Saudis and Pakistanis. They attempted a local revival of their "jihad"—simultaneously with their renewed campaigns of terrorism in Morocco, Algeria, and Western Europe. In the Balkans, their targets were the local traditional Muslims, as well as the Sufis.

Albanians were mainly hostile to the Wahhabis. The historian of Islam H. T. Norris has correctly observed, "Despite its small size, Albania and the Albanians . . . made an outstanding contribution to Sufi thought." As a Sufi territory, the Albanian lands are inside the body of Europe, less "Eastern," and easier and less expensive to visit than Morocco, Turkey, Turkestan, India, or Indonesia—to say nothing of Saudi Arabia and Iran. But the whole Sunni world is faced with Wahhabi expansionism. Within Albania itself, Wahhabi activism had remained minimally visible, concentrating on individual outreach (*da'wa*) in mosques but still backed up by a flood of fundamentalist literature into the country.

In Kosovo, although Saudi Arabia maintained a relief office in the capital, Prishtina, Wahhabis kept an even lower profile. Not only were Kosovar Albanians outspoken in their support for the United States, but a large number of Albanian Muslims in western Kosovo, the heartland of Kosovar Albanian patriotism, are Sufis, and Bektashi Sufis were leading participants in the Kosovo Liberation Army (KLA). In neighboring Montenegro and the Muslim-majority districts of South Serbia, the Wahhabi controversy was more open and even violent: Wahhabis disrupted regular religious activities and were involved in gunfire between ordinary people, as well as in fatal confrontations with local police. But in those areas the Wahhabis targeted Slav Muslims, not Albanians.

Kosovo includes the *turbe,* or tomb, of the Ottoman Sultan Murat, killed at the battle of Kosovo in 1389; the structure is a traditional place of Muslim pilgrimage, and I have visited it. The most prominent Balkan battleground in 2007 was the undeveloped but animated town of Tetova, in western Macedonia, which is particularly known for its Sufi traditions. Many local Albanians in the district are followers of Hajji Bektash. The Bektashis are without doubt the most influential Sufi order in the Balkans, and they are extremely opposed to any expression of radical Islam. Bektashis are also homicidally despised by Wahhabis, first because they are a liberal trend among Shia Muslims and, as seen in Iraq, Wahhabis loathe Shias more than they hate Jews or Christians; second because the Bektashis consume alcohol; and third because men and women are equals in Bektashi rituals, as they are in Turkish-Kurdish Alevi practices. Alevis also love Hajji Bektash. The Bektashi *babas,* as their teachers are known, have repeatedly declared to me that they are the "most progressive" element in world Islam.

Wahhabis and Bektashi Sufis in 2007 were locked in an armed standoff at the Bektashi complex known as the Harabati Baba *Teqe,* in Tetova. This large enclave of varied structures is famous throughout the region and appears on Tetova's municipal shield. In 2002, however, a group of Wahhabis equipped with automatic weapons took advantage of the post-Communist chaos in which property claims were left unsettled, as well as recent Slav-Albanian ethnic fighting in Macedonia, to occupy a major edifice inside the Harabati location. The seized building was formerly used for Sufi meditation.

I visited the Harabati *Teqe,* not for the first time, in March 2007. I was invited for the central Asian pre-Islamic holiday of Nevruz, a springtime observance favored by Sufis. The Bektashis had no friends in the Macedonian government who might rescue them from their assailants, and the Wahhabis, whose Kalashnikovs are never far out of sight, had proceeded to occupy more parts of the Harabati *Teqe.* Bektashis do not perform the normal daily prayers prescribed for Muslims, but the Wahhabis had taken over a guesthouse and dubbed it a mosque, broadcasting a tape of the Islamic call to prayer in a thick and indistinct voice. (Some Wahhabis seem to delight in a guttural and hasty recitation of the call to prayer, although traditional Muslims say that an unattractive call to prayer is against religion.) The radicals also seized a central building with glass windows and covered the panes with black paper, on the pretext that women praying inside did not want to be observed. They cut down some ancient trees, an act that enraged the Sufis, who are known for their devotion to nature.

The Albanian lands therefore witnessed three of the common tactics employed by Saudi-financed extremists seeking to export the bloody terror they wreaked in Iraq. In Kosovo, they burrowed deep undercover, like moles. Where they could, they preached and recruited, as in Albania. And where government was indifferent and their chosen enemies, especially the Sufis, appeared vulnerable, as in Macedonia, they invaded, occupied, and threatened.

In long discussions with the Bektashis in Tetova, I was repeatedly assured of their willingness to assist the United States and other democratic nations in rooting out Islamist radicalism. "We want to help, but we need help," said the Bektashi leader in Tetova, Baba Edmond Brahimaj, as he sketched out for me the network of extremist agitation in the region—from revived centers of fundamentalism in Turkey to cells, hidden unobtrusively in places like Peshkopia, a small, ancient town set near glacial lakes in the wild mountains of eastern Albania. The Bektashis daily watched their historic institution in Tetova fall under the control of fanatics bent on their destruction. Although they have many sympathizers, few were prepared to disrupt their own lives in a confrontation with the Wahhabis.

All over Europe, moderate Muslims no less than non-Muslims expected their governments to act against radical Islam, and all those waiting seemed destined to despair. Western European states appeared frozen in postures of accommodation, willful oblivion, ignorance, and simple denial of the reality: the radical Islamist enemy could not be beaten without an effective, determined Muslim counterjihad, assisted (but not directed) by Westerners.

I THEN RETURNED, AFTER many previous and lengthy visits, to Sarajevo in spring 2007, for the celebration of Rumi's eighth centennial. I found a city reminiscent of Barcelona during the Spanish civil war, described by George Orwell in *Homage to Catalonia* as suffering under a "horrible atmosphere produced by fear, suspicion, hatred." The Saudi-Wahhabis played a minor role in the Bosnian war of 1992–95 but attempted to use the aftermath of that combat, which left Bosnia prostrate, to turn the local Muslims, with their own Sufi and visibly life-affirming sensibility, into dour fundamentalists. After the atrocities of September 11, 2001, the Wahhabis seemed to have failed in Bosnia. But their strategy was different in Sarajevo from those seen in Tetova or Tirana.

The Bosnian capital is more European, more modern, more globally connected—and there, paradoxically, the colossal Saudi checkbook works even better than extremist rhetoric or direct confrontation does in poorer places. In developed cities, politicians and religious functionaries have more to gain or lose in their fight for place. In rural Albania, the Wahhabis may hand out money to ordinary people, but in Sarajevo, powerful individuals are for sale. Prominent Bosnian Muslim moderates had become, in 2007, hesitant to speak out or to associate themselves, as they previously did, with condemnation of Wahhabism, even though physical clashes in the region had fed an attitude of volatile resentment toward the Wahhabis in village mosques.

Wahhabis had successfully penetrated Bosnia's main Islamic institutions. Sadly, this was unsurprising to those who knew Bosnian religious history. The Bosnian scholar Jasna Samić, who had suffered the indignity of being accused of fundamentalism only because she (as did I) wrote for a local Muslim magazine, investigated why the Bektashi Sufis, now under Wahhabi assault in Macedonia, seemed to have left no trace in Bosnia. She concluded darkly,

> The general orthodoxy of "Sunnism" in Bosnia-Herzegovina had increased in the course of history: Bosnia became more "Sunni" with the coming of the Austrians [who took power in the land in 1878], and became yet more pronounced in [the former] Yugoslavia. Rigidity, intolerance, the authoritarianism of local clerics, formalism, and dogmatism (present in every area) along with ideas of orderliness and good manners, fear of lib-

eration, etc., finally expressed nothing more than anxiety over the loss of power. All this is comprehensible if one grasps that in this milieu the "semiliterate" dominate . . . Bosnian Sufis agree that Bektashism never had great success in Bosnia because of the strong presence of other [Sunni] orders such as the Naqshbandis and Qadiris, and the great influence of the clerics. It is likely that they could not root themselves in the region because of their non-conformism.

Ordinary Bosnians, however, tended to disregard the Sunni bigots and, even if they could not participate in Bektashism, sang and otherwise celebrated rebels, including a radical Sufi group, the Hamzevis. As a traditional Bosnian song acclaiming a Sarajevo bandit said, the ruling empire was built on evil, a Shia and radical Sufi concept.

And so, amid rumor and resentment, a Sarajevo commemoration of Rumi was held on March 30, 2007, at the Faculty of Islamic Sciences, a nineteenth-century neo-Moorish building on a high hill overlooking Sarajevo. Rešid Hafizović, who had emerged as a leading enemy of the Wahhabis, said, "[Rumi] calls for friendship, collaboration, peace and fraternal relations between people, invoking love towards all human beings as the supreme Divine creation, regardless of the religious, cultural, civilizational or spiritual garments in which each of us, as mundane beings, is clad. As a result, when Rumi died, his funeral was attended by mourners of many faiths: Muslims, but also Christians, Jews, Hindus and others. His words seem to have resonated with each of them on that sad day:

*Whoever you may be, come*
*Even though you may be*
*An unbeliever, a pagan or a fire-worshipper, come*

*Our brotherhood is not one of despair*
*Even though you may have broken*
*Your vows of repentance a hundred times, come."*

The lecture hall at the Islamic Faculty was crowded during Professor Hafizović's presentation, with no Wahhabi beards, bizarre outfits, or censorious comments discernible. The program included poems of Rumi set to the guitar, a style of religious performance that is extremely popular in the Balkans despite the Wahhabis' loathing of music sung to anything other than a primitive drum, even when its content is religious. The chorus repeated the most characteristic motif of Mevlana's work: "Only come." Special honor was extended to, and a series of commentaries were provided by, the ninety-year-old Hafiz Halid Hadžimulić, who has completed a translation of the *Mesnevi* into Bosnian and is the "grand-shaykh" of Bosnian Sufis. But in a fairly typical example of the clouded and unpredictable environment in Sarajevo, the old shaykh, so deaf his voice had become extremely high-pitched, had been absurdly accused of support for Wahhabism by local "post-Communist" gutter media. The city was filled with disinformation from all sides; radical Islam seemed to derange the Bosnia that loves Rumi.

Still, a novel aspect of the event was provided by a delegation of three Arabs, a teacher and two imams, from a Sufi school, the Al-Qasemi Academy, in Israel. Holders of Israeli passports and integrated into the Israeli social system, they offered a fresh view of the Middle East to the Bosnians. Perhaps the most surprising message brought by the Al-Qasemi delegation involved their description of the *Shariah* courts maintained by the state of Israel for resolution of disputes among Muslims. *Shariah* courts are scarce in the Balkans, and the explanation that Israel recognizes religious courts for Jews, Muslims, and, if they request them, Christians alongside its civil judicial apparatus, with the right of anybody to opt in or out of the alternative systems, was provocative to the Bosnian Muslims.

By welcoming their Israeli Arab brethren, Bosnians demonstrated that the spirit of Mevlana is a living and positive element in the culture of global Islam. Rumi—and Sufism—are more important for Muslims themselves than for Western readers looking for a few pages of easy enlightenment. Rumi, the "European," should symbolize a reborn, cooperative mentality in relations between Islam and the West. Yet in the streets of the Balkan towns, the terrorist enemy was once again present, and though recitations of Sufi texts may invigorate an alternative to extremism, they cannot suffice to defeat it. Wahhabi terrorism could not be allowed to be exported out of Iraq, whether to Sarajevo, or Surabaya in Indonesia, or the mosques and Islamic schools of Western Europe and North America, as it had radiated, once before, from Taliban-ruled Afghanistan.

Modern society is filled with nostalgia for the epoch of Rumi, the medieval Jewish Kabbalists, and the Christian mystic Llull, for their religious certainty no less than their cultural achievements. Until the ideal moment arrives when the world will again produce spiritually as well as technologically astute leaders, the sincerity, eloquence, and sensuality of Rumi will have much to say, to an audience not limited to mystical devotees and poets.

LET US NOW TURN farther eastward in search of the forerunners of the Bektashi Sufis who confront radical Islam in the Balkans—around a constellation of Islamic shrines in places as disparate as Hungary, Turkey, and Uzbekistan but centered on Turkestan in central Asia. In all their strivings, the Sufis we have discussed anticipated a reconcilia-

tion of East and West, of Islamic, Christian, and Jewish religious legacies. Among the Persians, Hallaj was associated with the personality of
Jesus in the minds of observers like Massignon, while Al-Ghazali cited
examples from the Gospels in his teaching. Ibn Arabi comes to us as
the earliest example of an illustrious, truly European Muslim, although
the Spain in which he lived, then as now, was distant from the heart
of the continent. Rumi, also Persian in origin, became known as
"European" because of his proximity to the Christian lands. Each of
these developments represented Islam looking outward as it refined its
metaphysics. This was a spiritual rather than a military attitude. But to
understand such a process, we must go to the central Asian Muslim
hinterland.

The early Turkish Sufis, Hojja Ahmad Yasawi (1103–1161?),
known to some as Kara Ahmet or "Black Ahmad," and Hajji Bektash,
brought a distinct vigor to Islamic metaphysics. Ottoman Islam stands
apart in history from the rest of the global Muslim community for several notable reasons. First, to emphasize, the Turkic people were not
conquered by the Arabs or Persians; they freely adopted Islam, giving
a definitive answer to those who dishonestly claim the faith of Muhammad was propagated only by the sword. A famous Turkish historian of
Sufism (and political figure), Mehmet Fuat Köprülü (1890–1966), declared that "dervishes, armed with an ecstatic religious love, introduced new beliefs among the nomadic Turks." But after the Sufis called
the Turks to Islam, the Turks began their career of conquest, and Sufis became their main exponents of the faith.

Some Turkish peoples, by contrast, became and remain Christians
(like the Gagauz of the western Black Sea coast and the Chuvash in
central Russia) or converted to Judaism (the Crimean Tatar Karaites),
while others held to the Buddhism of their Mongol cousins or to their
original shamanic religion. Although Turkish citizens are mainly

Sunni, the Turkish-speaking Azeris of Azerbaijan and neighboring lands are Shia, and as we see in the Turkish and Kurdish Alevi communities, some believers combine Shia Islam and Sufism with shamanism. Further, among the Turks, Islamic clerical hostility to Sufism was, at least at the beginning, largely absent. The persecutions inflicted on figures such as Hallaj were long unknown to them.

Energetic as they were, once the majority of Turks became Muslim, they drove across Asia, west into the heart of Christian Europe. They also pressed south into India, establishing the Mughal dynasty, named because of the mixed Turkish and Mongol ancestry of the conqueror Amir Timur (Timur Leng or Tamerlane, 1336–1405). The Turks were exceptional builders and left extraordinary monuments everywhere they went, including mosques, schools, bridges, palaces, and beautiful houses. They rescued the Jews expelled from Spain and Portugal at the end of the fifteenth century and helped erect hundreds of synagogues, religious schools, large burial grounds, and other properties for the use of the Jewish believers. Ottoman Islam, even with the retreat and defeat of its imperial power in the nineteenth and twentieth centuries, left a permanent religious presence—the Balkan Muslim heritage—in Europe, long after the end of Arab Islam in Spain.

The Turks conquered Constantinople, fulfilling a vision of the Prophet Muhammad that no Arab or Persian could attain. The Turkish entry into Europe merged three cultural types. The egalitarian, God-centered Semites (Hebrew and Arabic), with their widely distributed populations, and the teeming, hierarchical, priest-led Indo-European peoples—from the Nordics to the Persians—were now infused with the bloodlines of a vast shamanic culture. Although never unified in language or society, shamanism encompassed a single, wide stream—from the central Asian steppes west as far as the Balkans and east through Siberia. This great spiritual artery branched off in one direction to Manchuria and Korea, but also crossed the Arctic land bridge to the Western Hemisphere and extended through indigenous America, before the arrival of European explorers; it survives today in Native American cultures. The Turks breathed the same atmosphere as the Siberian hunters, the Arctic fishermen, the peoples of the Great Plains and Rocky Mountains in the American West, and even of the Sierra Madre Occidental in Mexico. One may think of the mountains of Albania, of Turkestan, of British Columbia and Colorado, of Chihuahua—and of their spiritual otherness—as alike.

Shamanism pervaded Turkish Sufism, instilling it with psychological openness, a deep love of freedom, and the fundamental values of a "steppe democracy," reinforcing the relevance of current Turkish, Kurdish, central Asian, and Balkan Muslim efforts toward the restoration of pluralism, and modernization, in Islam. In Turkestan, with its infinite sky, limitless empty land, and a backbone in the form of the "Mountains of Heaven"—the Tianshan range—thousands of holy men have lived: shamans, followers of the Iranian religions, Christians, Buddhists, and Muslims. Filled with the presence of ancient mysticism, day and night one seems to hear the murmur of spirits that have passed beyond.

With Hojja Ahmad Yasawi, the "saint of Turkestan," and his teachers, the great epoch of Turkish Islam, entirely expressed in Sufism, begins. It is said that notwithstanding his Islam, Hojja Yasawi maintained good relations with the shamans and Buddhists among his neighbors, and, like certain other forms of Sufism, the Yasawi tradition has fused Sunni and Shia Islam. His own instruction and methods, as well as the regulations he developed for his students, have had a lasting influence; his organizing principles were adopted by many Sufi orders. These rules include obedience, conviction, loyalty of the seeker to his teacher, and secrecy about Sufi teachings.

Baba Rexheb writes of Hojja Yasawi, "He lost his father when he was six years old. He then went to the city of Yasi, at that time the capital of Turkestan, and settled there. Upon completing his studies he moved to Bukhara where he met the great Sufi scholar, Yusuf Hamadani. Within a short time Ahmad Yasawi became, among his followers, the most important caliph [successor in teaching]. By Hamadani's request, Hojja Yasawi took his place after his death."

Abu Yaqub Yusuf Al-Hamadani, who died in the twelfth century, is believed to have also taught Abdul Qadri Jilani, of Baghdad, mentor of the Qadiri Sufis. Al-Hamadani is thought to have spoken Persian alone and not Turkish, and to have lived an extremely simple life, refusing any luxuries or contact with rulers or other prominent people. He is said to have been accompanied at all times by Al-Khidr, the "green man" or "spring man," an Islamic representation of eternal metaphysics, described as an immortal mystical companion to Moses but also associated with the Hebrew prophet Elijah. Al-Hamadani, in one of his most praiseworthy aspects, is reported never to have accused a Muslim of unbelief.

One of Hojja Yasawi's colleagues as a caliph of Al-Hamadani was Abd Al-Khaliq Ghujduwani (d. 1142), inspirer of another Sufi order, the Naqshbandis. Eventually, Hojja Yasawi, for reasons unknown, decided to move from Bukhara back to Yasi and left the rest of the circle of Sufis to the leadership of Ghujduwani. Baba Rexheb notes that "Hojja Yasawi had acquired great fame with his book of poems, *Divan-i Hikmat.*" The title is best translated as *Poems in Praise of Wisdom,* and its verses may have been composed by Hojja Yasawi's followers and successors rather than the Sufi himself. Hojja Yasawi's spectacular tomb complex in Yasi is known as the *Ka'bah* of Turkestan, a parallel to the Holy House in Mecca, and pilgrimages to it may be more important for Turkic Muslims than the ordinary Muslim *hajj.*

The Yasawi *turbe* is the most impressive in the system of shrines extending from eastern Europe to the steppe heartland—a physical representation of the pinnacle of Sufism in central Asia.

Turkish and Kurdish Alevis, as well as fortunate members of the Bektashi Sufi community in the Albanian lands, visit the smaller, more modest and traditional Sufi tomb of Hajji Bektash in the Turkish village where he died, which is named Hacibektaş for him. The Alevi writer Ali Sirin describes events in Hacibektaş, usually held on August 16–18, that have a festival atmosphere, including concerts and lectures as well as religious ceremonies. In the 1960s and 1970s, pilgrimages to the grave site were taken over by leftist secularists and socialist activists controlled the agenda. But in the 1990s, the Alevis regained control over the Hacibektaş observance and made it a forum for affirmation and defense of their spiritual identity. At Hacibektaş each year, hundreds of young Alevis line up in ball caps and polo shirts to pay homage at the *turbe*.

Albanian Bektashis are known to make the *hajj* to Mecca, but they also visit Hacibektaş, as well as the most significant Muslim tomb in Christian Europe, a sixteenth-century *turbe* in Budapest. This Sufi mausoleum in the Hungarian capital shelters the body of Gül Baba (d. 1541), the "father of roses," a Bektashi saint and companion of the Ottoman sultan Suleyman the Lawgiver, known to Westerners as the Magnificent. Suleyman's *Kanun*, or legal canon, based on Turkish customary law and distinct from *Shariah*, strengthened the system of justice in the Ottoman Empire, and he is honored by a plaque in the chamber of the U.S. House of Representatives. Some Islamophobes, if they knew of that bas-relief, would doubtless want to rip it off the wall. Whereas Serbian Christians have leveled the Islamic architectural heritage in the territories they conquered over the centuries, the Hungarians, notwithstanding their 175-year occupation by the Turks, have preserved the Gül Baba tomb as a national treasure.

The Hungarians may be inspired by the example of Sultan Suleyman himself. When the Lawgiver came victorious to the Hungarian capital and designated one of the churches as his personal mosque, a narrow-minded Muslim cleric called for the removal of a marble relief of Saint George slaying the dragon—an object supposedly forbidden in Islam. But Saint George has mystical standing for Muslims, being identified with Al-Khidr. Sultan Suleyman removed his own cashmere garment and covered the statue, ordering that no Muslim should look upon it and be offended, but also preserving it. The sultan may never have imagined the Christians would return to claim the church; or perhaps he did. But that Sufis go to the Gül Baba *turbe* in Budapest with nothing other than peaceful intentions is undeniable.

Albanian Bektashis honor Gül Baba in Budapest; Alevis visit Hacibektaş in Turkey to kiss the doorway at the tomb of the Sufi saint and to whisper prayers and supplications. Similarly, at the Hojja Yasawi shrine in Turkestan, in the shadow of its gleaming blue dome, couples and families walk to and fro, touching walls for blessings and watching one another circle around inside the mighty structure, built by Amir Timur and still unfinished, with rude logs protruding from its central archway.

Timur was sympathetic to Shia Islam, a historical item stridently rejected by the dictatorship of Islam Karimov ruling Sunni Uzbekistan, which seeks to replace Lenin with Timur as a Soviet-style unifying symbol. But many realities of the past are currently denied in central Asia. Under the dome of Hojja Yasawi sits an immense bronze cauldron weighing two tons, the *Taikazan*. It was used to prepare a sweetened grain pudding, called *ashura*, eaten to commemorate the martyrdom of Imam Husayn at Karbala, on the tenth of Muharrem in the Muslim calendar, which is a sacred day for Shias. The *Taikazan* at the Yasawi burial site is decorated with floral motifs and Islamic inscriptions describing the object as a gift of Amir Timur in 1399, with the name of the craftsman, Ustaz Abu'l-Aziz ibn Sharaf al-Din al-Tabrizi, and a blessing, "God is the Guardian."

IN JUNE 2004, I went to the *Ka'bah* of Turkestan—that is, to the tomb of Hojja Yasawi. Although I was invited to the region as a journalist, my main interest was as a pilgrim to the monument of this Islamic saint. While Hojja Yasawi remains the dominant figure among the Turkic Muslims of central Asia, the area is filled with evidence of the Islamic genius. Outstanding Muslim thinkers such as Ibn Sina, the great tenth-century physician known in the West as Avicenna, are claimed, along with Timur, by Uzbekistan.

The Uzbeks also consider their own such masters in the study of *hadith* as Imam ul-Bukhari (810–870) and Imam at-Tirmidhi (824–892). The neo-Stalinist Karimov government refurbished and expanded a sumptuous burial place for Imam ul-Bukhari. I had previously gone there, saw and touched the sarcophagus of the Imam, prayed, and received a blessing. The complex was then full of Uzbek couples waiting to get married; before they would have stood at a Communist monument to celebrate their love and their expectations. In 2000, Karimov opened a much smaller but elegant sepulcher, with a blue-tiled dome, for the theologian Abu Mansur Al-Maturidi (870–944) in the Chokardiza cemetery in old Samarkand.

Al-Maturidi is one of the most important writers on Islamic belief, with a conception of the Godhead that is rational and compatible with scientific inquiry. I had also gone to Al-Maturidi's dignified tomb and found the building empty; few in latter-day Samarkand apparently know who he was, and none would come to his monument to bless a wedding. Yet there I felt a spiritual intimacy greater than anywhere else among the many shrines and other holy sites I have visited—Jewish, Christian, indigenous American, Buddhist, or Muslim. Samarkand seems unique in the world: a place built to make description of it impossible. One may celebrate its cool breezes, thanks to its location in hilly country; one may enumerate its extraordinary structures and inventory their decorations. But in the only case I know of the truth of that particular cliché, Samarkand must be seen to be believed.

The authorities in neighboring Kazakhstan have taken a much less political approach than the Uzbeks to the celebration of local Islamic traditions, although they boast individuals of equal significance. Interest in the tenth-century political philosopher Al-Farabi, whose portrait appears on Kazakh currency, has been revived in many parts of the world, if only because his writings were studied and taught by the alleged inspirer of the neoconservatives, Leo Strauss, a philosophy professor at the University of Chicago. (Al-Farabi also greatly influenced Khomeini, creator of the twentieth-century Iranian Islamic republic.) It was amusing to find Al-Farabi's profile on Kazakh currency notes while the merit of his work was discussed, now and then, in Washington. I have visited Al-Farabi's birthplace in the abandoned city of Otrar, which has been a sandy and windblown ruin for many centuries.

Returning to the shrine of Hojja Yasawi, the memorial complex attracts half a million pilgrims each year, from Turkey itself as well as from Tatarstan in Russia and all the Turkic regions of central Asia: Kazakhstan, Turkmenistan, Uzbekistan, Kyrgyzstan, and even from the part of Turkestan controlled by China and inhabited by Uighurs. But diversions and distractions cannot be avoided in the journey to the Yasawi tomb. The central Asian Turks also honor a metaphysical figure nearly unknown in the West—Arystanbab, or Arslan Baba, another progenitor of Turkic Islam and among those identified as main teachers of Hojja Yasawi. Arystanbab is believed to have traveled from Otrar to Yasi to teach chemistry, or alchemy, among other arts and elements of metaphysics, to Hojja Yasawi. Legend holds that when Timur began work on the tomb complex of Hojja Yasawi, his efforts were obstructed by collapsing walls and other accidents until, in a dream, he was told first to erect a structure for Arystanbab.

With the steppes of Turkestan so sparsely inhabited, visiting these sacred places requires time and effort. I and my friend the local journalist Talgat Dairbek first flew by a local air service from Almaty, the pleasant Kazakh capital at the foot of the Tianshan on the Chinese frontier, to Shimkent in southern Kazakhstan, which seems lost in the Soviet past, with its small and comfortless airport. We were met by local officials and drove for two hours to what remains of Otrar, where we were treated to a traditional lunch of lamb, fresh fruit, and vegetables, accompanied by tea, fermented mare's milk (*kumys*), and camel's milk. We then went to the Arystanbab tomb, a small and obscure but delicate and intimate structure.

The light-colored brick shrine of Arystanbab is presumed to date from the tenth century. With two major domes and a single smaller one, plus towers at each corner of the structure, it felt to me like the tomb of Al-Maturidi in Samarkand; a primal source of spiritual power. Until the Communist Revolution of 1917, nobody traveled in Turkestan without visiting the Arystanbab *turbe,* and as I received a blessing from the resident shaykh there, I sensed the proximity of Al-Khidr. There is a second tomb of Arystanbab, or Arslan Baba, in Kyrgyzstan—the phenomenon of multiple shrines for a single saint is common on the Sufi route from the border of China to the Balkans.

Leaving the tomb of Arystanbab, we drove for two hours more to the Hojja Yasawi complex, near Turkestan City, the name now given to Yasi. The construction is dreamlike, with its high vault, arched entrance, and kufic (square Arabic) inscriptions from the *Qur'an* laid into the outer walls. In addition to his sarcophagus, which is built from a fine green stone, and the *Taikazan*, the complex includes a deep underground chamber into which Hojja Yasawi retired from the world at sixty-three—the age of the Prophet Muhammad when he died. The cellar above the chamber is decorated with the names of God and other inscriptions of metaphysical significance. And the shrine is filled with many types of live human faces.

One could hardly imagine a landscape less diverse, at first glance, than the expanses of Turkestan. But central Asia was used as a dumping ground by Josef Stalin, who deported whole nationalities there: thousands of Soviet Greeks and Bulgarians living on the Black Sea, hundreds of thousands of Soviet Germans, up to a million Soviet Koreans; the whole population of Lamaist Buddhist Kalmyks; as well as entire Muslim communities from Russia proper, including the Chechens, Ingushes, Balkars, Karachais, and Meskhetian Turks from the Caucasus, and the Crimean Tatars from their home on the peninsula for which they are named. This chapter in its history has given the often monotonous landscape a uniquely multicultural character.

Central Asia has another dark spot in its history: Kazakhstan was used by the Russians as a center for the testing of nuclear weapons, with severe consequences for the local population in the form of radiation-derived illnesses and birth irregularities. Yet regardless of its lonely landscape, or because of it, Turkestan remains a place of deep spirituality. Its Islam is pluralistic and progressive. There is no place in Turkestan, notwithstanding its "big sky" spaces, habits of hospitality, and huge energy assets, for Saudi-sponsored Wahhabism or any other variety of Islamist radicalism.

The Turkestanis themselves recite an ancient blessing, as follows:

*Thousands of saints in Turkestan*
*Thousands of saints in Turkestan*
*I pray for your aid.*
*Countless saints in Sairam*
*Thirty saints in Otrar*
*Most honorable Arystanbab*
*I pray for your aid.*

H. T. Norris writes that the pre-Islamic shamanism of the Turks "lasted long in their memory, subconsciously or consciously influencing the later Sufism of the *Yasaviyya,* the first Sufi order to be fully 'acclimatised' among the Turks." Mehmet Köprülü emphasizes that the early Sufis "address[ed] the people in a language they could understand: simple Turkish." To Balkan, Turkish, and central Asian Sufis, Hojja Yasawi and Hajji Bektash, although separated in time, are closely linked. The disciples of Hajji Bektash, like those of Hojja Yasawi, also used Turkish as a devotional language, in contrast with Arabic and Persian; this gave them great authority with the Turks. According to another investigator, Irène Melikoff, among the followers of the way of Hojja Yasawi as well as the Bektashis, "hymns are sung, and women participate in the ceremonies. Both orders share a belief in bird metamorphosis, a dove for Hajji Bektash, a crane for Yasawi."

Much of what Sufis believe today about Hojja Yasawi was developed by the historian Mehmet Köprülü, scion of a notable family of Ottoman grand viziers who were Albanians by ethnicity. Their original name was Qyprilli, derived from a Turkish word for "bridge builder," and they were known for their warm sympathies toward Christians, as well as for a family enthusiasm for Western education. Fazil Ahmad-Pasha Köprülü, who served as grand vizier to the Ottoman sultan Mehmet IV in the late-seventeenth century, founded the first private library open to the public, in Istanbul.

As noted, at sixty-three Hojja Yasawi withdrew from the world, living the remainder of his years in mystical retreat, known as *khalwa*. The deep chamber dug for him under his current tomb is intact and even comfortable; from there, he continued to teach, spreading the essentials of Islam to Turkic-speaking people who could not understand Arabic and Persian. He habitually told those who came to him, "Your intentions are your companions"—the traditional Islamic creed of Al-Ghazali, in which intentions count for more than external actions. The chamber is accessible to pilgrims today, another place of meaningful silence, along with the Al-Maturidi and Arystanbab shrines, in which the visitor is deeply impressed by Ahmad Yasawi's equal commitment to instruction of others and to isolated meditation.

The rules of his *tariqa*, for which the master of Turkestan is best remembered among Sufis, are recounted by Köprülü. All are aspects of obedience to the shaykh, including the honor of residing and eating with one's teacher. Hojja Yasawi projected the *tariqa* as a "fortified city" or *shahristan*, based on six principles: knowledge of the divine, generosity, honesty, certainty, trust in the Creator in providing materially and spiritually for the Sufi, and meditative introspection. The shaykh must also demonstrate six qualities: knowledge of religion, forbearance, patience, contentment, sincerity, and readiness to approach the disciple. The *tariqa* has six duties: seeking perfection while growing closer to the glory of God, desire for union with God, ceaseless fear of God, hope in the face of the worst situations, repeating God's name, and meditating on union with God.

There are also six common activities of the *tariqa*: Friday prayer, remaining awake until daybreak, guarding spiritual purity, seeking God's presence, calling on the power of God, and obedience to people following the correct path and to teachers. Then come six internal rules of the *tariqa*: to sit quietly, to remember one's inferiority, to respect all others as superior, to be respectful in the presence of saints and teachers, not to interrupt the shaykh, and to continually recall the secrets and miracles of the teachers. Finally, there are six recommended actions: to care for guests, to welcome guests regardless of their condition, to accommodate a guest without consideration of the length of a stay, to fulfill all the desires of a guest, to pray for Hojja Yasawi, and to pray for the current shaykh. Yasawi Sufi writings include more regulations for the behavior of Sufis, including advice on reading the *Qur'an*, and counsel that *dhikr*, the remembrance of God, be carried out with physical vigor in addition to recitation.

Köprülü noted that the disciples of Ahmad Yasawi spread across the steppe from the land of the Kazakhs to the banks of the Volga River. By the seventeenth century, when a classic Ottoman traveler and Sufi, Evliya Çelebi—who claimed he was descended from Hojja Yasawi—wrote an account of his own journey around the empire, the Yasawi inspiration had swept the Western possessions of the Ottomans, including the Balkans. Köprülü described Hojja Yasawi's *Divan-i Hikmat* as an encyclopedic work from various hands, lacking the great mystic depth of Ibn Arabi or the lyricism of Rumi. He cited, however, a verse that sums up the Sufism of Hojja Ahmad Yasawi:

*I seek my Creator day and night in the world.*
*I am freed from the four directions in the realm of being and*
   *becoming.*
*From four I reached seven, I did nine one by one,*

*From two I reached ten in the sphere of Saturn.*
*I crossed 360 rivers, I crossed 444 mountains,*
*I drank the wine of Unity, I entered the battlefield.*
*When I entered the battlefield, I found the field full.*
*I saw 100,000 mystics, all prancing in the field.*
*I ran among them and asked what I was seeking.*
*They all said, "It is in you." I was lost in amazement.*
*I submitted to pain, I plunged in the sea,*
*I saw the pearl in the shell, the jewel in the ore.*
*Poor [Hojja Ahmad]'s soul is both the jewel and the ore.*
*All of his place is in no-place.[3]*

Hojja Yasawi is associated by many Turkish readers with the outstanding medieval Anatolian poet Yunus Emre. The latter composed verses in the popular idiom of the thirteenth century but is supremely loved today in Turkey and central Asia.

Yunus Emre also attracts a Western audience, although it is not comparable to that of Rumi. One of his most famous verses reads:

*God's truth is lost on the men of piety;*
*Mystics refuse to turn life into a forgery.*

*God's truth is an ocean and the doctrines of faith a ship,*
*Few will leave the vessel to plunge into the sea.*

*At the threshold of truth, doctrine holds them back;*
*All come with open eyes to that door, but cannot see it.*

*Those who comment on the Four Books are heretics:*
*They read the text, but miss reality.[4]*

The Four Books are the scriptures recognized in Islam as God's revealed word: the *Torah* and *Psalms* of the Jews, the Christian *Gospels,* and the *Qur'an.*

HAJJI BEKTASH WAS the greatest mystical successor to Ahmad Yasawi as a Sufi teacher, on the road from central Asia to the Balkans. Hajji Bektash apparently intended to study Christianity in furtherance of Islamic missionization, but he is the inspirer today of Sufis proud to call themselves the most open and forward-looking community in Islam and the closest in heart to Jews, Christians, and Buddhists. Hajji Bektash came from the area of Khorasan, now on the border of Iran and Afghanistan, and the birthplace of Al-Bastami and Rumi. Khorasan was a center of ecstatic, intoxicated, rebellious, and self-denying Sufism, as well as of the most ancient pre-Islamic Iranian wisdom.

Two traditional volumes about Hajji Bektash have come down to us, both titled *Vilayetname,* or *Book of Sainthood*; one, the "small (*küçük*) *Vilayetname*" or *Makalat,* consists of his sayings, while the other, the "*Vilayetname* of Ferdowsi," recounts his life and was compiled by Uzun Ferdowsi, a Turkish author of the late-fifteenth century. Baba Rexheb wrote of Hajji Bektash that he was the son of a prominent and popular landowner and provincial governor; he "showed promise as a child and grew up wise and virtuous . . . a young man . . . liked by his peers." He was educated in Persian and studied under Luqman Perende, a disciple of Hojja Yasawi. He was inspired to leave Khorasan for Anatolia, or Rum, the same recently Islamized, formerly Christian territory to which Rumi was drawn. He settled at Karahuyuk, near Ankara.

Although Rumi is claimed first by Persians and Hajji Bektash by Turks, their shared origin in Khorasan gave them much in common.

The Western scholar J. Spencer Trimingham distinguishes between Khorasan and Baghdad Sufism. The Khorasanis leaned toward intoxication, while the Baghdadis were impelled away from it, and both Rumi and Hajji Bektash were less than "sober" in their Sufism. Bektashi sources include commentary on the relations between the two men. The "*Vilayetname* of Ferdowsi" records that Hajji Bektash once asked one of his disciples, Saru Ismail, what was inscribed in the student's heart. The acolyte answered that he had heated water for the great mystic to bathe in. "This is not the right moment!" declared Hajji Bektash, and he abruptly sent Saru Ismail through Anatolia to Konya, to demand of Mevlana a certain book that belonged to Hajji Bektash.

As Saru Ismail approached Konya, Rumi appeared and asked him what he desired. When he explained, Mevlana said, "Every day, Hajji Bektash enters into seven oceans and seven rivers. He has no further need to go into water. Why did you ask him to do so?" When the disciple insisted on asking for the book, Rumi replied, "All that is in the book is the advice I have just given you." Saru Ismail then returned to Hajji Bektash. This anecdote may have a striking but simple meaning: Hajji Bektash and his followers are notorious for ignoring the ritual washing and daily prayers observed by pious Muslims, and his reference to the book held by Mevlana may be an indication of the divine proof he adduced for such habits.

The "*Vilayetname* of Ferdowsi" also explains a curiosity that seldom rises to the level of a mystery among Western devotees of Rumi. That involves Shems of Tabriz: from where did he come to Mevlana and how had he acquired knowledge so great as to dazzle him? According to the Bektashis, Shems of Tabriz was sent to Rumi by Hajji Bektash.

Rumi and Hajji Bektash are often paired as representing a dual central Asian culture, Iranian and Turkish. The distaste expressed by

Hajji Bektash for the externals of ablution and prayer may reflect a steppe personality naturally drawn to independence of spirit and liberation of the soul as the heart of metaphysics. The group of Khorasan "missionaries" to which he belonged may have rebelled against the Muslim clerical class, as well as the discipline of other Sufis, and have been drawn into social protest. They seem to have been involved with Qalandarism, a nonconforming trend embodying extreme mystical intoxication, defiance of the world, self-denial and wandering, and contempt both for Muslim clerics and organized Sufism. Qalandarism has been associated with another chapter in Islamic history, the Malamati movement, which kept silent about its members' metaphysical dedication, refusing any identification with Sufism or even with prayer in public.

A great illumination of the Khorasanis came in their encounter, on their way from inner Asia to the edge of Europe, with Shia Islam and its insistence, in the examples of Imam Ali and Imam Husayn, on social justice. Early Muslim dissenters in central Asia thus found justification for their outrage at the corruption they witnessed in religion and statecraft. Yet they could not break away from Sunnism, even as, heading west, Khorasanis such as Rumi and Hajji Bektash adopted elements from other religions. Christian influences were reinforced in their journey to Anatolia. In their zeal for Islamic metaphysics, they seem to have viewed the wisdom of the other faith as a means to change the hearts of Christians and Muslims alike.

At the beginning of the twentieth century, the English traveler and historian F. W. Hasluck inventoried tombs and other locations, as well as rituals, shared by Christians, Muslims, and Jews in the Ottoman Empire. He found that although the Ottomans appropriated Christian churches including Hagia Sophia in Constantinople, popular Turkish Islam found ways to conciliate the different religions. Muslim children might be taken for baptism to increase their spiritual protection; Muslims would carry images of Christian saints. When bad weather and other disasters befell the peasants, Muslims, Christians, and Jews would combine in prayer. As with visitation of the tomb of Rabiya Al-Adawiyya in Jerusalem by non-Muslims as well as Muslims, many Christian and Jewish shrines were visited and protected by Ottoman Muslims. As indicated, the Christian Saint George is identified with Al-Khidr in Islam. The Bektashis, who are especially pleased about their good relations with Christians, boast that Orthodox Christian believers equate Hajji Bektash with Saint Haralambos, an early martyr. The Bektashis also claim a kinship with Catholics in that the Bektashi *babas* are celibate, a practice repudiated by ordinary Muslims.

The followers of Hajji Bektash further extended their intellectual horizons to include neo-Platonic philosophy, already absorbed into Islam and especially Sufism, and finally, a strange and dangerous (especially for its adherents) phenomenon called Hurufism, which preached a mystical interpretation of numbers similar to that in the traditional Jewish Kabbalah.[5] Hurufism also equated the form of God with that of humankind—a view rejected in mainstream Islam as a violation of monotheism and especially the uniqueness of God, to which nothing could be compared. But Hurufi identification of the divine and the human is vigorously present today in the massed choruses of Turkish and Kurdish Alevis in Germany who cry out in praise of humanity. Like Kabbalah and some radical Franciscan interpretations, Hurufism led its adepts to believe that numerology foretold great upheavals in the worldly order. The result in the Muslim lands was predictable: no cataclysmic overturn took place, but revolutionary movements appeared and popular rebellion subverted whole districts. Hurufism was viewed as seditious and was relentlessly suppressed in the Ottoman Empire; its members were burned alive "in the Christian style," according to the Turkish historian Ilber Ortayli.

But the Sufis who emulated Hajji Bektash seemed to have begun as radical missionaries, and through Ottoman history proved generous in sheltering other dissidents. They assimilated and protected Hurufis, as well as the forebears of today's Turkish and Kurdish Alevis. The Bektashi buried in Budapest, Gül Baba, was a distinguished Hurufi. The Bektashis also developed an early insistence on the participation of women, without veils, in religious and social rituals. Much later, they took up popular education and the use of other vernacular languages in addition to Turkish, such as Albanian. They professed Sunnism but practiced as Shia Muslims. The Bektashi order maintained these unorthodox attitudes by becoming a pillar of the Ottoman military; they were the chaplains of the Janissaries, or "new soldiers."

The Janissaries were originally taken as children from Christian families and were taught to serve as the guardians of the Ottoman state. With an interest in Christianity, the Bektashis became the appropriate medium through which the Janissaries would embrace Islam. After the passage of centuries, however, most of the Janissaries were offered by Muslim families for enlistment. As the most visible face of the Ottoman realm, the Janissaries had a considerable effect on Western European knowledge of the empire. For example, Janissary military musical bands influenced the composers of Vienna, including Mozart, whose remarkable work *The Abduction from the Seraglio* (1782) is set in Turkey and is deeply sympathetic to a Sufi interpretation of Islam.

Trimingham argues that the Turkish conquerors of Anatolia turned to wandering Yasawis, Qalandaris, Hurufis, and other nonconforming Sufis who had accompanied and inspired the armies on their road of conquest as the only "dynamic" element capable of consolidating Islamic rule. The Bektashi order accumulated great power in the Ottoman state, which did not, paradoxically enough, prevent them from participating in local uprisings against injustice. They were, put simply, wild and free, anticlerical but not antireligious Muslims, whether as defenders or opponents of the empire—the most ecstatic Sufis and most authentic apostles of Hallaj. They are perhaps the last significant historical example of a libertarian-revolutionary religious movement such as spread through the Judeo-Christian world[6] during the late medieval and Renaissance periods. The second great figure among the Bektashis, Ballem Sultan, restructured the order at the end of the fifteenth century and is credited with initiating into Bektashism the Ottoman sultan Bayazid II, who welcomed to his dominions the Jews expelled from the Iberian Peninsula. Ballem Sultan fully established the Bektashi order as a pole of the imperial system.

Much writing of great beauty is ascribed to Hajji Bektash, and many of his outstanding disciples, continuing to recent times, have been accomplished poets.

Hajji Bektash taught,

*Should the believer gain knowledge of God, everything would be pleasant.*

*He would feel neither happiness nor unhappiness. Therefore, O dervish, strive to reach the door of the house of God. If you do not choose that door, you will never find peace anywhere else. Whoever has passed through this door has never found another one . . .*

*Be careful! Walking toward God may, at times, cause one to move backwards . . . Once the spiritual approach occurs the distance traveled means nothing. If you were with me in spirit, you would be with me even if you were in Yemen. If you were not, even if you were beside me, you would be in Yemen.*

*Birds cannot touch the sky. They fly, however, high enough to escape hunters. The Sufi does the same by leaving the material world. Peace can be felt in the heart. Whoever stays in one place becomes a man; whoever travels meets men.*

*Whoever has known himself has known God.*

*A teacher without knowledge is like a bird without wings; a Sufi who does not invoke the name of God is like a tree without leaves. A teacher without knowledge is like Noah without the Ark; a dervish who does not mention God's name is like a body without a soul.*

*The road ends but its stages never do. There are two principal walks; one toward God, and the other to God. The former ends for it includes one's own disappearance and since nothing remains of him, his walk ends. The latter, the walk to God, wakes one to the world of God's secrets, which have no end.*

Hajji Bektash defined three sources of nourishment for the believer: sacred law, participation in the *tariqa*, and seeking God in one's own heart, or *haqiqa*.

The Bektashi Sufis are masters in perception of *wahdat ul-wujud*, the unity of being, and the doctrine that all creation is no more than a divine manifestation. This principle was eloquently expressed by the Albanian Bektashi author, patriot, and mystic Naim Frashëri (1846–1900) when he wrote,

*In the vast ocean the eye sees in each wave all of the seas.*
*Look then closely at each wave your eye can see.*

# 3

## The Wars Against Sufism

THE TURKS, WHO HAD accepted Islam, invaded Anatolia in the eleventh century. Their role as new rulers over a large Christian population drew their Sufis and their sultans to a spiritual compromise with the religion of Jesus. With a shamanic background, the original Turkish Sufis were ecstatic rather than "sober."

The sultans who created the Ottoman Empire—the most powerful Muslim state and the most extensive caliphate in Islamic history—did not base their rule on *Shariah* alone. As mentioned, they established a body of common law, *Kanun,* that paralleled the religious law of *Shariah.*

Much in the Ottoman experience is impressive, and offers apparent ways out of the current crisis of Islam. Sufi pluralism and tendencies toward an exalted spirituality, love of Jesus, and resistance to *Shariah*-centered literalism all represent alternatives to the stagnation imposed in Islam today by radical ideology.

But the Ottoman model disappeared a century ago, and in 1925 it was definitively overthrown by the dictatorial regime of Mustafa Ke-

mal, who was called Atatürk, "Father of the Turks." Mustafa Kemal
was a military hero in the national liberation war of 1918–23, when the
Turks, who had sided with the losing Central Powers in the First World
War, fought to prevent the full division of their country by the British,
French, Greeks, and small states on the eastern Turkish border. Many
Sufis served with distinction in the national war, but soon Mustafa
Kemal brutally suppressed the Sufi orders and other institutions of Ottoman Islam. Kemalism, as his political philosophy is known, represented militaristic secularism. In his most famous speech, attacking the
Muslim hold on Turkish consciousness, he assailed the wearing of the
fez, short pants, and other "Islamic" dress. Mustafa Kemal went on, "It
is a disgrace for a civilized nation to appeal for help to the dead . . . Is
it possible to call a group of people a 'civilized nation' while they let
themselves be led by the nose by a herd of shaykhs, *dedes* [an Alevi and
Bektashi title], *sayyids* [descendants of Muhammad] . . . *babas* and
emirs?" Mustafa Kemal had decided to write out of Turkish history the
entire spiritual patrimony of the nation, something that among European rulers only Communists have attempted.

In his personality, Mustafa Kemal was among the first Latin
American–style despots seen in Europe, but with forms of governance
borrowed from European state centralism. Imitating France, his authoritarian Turkish Republic not only banned religion from political
life but tried to create a single Turkish national identity by denying the
existence of millions of Kurds in the eastern regions of the country.
Hostility to the Kurds was aggravated by their refusal to abandon Sufism. The state compelled the Sephardic Jews of Istanbul and other
cities to become Turkish in culture, restricted the religious authority of
the Greek Orthodox church, which nonetheless retained its international seat at Istanbul, and refused historical honesty about the mas-

sacres of Armenians during the First World War. And so the Turkish Republic remains in its guiding principles today.

Militarist-secularist rule over many decades left a hole in Turkish culture where Islam and Sufism had been. Then, after seventy years, the people decided that since the secularists had promised them progress and delivered corruption and poverty, it was time to give religious believers a new opportunity to rule Turkey. Unfortunately, the long gap in Islamic culture had deprived the country of sophisticated religious education and systematic spiritual development, and the space for Islam was soon filled by "political Sufis," along with fundamentalist bigots of the kind that burned the Alevis to death in the Sivas incident of 1993.

In 2007, Turkey's reelection of the incumbent prime minister Recep Tayyip Erdoğan, identified with a "soft" Sunni fundamentalism, gave new importance to a low-level debate in Washington about foreign Islamic parties that claimed to respect democracy and secularism. But for Erdoğan's Justice and Development Party (AKP)—no less than its rivals in the Turkish military and secular state structures—pluralism was the positive element lacking in their outlook, rather than anything specific to politics or prayers.

Turkey after the long Kemalist period was divided between two forms of intolerance: a secular element that accepted Islam only under strict state-appointed monitors, and a religious faction that similarly restricted its approval to Sunnism. Neither respected Turkey's "controversial" minorities: the heterodox Alevis, who feared the AKP because it excluded them; the Kurds, whose situation was dangerous for Iraq and the U.S.-led Coalition there, as well as for Turkey itself; the small Greek Orthodox population; and the Armenians.

Many American commentators wanted to see "Islamic democratic" parties emerge across the Muslim world—notably in Egypt, with a presumed option of American accommodation with the radical Muslim Brotherhood (MB). Both Erdoğan's AKP and the Egyptian MB (the latter having provided the original structure of Hamas among the Palestinians) said what Westerners liked to hear. They affirmed that they opted for ballots over bullets, and since voting and renouncing violence were thrilling breakthroughs to most Americans observing the Middle East, the chance of supporting parties representing a "tame" Islamist ideology was attractive to many inside the Beltway.

In addition, the strident rhetoric and militaristic history of Turkish secularism seemed to blame Islam as a faith for the problems of Turkish politics, which played well with some sectors of Western opinion but was a risky conception if the Western democracies intended to defeat radicals inside Muslim countries. Nobody seriously suggested that the U.S.-led Coalition in Iraq should have made the eradication of Islam its strategic goal.

When they marked their ballots, many Turks voted for the AKP, because after experiencing enforced secularism, the people were aggrieved at those who swore that driving religion from the public sphere and rooting out the old manners and morals of the Ottomans would create a modern, efficient nation but then failed to make good on their promises of accountability and prosperity. Turkey ended up with an army prone to violence, a police known for extreme corruption, and political bloodshed between leftist and rightist nationalists. Worst of all, the Turkish army held on to its "right" to throw out governments of which it disapproved, which was hardly exemplary from the democratic viewpoint.

Officially, the AKP in its electoral propaganda asked for no more than an opportunity to administer the existing state in a more conscientious and clean manner. Its functionaries and apologists profusely denied any intent to reintroduce *Shariah*—a source of literal horror among many Turks—or otherwise expand the role of the mosque in Turkish life.

But would the "Islamic democrats" of AKP prove any better than their Kemalist predecessors in ruling Turkey? The country's combination of unstable factors meant that no outcome could be certified as secure. AKP supporters compared the movement with Christian-based parties in Germany, Austria, and the Netherlands, which have excellent records of fidelity to democracy—but also are products of compromises by and between the churches. The German Christian Democrats and Austrian (Catholic) People's Party arose in response to socialist labor movements, and they recognized or adopted many of the programmatic principles of the Left. The Dutch religious parties were born of a national reconciliation between Catholics and Protestants.

No such compromise between the AKP, the military, secular civilians, or, most important, religious and ethnic minorities was in sight in Turkey, and, if anything, the common Turkish nationalist and Sunni-centric habits of the secular military and the AKP had become more aggravated.

Neither the military secularists nor the AKP expressed any interest in recognizing the rights of the Alevi minority. Before the AKP came to power the Turkish Diyanet paid for new mosques and certified imams for the Sunnis but refused money for the Alevis to build their meeting houses, known as *cemevi*, or to train their clerics.

Neither the military secularists nor the AKP proposed to grant his traditional status to the Istanbul-based representative of the Christian Orthodox believers, Ecumenical Patriarch Bartholomaeus I. The Patriarch was required to be a Turkish citizen and had extremely limited official duties inside the republic. A Greek seminary and publishing house were closed. The secularists maintained this policy out of distaste for all religion, as well as because of Turkish nationalism. It was doubtful the Sunnis of AKP would rush to grant relief to the small community of Greek Christians.

Neither the military secularists nor the AKP had shown any interest in resolving the historical question of Armenian suffering in Turkey. The novelist Orhan Pamuk mentioned the Armenian events in writing and was threatened with a public trial—by the AKP government. And finally, and most dangerously, neither the military secularists nor the AKP indicated any willingness to concede ethnic rights to the Kurds. Military-secular tradition insisted that there were only Turks in Turkey and that Kurds were all terrorist secessionists; anybody who defended the Kurds was labeled a Marxist extremist. Turkish troops and attack aircraft had been sent to the border of Iraqi Kurdistan, and both the military and the AKP adopted a threatening tone toward the U.S.-led Coalition in Iraq, which could produce a shooting war between NATO partners. Both the Turkish military and the AKP also fed growing anti-American propaganda of the crudest kind.

Perhaps worst of all, the AKP's Sunni fanatics sought to export their ideology to the former Ottoman provinces in the Balkans (some of which, such as Bosnia-Herzegovina and Albania, have no Turkish-speaking communities that might normally be interested in politics in Turkey) and the Turkic areas of central Asia. For Turkey to become a respected, modern nation, it was time for it to give up all forms of ideological politics: militaristic secularism, an ultranationalist definition of rights, and Sunnicentrism. Turkey needed a government about which there would be no doubts, because it would stand above and seek to heal—rather than stand upon and aggravate—its dangerous differences. But there was no clear evidence that the AKP could provide such a government.

. . .

WHAT ROLE COULD SUFISM play in alleviating the Turkish stalemate between secularism and a new fundamentalism? Mustafa Kemal had banned the Sufi orders, and the Bektashis, one of the core intellectual bodies of Ottoman Islam, then relocated themselves to Albania, becoming totally Albanian in culture. Other orders maintained a quasi-underground existence inside Turkey. The Naqshbandi Sufis had held a status in the Ottoman state so high that it was impossible for the Kemalists to thoroughly repress them. The nineteenth century in Turkey has been called the Naqshbandi era; and after the arrival of secularism, Naqshbandis participated in protests against the Kemalist order but also infiltrated all levels of the new society. Sufis therefore remained prominent and even pervasive in Turkish life, although under duress, and served as a cultural and social "third alternative" to secularist and clerical authority. Sufism in the Turkey of the future could be no less significant in opposing an Islamist state than it might be in Saudi Arabia or Iran. But first the powerful Naqshbandis, who are *Shariah*-centric Sufis, would have to prove respect for the rights of Alevis and other nonconforming Muslims.

The Naqshbandis are, with the Qadiris, probably the world's largest *tariqas* in numbers. The historian Hamid Algar calls these two the "universal" Sufi orders. Throughout their later history, Naqshbandis are known for three things: disagreement over their origins, involvement with political power, and an adherence to *Shariah* that may define them as "Sufi fundamentalists." Widely recognized modern Sufis in Turkey have included Said Nursi (1877–1960), who began as a student of the Naqshbandis but then claimed direct guidance from the twelfth-century shaykh Jilani. Mehmed Zahid Kotku (1897–1980), his son-in-law Mahmud Esad Coşan (1938–2001), and Fethullah Gülen (b. 1938) gained political influence while representing Naqshbandi variants. Late in the 1990s it was announced that the family of the Turkish president Turgut Özal, who died in 1993, was Naqshbandi. Turkish Sunni politicians of the 1990s included many more Naqshbandis.

Said Nursi, Kotku and Coşan, and Gülen all sought to modernize Islam by applying Sufi concepts. Said Nursi's followers stress his devotion to scientific studies and his belief that scientific discoveries reinforce rather than undermine religious belief. With the coming of the Turkish Republic, Said Nursi underwent an intellectual rebirth. The "old Said" had been one among many Islamic preachers in Turkey; but although he supported political reform of the Ottoman order, he was disillusioned with the extent of Kemalist changes and a "new Said" emerged. He dedicated himself to prayer, study, and meditation, became isolated from the public, and was subjected, after 1925, to internal exile and other persecution by the state.

The writings and lives of recent Sufis such as Said Nursi are marked by a defensive spirit, as they strove to protect their mysticism from attacks on Islamic metaphysics by fundamentalists, then by modernists. Unlike Rumi and Hajji Bektash, the twentieth-century Turkish Sufis lacked the freedom to follow their individual inspiration along the brightest, star-strewn pathways of beauty and exaltation. Between the great ages of the Sufi masters and the end of the Ottoman caliphate, the heart of Sufism was scarred. Paradoxically, foreign academics, fundamentalist reformers, and Muslim modernists alike blame the centuries in which the Islamic world fell behind the West in economic and political development on Sufi dominance over the Muslim mind. But modernizing Sufis, along with the fundamentalists, found the cause of Islam's difficulties in *lack* of belief rather than *excess* of it. To the fundamentalists, the Sufis were near-atheists. The Sufis rejected such claims, arguing that their belief was more intense than that of the fundamentalists. To the modernists, the Sufis represented credulous acceptance of backward customs.

Differences in the speed of modern development between West and East are too complex to be dealt with in passing. (It should be noted, however, that non-Muslim societies like China have faced as many or more challenges than the Islamic world in adapting to modern inventions and institutions.) But Sufism cannot be held responsible for the historical and geographical accidents that focused Islam on ancient, overcrowded, and long-inert regions, where progress had always been slow.

To Said Nursi, diminishing belief was the main problem faced by Muslims and, by implication, humanity in general. While suffering under the new Turkish state, the "new" Said Nursi began a monumental work in support of religious belief and metaphysics, the *Risale-i Nur* (*Treatise on Light*). Al-Ghazali had long before stressed that mystical knowledge of God and the universe leads to human happiness, but Said Nursi reordered the equation in attempting to answer a world hungry for serenity: happiness could come only from knowledge and faith. Like other Islamic ideologists who sought to reconcile religion and science,[1] Said Nursi argued that all of the universe is contained in divine "signs."

He engaged with the Sufism of Ibn Arabi, admitting that the work of the Greatest Master described things that could not exist in the world as we perceive it. Said Nursi taught that the universe is organized in levels of complexity that resemble those of modern physics. Some mystics would see more deeply and further into the components of nature than others. The things they beheld—Said Nursi cites visions of "seven levels of the earth" as described by Ibn Arabi—could not be confirmed by science. "Those strange levels are not found on our globe," the Turkish commentator wrote. But the perceptions of an ecstatic Sufi could only be accounted for by principles of faith as explained by religious scholars. For Said Nursi, "the balance of all illuminations, mental states, visions, and unveilings" are to be found in the *Qur'an,* the *hadith,* and the explanations of "purified, exacting scholars."

Said Nursi was a *Shariah*-centered Sufi, but he was not narrow-minded. Answering whether a Sufi path could exist "outside" the practices of the Prophet and *Shariah,* he wrote, "There are such paths, and there are not. There are, because some of the highest Saints were executed by the sword of the *Shariah.*" He believed that enlightenment was accessible only through religion (and specifically Islam), but he also taught that "ecstatics and those immersed in divine contemplation" who fall away from *Shariah* incur no guilt unless they deny the validity of religious law. He classified those who pursue Sufism outside *Shariah* as "either overwhelmed by their mental state, immersion, or ecstasy or intoxication" or "dominated by some of their subtle faculties that do not heed the injunctions of religion nor listen to the will." Their resistance to *Shariah* would be involuntary, not defiant. But Said Nursi strongly criticized those who were indifferent to *Shariah* as a set of "dull formalities."

Although Said Nursi was a suspect figure among Turkey's secularists for the rest of his life, his writings circulated widely in secret, and by the 1950s he had a large following of *"Nurcu* circles," or Followers of Light, today estimated at up to six million members. The heritage of Said Nursi is one of ideological polemics for religion in general rather than of ecstatic transcendence. He defined the aim and goal of the Sufi as "knowledge of God and the unfolding of the truths of faith—through a spiritual journey with the feet of the heart under the shadow of the Night Journey of Muhammad, to manifest the truths of faith and the *Qur'an* through 'tasting' . . . and certain enhanced states . . . to an extent through direct vision . . . an elevated human mystery."

Mehmed Zahid Kotku, a Naqshbandi, emerged as the spiritual guide of new Islamic parties that first appeared in Turkey in the 1960s and 1970s calling for the return of religion to politics. He became known as *Hocaefendi* (pronounced *"Hojja Effendi"*). Like Said Nursi, he was a modernist regarding science. His ideology called first for the moral and spiritual transformation of Turkish society, and he warned against hastily demanding an Islamic state. He also advocated education, entrepreneurship, and investment, but he defined freedom in terms of inner cultivation. He successfully recruited the prime minister Necmettin Erbakan, who was removed from power by the Turkish army in 1997 as an Islamic militant, as well as the previously mentioned president Turgut Özal, who had also been prime minister. Erbakan was and remains despicable for his ignorant and hallucinated anti-Jewish views borrowed from the Wahhabis but even more deranged—for example, denouncing the traditional Kabbalah as a conspiratorial doctrine when in reality it introduced Islamic metaphysics into Judaism.

*Hocaefendi* Kotku was a great devotee of prayer at midnight. He described the "bondage of the Divine Audience" in Sufism:

> *Think of and imagine the heart . . . It is the place to which the Divine looks and attention is directed and concentrated. Allah, the Highest and Most Exalted, observes deep in the hearts of His servants and manifests Himself there. The heart is the place of spiritual illumination, and we join that place with its bright glow. Our surroundings are all illuminated with that bright light . . . And we imagine that there, in front of us and written in brilliant letters, stands the name of ALLAH, may his glory be exalted. We then recollect the most beautiful attributes of Allah . . .*
>
> *After meditating for a while in such a mood we say "O Allah . . . The earth belongs to you . . . The heavens belong to*

*you . . . Whatever there is in heaven and on earth is yours . . .*
*Whatever in existence is yours . . .*
    *"Please forgive me, O Allah."*

Kotku led a Naqshbandi circle that met near the Iskenderpasha mosque in Istanbul. His son-in-law and successor as leader of the Iskenderpasha group, Mahmud Esad Coşan, carried the message of a modernized, business-model Islam even further, promoting Turkish Islamic media as well as new technologies. But Coşan also showed pronounced anti-Western attitudes, condemning Kurdish nationalism, Alevi self-expression, and the war in Bosnia-Herzegovina in the 1990s as elements in a Western conspiracy against Turkey.

These forms of Sunnicentric "political Sufism" seem to have wandered very far from the metaphysical insights of Ibn Arabi, Rumi, or Hajji Bektash. Yet there was a social content in Sufism, calling for the transformation of society, very early. The Turkish and other Naqshbandis stand out in explicitly seeking political power as a means for moral and spiritual improvement of society. In this, they resemble Islamist ideological groups in the Arab world and Iran.

The last Turkish Sufi to gain national and international renown is Fethullah Gülen, who has lived in the United States since the 1990s. Gülen leads a large religious movement that restates the arguments of Said Nursi, and which appears omnipresent among Turkish Sunnis both in the country and as emigrants in Europe and America. He has emphasized interfaith dialogue with Christian and Jewish theologians but has been viewed with great suspicion by Turkish secularists. He has assumed the title *hocaefendi* for himself.

We will later consider the origins of the Naqshbandis, who have a much longer history in the wars against (and within) Sufism. First we must turn back to the catastrophe of Baghdad in the year 1258—the fall of the great Muslim Arab metropolis to the Mongol conqueror Hülagu, grandson of Chinggis Khan.

SUFIS SUCH AS HALLAJ and Suhrawardi had paid the full price for their mystical dissidence. But criticism of Sufism among Muslims again became violent after the trauma of Baghdad. Ethnic cousins of the Turks, the Mongols long remained faithful to shamanism, Manichaeism, Eastern Christianity, and, finally, Buddhism. By the thirteenth century they had conquered the wide Iranian culture zone and eastern Iraq. Hülagu, a Buddhist, was chosen as *khan* of Iran and was assigned several tasks, including the destruction of the Baghdad caliphate and invasion of Syria. The Mongols, some of whose commanders were Christian, were contemptuous of the Muslims, and the campaign of Hülagu encompassed such cruelties at the taking of Baghdad that Muslims everywhere thought the world was ending. The Baghdad caliphate claimed authority over all Sunnis but could not muster them for defense; the Sunnis in Baghdad accused the Shias of siding with the invader. The city was taken after less than a month, and thousands of its inhabitants were killed. The Mongols wrecked the world-renowned libraries of Baghdad, and it is often said that after the river Tigris turned red with blood, it was black with ink. Many Christians in Mesopotamia celebrated the fall of the caliphate, complaining that Baghdad had swallowed the riches of the world. To them, to Arab Muslims, and to many modern historians, the great age of Islam had come to a close.

Hülagu, although a Buddhist, described the successors to Chinggis Khan as divided between his own branch, which favored the Christians in Iran and Iraq, and the northern *khans* who supported the Muslims on the Russian and central Asian steppes. Not all Christians were convinced of Mongol sympathy for them; when the Mongols assaulted

Syria and Palestine, some crusader knights saw the newcomers as worse than the Muslims. And the horrors of Baghdad left those descendants of Chinggis who were well disposed toward Islam as new enemies of Hülagu.

Islam recovered from the destruction of the Baghdad caliphate, proving both its Mongol and Christian enemies wrong. The Mongol rulers of Iran and Iraq were, like their Turkic relatives, destined to come into Islam by the Sufi path. Even Hülagu had been a patron of Persian literature, and the Iranian art of miniature painting was influenced by Chinese styles. But the entry into Islam of the Mongol rulers of Iran and Iraq did not come immediately after the capitulation of Baghdad. Almost forty years had passed when, in 1295, Ghazan Khan (1271–1304), great-grandson of Hülagu, took power in Tabriz, the capital of Mongol-ruled Iran and Iraq, as well as the place of origin of the enigmatic Shems, companion of Rumi. Ghazan Khan was born a Buddhist but became Muslim. He had served as Mongol ruler in Khorasan, the birthplace of Al-Bastami, Rumi, and Hajji Bektash, and famous, as we have noted, for its ecstatic spirituality. The circumstances of Ghazan Khan's becoming Muslim are debated, but it is unarguable that he restored the power of the faith of Muhammad in Iran and Iraq.

Ghazan Khan was known for many virtues, which included military courage—at one battle he is said to have remained fighting alone after his soldiers deserted him. He was an efficient administrator, and though committed to re-Islamization of the territory he ruled, he restrained those Muslims who wanted revenge on the Christians and Buddhists living among them for the atrocities inflicted on the Muslims after the fall of Baghdad. Ghazan Khan rehabilitated agricultural lands that had been devastated by the Mongol invasions, and he was praised as the first Mongol ruler who preferred construction of new mosques, schools, and other buildings to arbitrary destruction.

The Islamic order created by Ghazan Khan was pluralistic. Jewish influence in it is also debated but cannot be excluded. Even before him Muslims were granted recourse to *Shariah* law, although Mongol customary law was supreme in his state. But above all, the court of Ghazan Khan favored Sufism so much that Trimingham states flatly, in a parallel to his description of Turkish policy in Anatolia, "With the accession of Ghazan Khan . . . Sufis replaced the *ulema* [Muslim clerical] class . . . as the significant representatives of the religion . . . in a new way and after their death they continued to exercise their influence. The shrine, not the mosque, became the symbol of Islam. The shrine, the dervish-house, and the circle of *dhikr*-reciters became the outer forms of living religion . . . And this continues."

But unlike the central Asian Muslims, both Turkish and Mongol, who were in the ascendant, Arab Islam had suffered a sharp decline with the obliteration of the Baghdad caliphate. The Arab response to the profession of Islam by the Mongol rulers in West Asia was hostile. Ghazan Khan was accused of remaining an unbeliever, notwithstanding his acceptance of Islam and reestablishment of it as the dominant faith in Iran and Iraq. The allegation of unbelief was made by a former Sufi, Taqi al-Din Ibn Taymiyyah (1263–1328). Ibn Taymiyyah represented no less a significant development in the long perspective of Islamic history than the fall of the Baghdad caliphate. He was marginal in his time but is idealized today—especially by the radicals of Al-Qaida and other Wahhabi fanatics.

Ibn Taymiyyah argued, in opposition to the principle of Muhammad himself, that pronouncing the *shehada* or Islamic declaration of faith ("I affirm there is no God but God; I affirm that Muhammad is God's Prophet") was insufficient to make someone Muslim. According to Ibn Taymiyyah, believers must prove their Islam by living under exclusive and narrow *Shariah*. Here Ibn Taymiyyah also repudiated the wisdom of Al-Ghazali, who had established that internal belief was more important than external observance. Since Ghazan Khan, in the manner of the Turks with their *Kanun,* allowed *Shariah* and Mongol customary law to coexist, the ruler was not to be considered a Muslim. Rather, Ibn Taymiyyah demanded jihad against him, much as Al-Qaida declares war on today's Muslim political leaders who do not accept their interpretation of religion.

In the thirteenth century, except for Sunni persecution of Shias, these habits were still rare in Islam—especially the allegation that a Muslim could be judged an unbeliever regardless of public affirmation of One God, the message of the *Qur'an,* and the prophecy of Muhammad. But equally novel were the attacks of Ibn Taymiyyah on the Sufis, which are correctly identified by historians of Islam as the first sustained, although failed, campaign against Islamic metaphysics in general. Although the views of Ibn Taymiyyah did not immediately prevail, he was taken up again five hundred years later by Muhammad Ibn Abd Al-Wahhab, the second important Muslim persecutor of the Sufis. Ibn Taymiyyah was a confused individual, of a type known throughout history. He had been a Sufi but turned against them with exceptional venom and cannot be described as a representative of Sufi metaphysics. He insisted on the pious argument that Sufism was acceptable only as a form of self-purification, but added that all features drawn from popular religiosity or other religions must be mercilessly rooted out. In the six and a half centuries of history preceding him, Islam had absorbed many such elements. But Islam was strengthened, not weakened, in that period. The rage of Ibn Taymiyyah was a purely Arab anger at the "new Islam" of the central Asian peoples, who would not give up their legal standards, their shamanic and related customs, or their comprehension of Christianity, Buddhism, and the Chinese religions.

Though he had once been a Qadiri Sufi, Ibn Taymiyyah became the adversary of the greatest Sufis (including Ibn Arabi, whom he condemned as an unbeliever). His Sufism is ignored by his fundamentalist Muslim admirers today, who view him merely as an enemy of Islamic mysticism. In the West, superficial hatemongers who want to blur the sharp lines between the extremism of Ibn Taymiyyah and the Sufi vision cite his Sufi involvement to claim that Sufi criticism of him as a preacher of intolerance and violence is without substance and that violent fundamentalists and peaceful Sufis are equally bad—all of them being Muslims. But Ibn Taymiyyah was neither the first nor the last Muslim to legitimize Sufism only in a cage of *Shariah*; neither the first nor the last figure to advocate division of the community in the name of unity; neither the first nor the last believer, whether Islamic or otherwise, to call for religious reform and to accuse all others in the faith of corruption; neither the first nor the last personality to act or write in self-contradiction.

Ibn Taymiyyah is despised by traditional Muslims for other deviations from mainstream Islam; conversely his ideas have been presented as returning Islam to its original purity at the time of Muhammad, although the conceptions of Ibn Taymiyyah were his own and had no precedent in the life of the Prophet or his immediate successors. But Ibn Taymiyyah is mostly recalled for his unrestrained hatred of Sufis and Shias.

One of the most widely read and characteristic diatribes of Ibn Taymiyyah against Sufis took place when he encountered the thirteenth-century Muslim legal authority Ibn 'Ata' Allah Al-Iskandari, a Sufi and mosque preacher in Cairo. Ibn Taymiyyah attacked Ibn Arabi, denouncing the theory "that all existence is one in being (*wahdat ul-wujud*) and other such things to which your Shaykh summons people: this is clearly godlessness and unbelief." Elsewhere,

Ibn Taymiyyah had praised Ibn Arabi's works except for *Fusus al-Hikam* (*The Seals of Wisdom*), which he condemned, and which some intimidated Sufis today, eager to defend themselves against fundamentalist attack, downgrade to a minor work. The *Fusus*, nevertheless, has unchallengeable standing as one of Ibn Arabi's greatest achievements.

Ibn Taymiyyah also attacked the Sufis for "the insertion of the ideas of idolaters such as the Greek philosophers and the Indian Buddhists" into Islam, as well as the belief that human beings can attain union with God. He assailed the Islamic custom of *mawlid*[2] in celebration of Muhammad's birthday, and in his convoluted manner decried it as a practice imitative of the Christian feasting in honor of Jesus; yet he praised Muslims for the love of the Prophet expressed in *mawlid*. (His later imitators mainly forbid the practice and those who engage in it, allowing no such expression of love of Muhammad.) He reviled prayers addressed to God asking for intercession by the Prophet. And he abused other Sufis such as Hallaj. But he lacked the power to overcome the by then established Islamic principle that the belief of the heart is judged by God alone, and that the sincerity of the metaphysical believer could not be judged heretical on the basis of external practice. Celebrations of the Prophet's birthday became more popular, Muslims increased their intercessory prayers to God for the grace of Muhammad, and the genius of Ibn Arabi and of such tragic figures as Hallaj was defended. The anti-Sufi insults of Ibn Taymiyyah were a trivial feature in Islamic thought during his life.

FIVE CENTURIES PASSED BEFORE the appearance of a figure even more threatening to Sufism than Ibn Taymiyyah. By then the world of Islam was obviously weakened by Western advances. An obscure proponent of a fundamentalist purge in Islam read deeply in Ibn Taymiyyah, but with a more ambitious spirit. Ibn Taymiyyah attacked the Sufis and others he despised, but he did not argue that the whole community of Muslims had fallen into disbelief. That bizarre charge was introduced by a simpleton from the wilderness of Najd in east-central Arabia named Muhammad Ibn Abd Al-Wahhab (1703–1792). His creed, Wahhabism, is now known to the whole world, as the inspirer of Al-Qaida on September 11, 2001, as well as in Iraq and everywhere else the terrorist conspiracy sheds blood. Ibn Abd Al-Wahhab considered himself a reformer of Islam, and non-Muslims or Muslim dissidents who call for a "Muslim Reformation" today seldom understand that religious reform means very different things to liberal-minded protestors and literal-minded purifiers. Ibn Abd Al-Wahhab was of the latter kind. And it is mainly because of Ibn Taymiyyah and Ibn Abd Al-Wahhab that what was described after the U.S.-led intervention in Iraq as the "Iraqi resistance" against Americans became the "Sunni insurgency"— and then fell under Al-Qaida control, turning into the Wahhabi jihad, or Saudi second invasion of Iraq, financed from Riyadh, against Sufis and Shias.

Like Ibn Taymiyyah, Ibn Abd Al-Wahhab seems to have spent some time with Sufis, and this fact has also been used by slothful Western authors to argue that there is little difference between the violence of the Wahhabis and the metaphysics of the Sufis. The claim is absurd. Ibn Abd Al-Wahhab gained very little from his brief involvement with Sufism. His manifest intent was that of a radical "cleansing" through blood. He was convinced that Islam was threatened from within and fanatical about his belief that he alone had the prescription for its rescue. Islam must, he exhorted, expunge everything spiritual it had encompassed since the time of Muhammad and his successors, especially anything associated with Sufism. The Shias were unbelievers and must be exterminated. In the minds of his later admirers, the attitudes of Ibn

Abd Al-Wahhab would justify not only mass murder in twenty-first-century Iraq but the entire global assault by Al-Qaida on Christians, Jews, Hindus, and Buddhists, in addition to Shia and Sunni Muslims who rejected Wahhabism.

Ibn Abd Al-Wahhab did not spend much time on Christians and Jews except to accuse Muslims of unacceptably imitating them and to defame Jews as corrupt. But they were *very* thin on the ground in the area of Arabia where he lived most of his life. He was more intent on wiping out the Sufis, Shias, and others who according to him were no longer Muslims. The father of Wahhabism was not much of a scholar, and his main "contribution" is a little book called *Kitab al-Tawhid*, or *The Book of Monotheism*. There he expressed the core of his doctrine: it was not enough for a Muslim to publicly declare belief in One God. A Muslim must also actively repudiate any "worship" of other objects "beside Allah." A Muslim who did not affirm such a denial or who failed to repeatedly verbalize it had become an unbeliever and could be killed, his property seized and family members humiliated and raped.

The self-importance of Ibn Abd Al-Wahhab knew no bounds. At a time when the Ottomans had failed in their second siege of Vienna and when the Christian powers had enriched themselves by global exploration, pillage of the gold and silver of the New World, seizure of indescribably vast lands, and the enslavement and transportation of Africans, Ibn Abd Al-Wahhab believed that only the persecution of Muslims he deemed to have fallen into unbelief mattered. Soon, the descendants of Ibn Abd Al-Wahhab had formed a compact with the local bandit clan of Al-Sa'ud, under which the two families would marry among each other. They adopted a theological and political scheme in which the descendants of Ibn Abd Al-Wahhab would administer religious affairs and the house of Sa'ud would govern the state. The Ottoman court recognized the plan as subversive of the

Sunni order and banned the Wahhabi sect. But after spilling a considerable quantity of blood and stealing great amounts of treasure in Arabia and Iraq, on the pretext that they alone were legitimate interpreters of Islam, the Wahhabi-Saudi conspiracy produced the kingdom of Saudi Arabia in 1932, and after that came the oil, and the money, and Al-Qaida.

The miserable *Kitab al-Tawhid* is little more than a handbook for interrogation and punishment of "thoughtcrime" suspects, to borrow the term invented by Orwell. Prayer to God in honor of Muhammad is outlawed as blasphemy against monotheism. Muhammad is downgraded to being the messenger of God and nothing more. Muslims who praise Muhammad are, as in the vocabulary of Ibn Taymiyyah, equated with Christians, who made Jesus into God's son. But for Ibn Abd Al-Wahhab, Muslims expressing their love of the Prophet are to be wholly excluded from Islam. Erection of tombs and memorials to righteous Muslims, and praying at such sites, equals the worship of idols and is forbidden. So is the wearing of Sufi garments. Use of amulets (such as the "hand of Fatima" or "five" widely seen in North Africa and adopted by Jews who lived in Morocco, or charms against the evil eye) or anything else that could be construed as magic or reading of omens must be punished severely. So must acquisitiveness toward wealth—certainly ironic considering that the rulers of Saudi Arabia, where Wahhabism is the state religion, have shown no reluctance to accumulate and spend. All such habits were attacked by Ibn Abd Al-Wahhab as "unacceptable innovations" (*bidas*) that had impermissibly adulterated the original faith of Islam. He had a deranged talent for heresy hunting; he denounced those who complained about the weather for denying God's will.

Ibn Taymiyyah and Ibn Abd Al-Wahhab have been compared, even by their enthusiastic defenders, with the most destructive phenomenon in early Islam, a group known as the Khawarij or Kharijites (from an Arabic word meaning "rebels" or "renegades"). The Kharijites, like Ibn Taymiyyah and Ibn Abd Al-Wahhab, accused the majority of Muslims of insufficient piety and called all who disagreed with them unbelievers. The Muslims have preferred to forget the Kharijites, though a moderate version of their interpretation, Ibadhism, is official in the Gulf sultanate of Oman. Historical details on them are scarce, and ironically, one must turn for an account of them to a fundamentalist predecessor of Ibn Taymiyyah, the Baghdad-born religious writer Ibn Al-Jawzi (1126–1200).

Ibn Al-Jawzi was a true hater, especially of Shia Muslims. His ranting against them is so virulent that an excerpt of his work *Talbis Iblis* (*The Devil's Deception*) is distributed today in such vulnerable places as American prisons by Sunni-Wahhabi extremists. Ibn Al-Jawzi also opposed Al-Ghazali. But his book is useful for its description of the Kharijites, who indeed resemble the Wahhabis of today. After Muhammad divided a shipment of gold sent to him from Yemen by his son-in-law Ali Ibn Abi Talib, separating shares of it among four of the Prophet's companions, some grumblers complained at not being included in the distribution of wealth. Muhammad asked why they would not trust him, and "a man with sunken cheekbones, a protruding forehead, thick beard, and a shaven head" called out to Muhammad to fear God, that is, to show honesty.

The companion who arrogantly cautioned the Prophet of Islam against corruption was named Dhul-Khuwaisara at-Tamimi, and his kin organized a rebellion against Muhammad's son-in-law Ali once the latter had become caliph. The Kharijites were so assiduous in prayer, it was said their foreheads became calloused. Their constant recitation of the *Qur'an* made their camp sound as if it were a huge beehive. And when they fought against Ali, they shouted, "Prepare for paradise and

God," in the manner of today's jihadists. A Kharijite named Ibn Muljam assumed leadership of the group, called on them to give up their lives in battle against those they considered to have strayed from Islam, and murdered Imam Ali—in a mosque, it is said. With this deed began the great schism in Islam between Shias, who consider themselves "the party of Ali," and Sunnis. The Kharijites continued to disturb the Arabian Peninsula for decades. *Takfir*—excommunication—was their preferred method of argument; they called anybody who disagreed with them a polytheist, and those who did not fight alongside them were further labeled unbelievers. They also legitimized the slaying of Muslim women and children as alleged polytheists. Ibn Al-Jawzi commented justly of them that they considered the murder of children acceptable but eating a date without paying for it a great sin. They prayed through the night, yet they killed Ali and massacred the Muslims. It is unsurprising that the Wahhabis of Al-Qaida should be compared with them.

Ibn Taymiyyah and Ibn Abd Al-Wahhab remain the two most famous enemies of the Sufis, but in the nineteenth century a new, modernizing trend rose in Arab Islam that criticized the Sufis but did not incite violence against them. Like Ibn Taymiyyah (whose writings were revived at the end of the nineteenth century) and Ibn Abd Al-Wahhab, the Arab reformers claimed to return to the original, undiluted Islam of Muhammad and the three centuries of leading Muslims after him. These nineteenth-century Muslim modernists called themselves Salafis, after the Arabic term (*aslaf*) for the early generations of Muslims after the Prophet, that is, his Companions and his Successors. Ottoman Muslim theologians, who had rejected the pretensions of the Wahhabis, argued that it had never been acceptable for Muslims to compare themselves in virtue to the Prophet and the *aslaf*. A more accurate term than "Salafis" would be "Islahis," meaning reformers. The best-known nineteenth-century Islamic reformers were an Iranian, Jamalud'din Al-Afghani (1838–1897), and his Egyptian disciple, Muhammad Abduh (1849–1905). They were succeeded in the original "Salafi" movement by a Syrian, Rashid Rida (1865–1935).

The title "Salafi" has been appropriated by the Wahhabis as a cover, since the Wahhabis know that the blood and fire to which they have subjected the Muslim world have made them hated under their own banner. Wahhabis call themselves "Salafis" in the same way that totalitarian leftists call themselves "progressives" although the admirers of Stalin or Castro have had nothing in common with the Americans who once voted for Theodore Roosevelt, the greatest of the true Progressives. Unfortunately, in the aftermath of September 11, 2001, it was common to see and hear Western governments, media, think tanks, and other institutions taken in by Saudi propaganda and Western academic assertions that there was no such thing as Wahhabism— just plain Islam, allegedly practiced in its pristine form by the current "Salafis."

Al-Afghani was the most flamboyant of the nineteenth-century reformers, a pan-Islamic revolutionary who wandered the Muslim and Christian lands seeking to regenerate the Muslims and combat European imperialism. He had much in common with the pre-Marxist Russian revolutionaries of his time, such as Aleksandr Herzen and Mikhail Bakunin. Most of the nineteenth-century Muslim reformers condemned aspects of Sufism, which they equated with a disintegrating Ottoman order, as allegedly keeping Islam in a backward condition. To many of them, Sufism was alien to Islam as well as decadent, although unlike Ibn Taymiyyah, they made exceptions for Al-Ghazali and other outstanding theologians. Some of the modernists were Sufis who had shifted from the metaphysical thought of Ibn Arabi to the purism of Ibn Taymiyyah; but other dissenters, basing themselves in

Ibn Arabi, blamed the domination of clerics for the decline of the Islamic world.

THE NINETEENTH-CENTURY "SALAFIS" did not make war against Sufism except by the tongue and the pen. Within the Sufi environment, however, the ever-present division between the "sober," *Shariah*-compliant Sufis and ecstatic, liberated Sufis became violent. The Naqshbandi Sufis emerged as preeminent guardians of religious conformism among the Sufis. They are the only *tariqa* insisting that their line of descent begins with the first caliph after Muhammad, Abubakr, the greatest caliph for the Sunnis. The Naqshbandis probably originated as imitators of Abd Al-Khaliq Ghujduwani, the twelfth-century associate of Hojja Yasawi, but while the Yasawi Sufis moved in the free-spirited direction of Turkish culture, the Naqshbandi Sufis set out to eradicate Buddhist elements from central Asian popular Islam, to supposedly "purify" it of the mysticism inherited from "thousands of saints in Turkestan."

Politics and rivalries have clouded the history of the Naqshbandis, making even their name controversial. *Naqshband* refers to a seal upon the heart; Ghujduwani taught Sufis to constantly repeat a silent *dhikr*, audible only to oneself, that should impress itself on the heart. Today's Uzbek authorities, who claim Ghujduwani as one of their "great ancestors," argue that the emphasis on repetition comes from an Uzbek saying that one should measure seven times before cutting cloth. This explanation is similar to another definition of the name Naqshband, referring to the trade of the fabric weaver pursued by the guide of the order two hundred years after Ghujduwani: Bahauddin Naqshband (1317–1389), whom many Naqshbandis identify as their founder and who is called "the Imam of Sufism" by some Muslims. Uzbek government literature praising Bahauddin Naqshband celebrates his teaching that mystics should live in the world, occupy themselves with regular employment, and put the interests of others before themselves—a kind of Sufi collectivism not unlike idealized Soviet Communism. Karimov's Uzbek government has rehabilitated the tomb of Bahauddin Naqshband in Bukhara.

Uzbek sources confirm that Ghujduwani was, like Ahmad Yasawi, a student of the wise Abu Yaqub Yusuf Al-Hamadani but add that like Rumi and Hajji Bektash, Ghujduwani was a product of Khorasan and its tradition of disaffection with the Muslim clerics. In "rebel" Khorasan, the Naqshbandis became ultraconservative, and turned to an extreme adherence to *Shariah*. In their insistence on *Shariah*, the Naqshbandis were not very different from Ibn Taymiyyah, and some Naqshbandi literature gives the impression that they want to claim Ibn Taymiyyah while also criticizing him. Bernard Lewis compared Naqshbandi shaykhs who fought the tsarist Russians in the eighteenth-century Caucasus with their contemporaries in the Wahhabi movement as "purifiers" of Islam. Although the Wahhabis despise Sufis and the Naqshbandis hate the Wahhabis, in terms of living Islam they most often provide a mirror image of each other, equally intolerant in their attitudes. The late Grand Mufti of Syria shaykh Ahmad Kuftaro (1915–2004) was a Naqshbandi enemy of the Wahhabis but also issued a *fatwa* supporting suicide terror in Iraq after 2003. Lewis's original perception was surer than I, for one, thought it to be.[3]

Naqshbandis spread throughout the Muslim world, from the Balkans to Southeast Asia. They produced a series of Sunni revivalists, including Ahmad ash-Faruqi Sirhindi (1564–1624) in India and Khalid Al-Baghdadi (1779–1827), a Kurd who went to India to study. Sirhindi spread the idea that Sufis should approach rulers intimately to keep them away from Hindu and other syncretic practices, and to reassert the priority of *Shariah* in Muslim-ruled countries. Sirhindi preached that after the resurrection of the dead they would be questioned by God about their adherence to *Shariah,* not their Sufism. (The unimaginably greater Al-Ghazali thought otherwise.)

Like Ibn Taymiyyah and Ibn Abd Al-Wahhab, Sirhindi proclaimed that the Naqshbandi Sufis were identical in teaching with the Prophet's Companions. Al-Baghdadi, a former Qadiri Sufi who brought a number of leading Kurdish Qadiris into the Naqshbandi order, made this attitude, as well as hostility to Shias and Westerners, the basis for Naqshbandi dominance in the Ottoman court. The Naqshbandism of Sirhindi and Al-Baghdadi has been described as an intrusion of radicalized Indian Islam, which was in conflict with the Hindus and the British, into the Ottoman Empire. In this way it reproduced the original intolerance present in the anti-Buddhist mission of the Naqshbandis. Al-Baghdadi compared himself with the *aslaf,* and he could be called a "Sufi Salafi." The outcome has been the same in many places: Naqshbandis ascendant in current Turkish politics; Naqshbandis benefiting from the Uzbek dictatorship of Karimov; Naqshbandis currying favor from Prince Charles of England. All such politicking is done in the name of classical Islam—but it is a form of the traditional faith that also upholds *Shariah*-compliant, "sober" obedience to a narrow and rigid interpretation of religion.

The Naqshbandis are justly proud of their role in the Caucasian Muslim resistance to Russian tsarism in the nineteenth century—the irregular war led by Imam Shamyl (ca. 1800–1871)—and they and the Qadiris are best known as jihadist Sufis. But they also have a serious blot on their relations with other Sufis: their complicity in persecution of the Bektashis. We have already noted how the dominance of the *Shariah*-centered and "sober" Qadiris and Naqshbandis has been blamed for the failure of the Bektashis to thrive in Bosnia-Herzegovina. In

1826 the Ottoman ruling class made the first serious attempt in Turkey to suppress the Bektashi order, the chaplains of the Janissaries. Turkish historians, scholars of Sufism, and Naqshbandis have tried to downplay these events, but they were deeply harmful to Turkish society, and represented an important landmark in the country's history. Not only had the Bektashis helped bring the Turks into Islam and establish Ottoman power in newly conquered lands, but their preaching and writing in the Turkish language made them ethnic heroes. They had also established spiritual ties with non-Muslims, were extremely liberal and pluralistic, and were especially popular among the poorer classes. The Bektashis were what they had always been: libertarian Islamic revolutionaries, even when serving the Janissaries.

History reveals an exact opposition between the Bektashis and the Naqshbandis, much more than between the Naqshbandis and Wahhabis. Where the Bektashis stood for harmony with non-Muslims, the Naqshbandis hated them; where the Bektashis disregarded *Shariah*, the Naqshbandis defended it. The Bektashis sympathized with Shias and honored Imam Ali; the Naqshbandis despised Shias. Finally, the Naqshbandis believed in a single caliphate uniting the disparate cultures of Turkey, Iraq, India, and Southeast Asia; they were not devoted to the Turkish language or customs. The Naqshbandis were long a minority at the Ottoman court, where the Mawlawi order of Rumi was more favored, but the strict views of the Naqshbandis came to coincide paradoxically with the immediate interest of the court, which needed to satisfy Western and local demands for abolition of "archaic" institutions like the Janissaries. Modernizing "liberals" allied with Sufi fundamentalists in a war against liberated Bektashis; anti-Bektashi "reforms" demanded by defenders of *Shariah* were allegedly modernist but would make the state more rather than less Islamic in law. Trends in Islamic history collided in Constantinople; the Ottoman Empire was in an increasingly fatal and confused conflict with itself. The internal division of the Ottomans was extremely complex and cannot be reduced to a simple paradigm.

But the Janissary corps was abolished as a concession to the West, and soon the Sunni clerics and some Sufi shaykhs met in Constantinople to decide the fate of the Bektashis. The clerics accused the Bektashis of irreligion, heresy, and contempt for the *Shariah*, but introduced no evidence. Many Bektashi *babas* were executed or murdered, and others were sent into internal exile in places known for Sunni fundamentalism. The extensive *tekkes* and other properties of the Bektashis were seized by the state and handed over for administration by the Naqshbandis. The Naqshbandis had participated in a crime against the spirit of the Bektashis, one of the most distinguished and honorable Sufi orders.

The Bektashis, however, proved capable of survival. Since Sufis often belong to more than one order, some Bektashis were also Naqshbandis, and some Naqshbandis who had taken over Bektashi institutions "in the name of *Shariah*" were also Bektashis. After a quarter-century, the properties of the Bektashi Sufis were returned to them and their liberty had been restored. But many *babas* had been martyred in conditions remembered and retold in Turkey and the Balkans today.

The Wahhabi war *against* Sufis in Arabia continued simultaneously with the war *between* Sufis in the Ottoman Empire. But just as Naqshbandi Sufis came from India to Turkey to support "sober" and *Shariah*-compliant Sufism, Moroccan and West African Sufis stepped forward to defy Wahhabi preaching. West Africans are among the most interesting and least appreciated Sufis in the Muslim world, as well as in Western literature on Islamic mysticism.

The Idrisi Sufis were a product of North Africa and shared the

Wahhabi appeal to "cleanse" Islam. At the same time, they confronted the Wahhabis in defense of Sufism. Their great shaykh, Ahmad ibn Idris (1749–1837), born in Morocco, then traveled to the parts of Arabia that had been seized by the Wahhabis to debate with them. Ibn Idris put forward an eloquent argument against the fundamentalist urge to constantly expand the inventory of forbidden practices in Islam. He quoted a *hadith* of Muhammad: *"The Muslim who committed the greatest offense against Muslims is the man who asked about something which had not been forbidden but then became forbidden because of his question."* To act in the manner of the Wahhabis, seeking practices to ban and people to punish, would unacceptably increase the burden on the Prophet and the whole Muslim community. This *hadith* could stand as a central argument in the long history of tension between clerics and mystics in Sunni Islam—and embodies the issue that has taken so many Muslim lives in Iraq and elsewhere.

# 4

## Sufis in Today's Muslim World

SUFISM IN MUSLIM COUNTRIES is obviously the most significant element in its existence. Mystical Muslims are found in French-speaking West Africa, Morocco, Libya, Egypt, Sudan, Syria, Lebanon, Israel and the Palestinian territories, the Balkans, Turkey, central Asia, Iraq, Kurdistan, Saudi Arabia, Iran, Afghanistan, Pakistan, India, Malaysia, and Indonesia—throughout the Islamic world. For the outsider, the complex network of Sufi orders may seem confusing, but Sufi adherents learn and participate in the "system," and after a brief study the different histories and habits of the orders are easy to grasp.

In the Ottoman state, the authority of twelve Sufi tariqas was recognized: the Yasawis, Qadiris, Rifa'is, Kubrawis, Suhrawardis, Bektashis, Mawlawis, Sa'adis, Halvetis, Naqshbandis, Bayramis, and Zaynis. The Bosnian scholar Hafizović has identified a slightly different list of twelve "orthodox" Sufi orders: the Qadiris, Shazalis, Kubrawis, Mawlawis, Chishtis, Nimatullahis, Naqshbandis, Suhrawardis, Rifa'is, Halvetis, Nurbakshis, and Tijanis. The second list bars the heterodox

Bektashis but includes the Tijanis, who were never "accepted" under Ottoman authority. We have already examined some of these and will here take up all of them, although in neither of the stated inventories.

A third, extended roster of eighteen Sufi orders, some of them almost completely unknown to scholars, was compiled by the nineteenth-century Bektashi poet Turabi Ali Dede. The text in which it appeared was transcribed for me by the Bektashis of Tetova in Macedonia and merits study, but such is beyond the scope of the present work. In Sufism, official recognition has little enduring meaning, considering the extraordinary proliferation and diversity of metaphysical phenomena throughout the Muslim world. What were once a dozen major *tariqas* now seem a dozen times that number.

But however complex and prolific the maps of the Sufi constellation may be, the organized orders are always based on a *silsila* or line of saintly descent. In the underground chamber to which Hojja Ahmad Yasawi retired late in life beneath his magnificent mausoleum in Turkestan, there today appears a chart of the main Sufi *tariqas* and the *silsila* claimed by each of them. The diagram shows Imam Ali Ibn Abi Talib, the fourth caliph and ideal of the Shia Muslims, at the center of display, with all *tariqas* but one—the Naqshbandis—originating with him. The Sufi family tree in the Hojja Yasawi tomb is not arranged chronologically, but the bottom or root position is occupied by three groups. First, and in the center, the Yasawis, in the twelfth century—understandable in that monument. To the left appear the Bektashis, in the thirteenth century, linked by the relationship of Hojja Yasawi and Hajji Bektash. Proceeding upward from the Bektashis on the left side of the chart we find the Halvetis of the fourteenth century, then the individuals Junayd Al-Baghdadi and, related to him by metaphysical association, Al-Ghazali. Suhrawardi comes next, in the twelfth to thirteenth centuries.

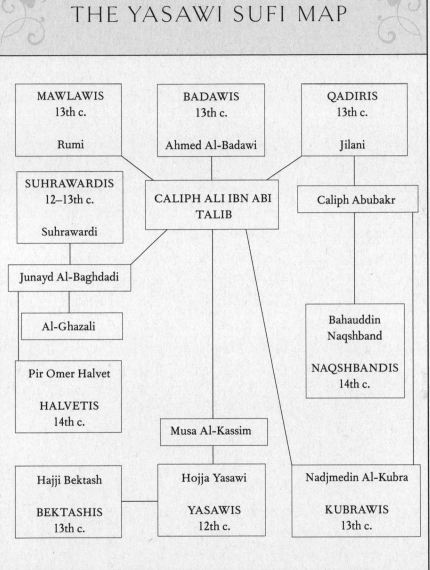

# THE YASAWI SUFI MAP

| MAWLAWIS 13th c. Rumi | BADAWIS 13th c. Ahmed Al-Badawi | QADIRIS 13th c. Jilani |
|---|---|---|

SUHRAWARDIS
12–13th c.

Suhrawardi

CALIPH ALI IBN ABI TALIB

Caliph Abubakr

Junayd Al-Baghdadi

Al-Ghazali

Bahauddin Naqshband

NAQSHBANDIS
14th c.

Pir Omer Halvet

HALVETIS
14th c.

Musa Al-Kassim

Hajji Bektash

BEKTASHIS
13th c.

Hojja Yasawi

YASAWIS
12th c.

Nadjmedin Al-Kubra

KUBRAWIS
13th c.

On the opposite, right side of the diagram, the third foundational position, alongside the Yasawis and Bektashis, is occupied by the thirteenth-century Kubrawi Sufis, an order that spread from the Iranian culture zone to India. The poet and biographer Farid'ud'din Attar was taught by a Kubrawi shaykh. The Nurbakshi Sufis are another Iranian order growing out of the Kubrawi *silsila*. In the underground chart at the Yasawi tomb a line is drawn from the Kubrawis to one of the three *tariqas* at the top of the group: the Qadiris. The Yasawi map shows only the Kubrawis and Qadiris linked to both Caliph Abubakr and Imam Ali. Alongside them, since the fourteenth century, Naqshbandis derive from Abubakr alone, and they are shown almost as a separate body, except for a common line with the Qadiris. Leftward from the Qadiris on the subterranean outline stand two other *tariqas* with great authority in the world of Sufism: at the center, the Badawis beginning in the thirteenth century, distributed throughout the Arab countries, and the Mawlawi order of Rumi.

The four most significant *tariqas* in today's Muslim world include only two on the wall of the Yasawi underground chamber: the Qadiris and the Bektashis. Apart from them, the Nimatullahi order in Iran, which is rigorously Shia, and the Alawis/Ba'Alawis originating on the Red Sea and Gulf coasts of the Arabian Peninsula (not to be confused with the Turkish and Kurdish Alevis or the Syrian Alawites[1]) are key elements in the future of Islam. Each of the four has its niche: the Qadiris as an activist body throughout the Muslim world, the Nimatullahis as Iranian reformers, the Alawis as a force in Saudi Arabia for restoration of a pluralistic Islam and disestablishment of Wahhabism as a state sect, and the Bektashis as modernists, mainly in Europe.

Let us begin, then, with the Qadiris, Nimatullahis, Arabian Alawis, and Bektashis.

*Qadiris:* We have already encountered the Qadiris, and their identification with the Persian proponent of strict Muslim observance, Abdul Qadri Jilani, whose beloved tomb in Baghdad was bombed in 2007 by Wahhabi terrorists. His influence was immense; in the words of Baba Rexheb, his beliefs "permeated Muslim society as far as India." But the Qadiri order itself was delayed in its appearance, and there is even some doubt whether Jilani was an authentic Sufi. Highly disciplined in their devotion to the external practice of Sunni Islam, the Qadiris went beyond India, penetrating Indonesia in the farthest east and West Africa in the other direction. The Qadiris are known for jihad fighting in defense of Islam and *Shariah* in places as diverse as Algeria, Kosovo, and Chechnya.

The nineteenth-century Sufi and leader of early Algerian opposition to French conquest, Abd Al-Qadir Al-Jazairi (1808–1883), famously taught that jihad is the most difficult duty a Sufi can fulfill. Al-Jazairi himself preached and showed by example that protection of non-Muslim civilians (in this instance, French colonists) was required from Muslims fighting a Christian invader. He traced his Sufi inspiration to Ibn Arabi and interpreted his own experiences through his study of the Spanish Sufi's insights. Al-Jazairi concluded that the future of Islam lay with acceptance of the technological and social changes seen in the West. Yet Al-Jazairi was one of the two most beloved personalities among the nineteenth-century Muslims, along with the heroic combatant against the Russians in the Caucasus, Imam Shamyl, a Naqshbandi. Al-Jazairi and Shamyl were adulated as heroes by the whole Muslim world, while "Salafi" reformers such as Al-Afghani were considered adventurers.

Some of the most eminent Qadiris strayed far from a "sober" and *Shariah*-centered Islam, with which they have come to be identified. Whereas an eleventh-century "fundamentalist" Sufi, Abdullah Ansari, refused to condemn Hallaj, Abd Al-Qadir Al-Jazairi declared in a poem titled *"Wahdat ul-wujud"* (Unity of Being):

> I am God [ana ul-haqq], I am a creature; I am the Lord, I am a
>   servant;
> I am the Throne and the mat worn down by feet;
> I am hell and I am a happy eternity;
> I am water, I am fire; I am the air and the earth;
> I am "how many" and I am "how"; I am presence and absence;
> I am essence and attribute; I am proximity and distance;
> All being is my being; I am the only, I am the One.

The jihad traditions of the Qadiris led some of them in 2004 to join fighting against American-led troops in the Iraqi town of Fallujah, and Sufi singers incited local Sunnis there to attack the Coalition forces. But Wahhabi terrorists then arrived in the city and began killing the Sufis for selling CDs and listening to music, which the Wahhabis condemn, as well as for the traditional Sufi prayers at tombs and meetings for *dhikr*, equally or more obnoxious to the radicals. In Fallujah, the Wahhabis were more concerned with slaying Sufis and women without full body covering than with fighting the Americans. Execution orders after the killing of "offending" men and women were posted as flyers in the streets. When U.S. and Coalition troops took Fallujah, they were welcomed by the Sufis for rescuing them from "the Taliban." As many Iraqis would point out, even those inflamed by nationalism and anxious to fight the U.S. intervention were not fanatical enough to accept a Wahhabi tyranny, and few Iraqis were willing to blow themselves up in suicide bombings. Such reluctance partly explains why so many of the foreign fighters in the "Sunni" terror inflicted on Iraq were Saudi subjects.

*Nimatullahis:* In Iran, where Sufi classics form the greater part of the national literature, the Nimatullahi order is the main *tariqa*. It was founded by the fifteenth-century poet Nurud'din Nimatullah Veli, known as Shah Nimatullah. Shah Nimatullah's poetry is much read and appreciated in Iran today. Here is one of his verses:

*Come, my heart and my soul is filled with love for the dervishes.*
*Come, for the king of the world is a beggar compared with the*
*    dervishes.*

*I swear by the feet of the poor dervishes and by the life of the*
*    Master,*
*That the dust thrown in the air by the feet of dervishes is like kohl*
*    for my eyes.*

*Enter into the place where the Archangel Gabriel[2] has no access;*
*That is the place of solitude of the dervish.*

*The voice of the chanting of the lovers and the joy of our*
*    gathering*
*Are examples of the presence and emanations brought by the*
*    dervish.*

*Lift a glass full of the dregs of grief to toast the eternal*
*    cupbearer,*
*For the glass with these dregs is the best remedy for a dervish.*

*Although I love a dervish who made my heart bleed*
*It is joyful to me, for this suffering is caused by a dervish!*

Shah Nimatullah studied with the Qadiris, but his order is believed to have begun as a branch of the aggressively Sunni Naqshbandis. The Nimatullahis converted to the Shia way of Islam, yet anti-Sufi elements inside Shia-ruled Iran today accuse the order of remaining Sunni. The Nimatullahis in Iran adhere to strict Islamic law according to the Jafari Shia interpretation.

They have many branches, one important community being the Nimatullahis of Gonabad, an area in the fabled Khorasan known for producing saffron. The Nimatullahi-Gonabadis were organized at the end of the nineteenth century by Hajji Mollah Sultan Mohammad Gonabadi. Ayatollah Khomeini wrote in praise of the Gonabadis; their current leader is Nur Ali Tabanda. A competing Nimatullahi figure, Javad Nurbakhsh, lives in Britain in exile as a former supporter of the Iranian shah. His writings, however, are widely read and admired in Iran. While the Gonabadis are known as religious, the followers of Nurbakhsh are not.

*Hejazi and Southeast Asian Alawis and Ba'Alawis:* These are, again, neither Turkish and Kurdish Alevis nor Syrian Alawites but a powerful force in Arab and Southeast Asian Sufism. The Alawi *tariqa* was founded in Hadramaut on the south coast of Arabia by Muhammad bin Ali Ba'Alawi (1178–1255). He traced his Sufi descent back to Muhammad himself, but also to Imam Ali, Junayd Al-Baghdadi, and Al-Ghazali, through the Shazali Sufi order. The Alawis functioned secretly for five centuries. The most important Alawi figure in modern times was Sayyid Muhammad ibn 'Alawi Al-Maliki, known as Sayyid Al-Maliki. He was the author of more than one hundred volumes on Islam.

Sayyid Al-Maliki was a leading representative of the Hejazi tradition in Arabia—the culture of Mecca and Medina before its twentieth-century takeover by Wahhabism. Because of his opposition to the Wahhabis, he was dismissed from a professorship at the religious university of Umm ul-Qura in Mecca. He was arrested and deprived of his passport and, therefore, the right to leave the kingdom. But he had visited Indonesia, Morocco, and South Africa, where he taught Sufism to many believers. He also had Sufi disciples in the United States. He became a spiritual mentor for foes of Wahhabism around the world as the unofficial, alternative, anti-Wahhabi "Chief Scholar" of Saudi Arabia.

Sayyid Al-Maliki never showed anger to his Wahhabi oppressors. He answered them with a superior knowledge of Islam and pointed out their own doctrinal weaknesses, which were many, since the Wahhabis are known for improvisation rather than scholarship. And so he was silenced. For some time before his death I was warned by Saudi reformers not to write too much about him in the Western media, not to call attention to him, as he would attract more repressive actions. But since his death in 2004 he is now beyond such concerns.

Dr. Irfan Al-Alawi, an expert on the Islamic heritage of Arabia, was an associate of Sayyid Al-Maliki's. He wrote of him, "Sayyid Muhammad ibn 'Alawi Al-Maliki was born in 1947, a descendant of the prophet Muhammad (Blessings and peace be upon Him) through Imam Hasan, a grandson of the Prophet." Al-Maliki's family were jurists of the Maliki school of Sunni *Shariah*, which is prevalent in Arab countries and West Africa but has been subjected to suppression in the Saudi kingdom. As Al-Alawi commented, the shaykh's family had

an ancestral residence in the Holy City of Mecca. His grandfather was the Qadi [chief judge] of Mecca and an Imam of the

Haram [Grand Mosque of Mecca], the site of the *Ka'bah*. The Maliki residence was close to the Haram, next to Bab al-Salaam [the Gate of Peace], and there our shaykh was born.

At school in Mecca, his first and most important teacher was his father, the illustrious Sayyid Alawi . . . our shaykh's grandfather, Sayyid Abbas, [was the] son of the great saint Muhammad Al-Maliki Al-Idrisi.

Throughout his life, Sayyid Al-Maliki remained very close to the Ba-'Alawi Sufis. There were always young 'Alawis among his students . . . When he spoke, Sayyid Al-Maliki's words assuaged troubled hearts, uplifted souls, stirred up the love of God and His Prophet in people, and increased their knowledge.

Sayyid Al-Maliki was also dedicated to protection of Islamic heritage against Wahhabi demolition, which has been extensive in Saudi Arabia. The Wahhabis prohibit preservation of tombs, early mosques, and other structures associated with Muhammad, his Companions, and Islamic saints. Wahhabi destruction in Mecca and Medina has included leveling the house Muhammad lived in, which seems bizarre enough to Westerners but genuinely outrageous to traditional Muslims.

The Sufi translator G. F. Haddad in his valuable contemporary chronicle *From the Two Holy Sanctuaries: A Hajj Journal* praises Sayyid Al-Maliki and claims to derive legitimacy from his association with him. But Haddad, a "fundamentalist" Naqshbandi, has also tried to enclose Sufism in a framework of orthodoxy. This is typical behavior today among the Muslim Sufis who want to defend themselves from the homicidal mania of Wahhabis and other radicals by proclaiming their own superior adherence to narrow *Shariah* rather than to legal and intellectual pluralism. These orthodox and, naturally, "sober" Sufis become demonstrative if not exhibitionistic in their piety and, in the case of Haddad and others, turn to ideological Islamism and anti-Western attitudes.

There is little to suggest that Sayyid Al-Maliki intended his thought to be kept within narrow boundaries, although he defended traditional Islam against the Wahhabis. In favoring the *mawlid* celebration of the birth of Muhammad, he rejected Wahhabi charges that honoring the Prophet's birthday was an "unacceptable innovation" (*bida*) in the religion of Islam, which must not change from its original form. That was the Wahhabi posture from the emergence of their extremist movement out of the void of east-central Arabia in the eighteenth century. But as Sayyid Al-Maliki and other opponents of Wahhabism since Ottoman times have said, if Muslims reject all innovations since the era of the Prophet, they must abandon the written *Qur'an,* the production of books of knowledge, the erection of minarets at mosques, the construction of schools, hotels, hospitals, first aid centers, and jails, and use of modern weapons. Should the Muslims of Bosnia-Herzegovina, Sayyid Al-Maliki implied, have fought Serbian aggression using only bows and arrows and spears when faced with artillery, rocket bombs, tanks, jet aircraft, and other sophisticated military equipment?

To Christians and Jews it is obviously perverse that Muslims could be prohibited from praising and expressing love for their Prophet by commemorating his birth. But under Wahhabi rule, *mawlid* for the Prophet was permitted only behind the walls of private homes in the Saudi kingdom, and only in the past decade. Sayyid Al-Maliki also called attention to a positive parallel between honoring Muhammad and Jesus, recalling that in narratives of the Night Journey of Muhammad to Jerusalem and the heavens, it is said that the Prophet of Islam, accompanied by the Archangels Michael and Gabriel (Jibril), passed over the town of Bethlehem, and Muhammad prostrated twice in prayer to mark the birth of Jesus.

In 2005, I visited one of the world's great Sufi communities at the Ba'Alawi Mosque in Singapore. The site is a small, sacred precinct, open to the breezes, since the environment is tropical. I came to prayer on the evening when *Isra wa'l Miraj*, Muhammad's Night Journey, was commemorated. I was invited to the *minbar*, or pulpit, where, surrounded by hundreds of Malay faces and speaking in English, I quoted from Sayyid Al-Maliki's narration and explanation of the Night Journey, *The Resplendent Lights of the Night-Journey and Ascension of the Best of Creation*. In that text, Sayyid Al-Maliki explained that, in addition to honoring Jesus, the angel Gabriel had commanded Muhammad to pray at places associated with Moses, including Midian and Mount Sinai.

In one of the most affecting examples of the Muslim affinity for the Jewish patriarchs and prophets, Sayyid Al-Maliki, like other commentators on the Night Journey, recounted the following:

> [During the Ascent] Muhammad saw a man talking loudly and angrily. Muhammad demanded from Gabriel to know who the man was, and Gabriel responded, "That is Moses."
>
> Muhammad asked, "To whom is he speaking harshly?" Gabriel replied, "To God."
>
> Muhammad asked, "How can Moses rudely admonish God?" And Gabriel said, "Almighty God is used to the brusque manner of Moses."

In the Ba'Alawi Mosque of Singapore, the Sufis honor another Muslim saint, Sayyid Umar bin Abd Al-Rahman Al-Attas, who died in south Arabia in 1660. Arabs from the Ḥadramaut coast via Indonesia were a major element in the rise of Singapore as a nineteenth-century trade center. They brought their mysticism with them, as embodied in a *ratib* or collection of invocations produced by Sayyid Al-Attas known as *The Rare Gift and the Key to Opening the Door of Union*. The text refers to mystical union with God and consists of seventeen invocations, which together make up one of the most powerful examples of Sufi *dhikr*. Recitation of the *ratib*, it is said, synchronizes one's breath with God. It concludes:

> *I seek forgiveness from God* [said eleven times]
> *I am repentant to God* [three times]
>
> *O God! (Grant me to die) by it—*
> *O God! (Grant me to die) by it—*
> *O God! (Grant me to die) by a*
> *Goodly ending.* [repeat three times]

We will further discuss the life of Sayyid Al-Maliki of Hejaz in the succeeding chapter, which includes analysis of Saudi Arabia's current situation. It would appear that the Ba'Alawis have transcended the division between the "sober" and intoxicated Sufis. This seems eminently appropriate to the hot nights of Singapore.

*Bektashis and Turkish and Kurdish Alevis:* After examining three leading *tariqas* that put *Shariah* first, and notwithstanding the exalted recitations of the Ba'Alawis, it is striking how far the Bektashis and their Alevi cousins have marched from "sober" and *Shariah*-centered Sufism. Rather than narrow observance, they boast an openhearted form of Islam, anticipated by many Sufi masters but most especially by Al-Ghazali. There are, today, millions of Albanian Bektashis and tens of millions of Turkish and Kurdish Alevis. They have maintained their communities because they have, *in visible reality*, "marched" rather than, as the *Shariah* fanatics would have it, "strayed" from an outlook of extreme outward piety. In the Ottoman Empire, they marched with the Janissaries, a basic institution of Turkish rule, and in the Albanian lands they have fought for liberal and secular ideals. Some Bektashis marched in the Albanian Partisan forces that fought the Nazis in the Second World War—the famous Bektashi Babas Faja Martaneshi and Fejzo Mallakastra, who wore their Bektashi robes and felt crowns into battle, in the same manner that their predecessors had in the ranks of the Ottoman forces.

As previously noted, Bektashis also fought in the Kosovo Liberation Army (KLA). In Turkey, the Alevis march with secularists against the imposition of Sunnicentric governance. Who is to say that the Bektashis and Alevis are not as Islamic, in their own way, as the "*Shariah*-centered" Sufis of the Qadiri, Nimatullahi, or Ba'Alawi orders? Why today should the "sober" Sufis dissociate themselves from the intoxicated Sufis of the Bektashi and Alevi kind if it is only out of fear of fundamentalism? Qadiris, Nimatullahis, Ba'Alawis, and Bektashis—each represents a specific face of Islamic metaphysics through the centuries, from the tempered fortitude of the Qadiri *tariqa* to the Shia enthusiasm of the Nimatullahis and the sublime speech of the Alawis to the joyful libertarianism of the Bektashis. All the rest among the Sufis are variants of these four streams.

*Mawlawis:* Mawlawi Sufis appear in many forms. "Whirling dervishes" from Konya, location of Rumi's much-visited mausoleum, travel around the world as a folklore entertainment group. In the West, the popularity of Mevlana's poetry has made a New Age version of his order attractive. Mawlawi *tekkes* also exist throughout the Ottoman cultural area, including in Kosovo. They tend, however, to be more reserved in their public activity.

Many Bosnians believe that after they were conquered by the Ottomans in the fifteenth century, spiritual authority in their country passed from a *djed* or elder in a semilegendary independent Christian "Bosnian Church," to a Mawlawi shaykh. It is said the transfer took place at a holy site of the Bosnian Church, which became a Mawlawi *tekija,* in the area of Sarajevo called Bembaša, an inviting setting on the Miljacka River, which then turns to flow straight through the city. Bembaša became a motif in classic Bosnian love songs, with a handsome young man going there and encountering beautiful girls who tease him, and is still known as a place where lovers walk together. This may be a survival of ancient local culture: the home of magical, capricious female spirits became the place of Christian worship and then of Sufi devotions, while remaining associated with passion. The Mawlawi *tekija* at Bembaša was open until at least the middle of the twentieth century.

*Halvetis:* Followers of Pir Omer Halvet (died ca. 1397 at Caesarea in Israel), this *tariqa* gave rise to many later orders. New *tariqas* emerging from the Halvetis included the *Cerrahis, Bayramis,* and the disciples of *Gulsheniy* (a follower of Ibn Arabi) and of *Niyazi Misri,* an important poet who had significant contacts with Jewish mystics of his time. The Halveti and post-Halveti orders remain a powerful component of Islamic culture. Their distinguishing characteristic was originally the seclusion (*khalwa*) of adherents, with intense repetition of God's names, though it is unclear how many Halvetis actually practice *khalwa* today. A process of outer purification, in which one asks for God's forgiveness for sin, precedes an inner purification with the suppression of temptation and lust by prayer.

There are many Halveti *teqes* in Albania and Kosovo. Indigenous Sufism in the eastern Adriatic area was first established in the north Albanian city of Shkodra, founded as Scodra in the fifth century before the birth of Jesus. Shkodra was subdued by the Ottoman sultan Mehmet the Conqueror after a forty-day siege in 1478. The Turkish armies had won the Battle of Kosovo in 1389, and, even before that, Turks serving as mercenaries for Christian rulers had introduced Islamic metaphysics to the region. Shkodra remained mainly Catholic throughout the Ottoman period, which ended in Albania in 1912; its Catholic cathedral was the largest in the Balkans. The first Bektashi *teqe* in the western Balkans was founded in Shkodra, although there is no Bektashi presence in the city today.

I have a recollection of Shkodra in which art, architecture, nature, politics, and spirituality intersect. The Ottomans left many monuments in the Balkans, among them numerous bridges. Between the main town of Shkodra and the outlying village of Bahçallëk, across the swift waters of the Kir, a tributary of the Drin River, a stone bridge was built, slowly, over the centuries. It had an undulating, rather surrealistic quality, like many Ottoman bridges in the Albanian lands. As with Bembaša in Sarajevo, the Bahçallëku Bridge became a place young men and women would meet and flirt, walking in the cool river air. In the early nineteenth century, the English author and artist Edward Lear, best known in the Anglo-American world for *The Owl and the Pussycat* and other nonsense verse, but much more famous in the Balkans for watercolors executed during travels in the region, drew a wonderful image of the Bahçallëku Bridge.

The stone bridge with its dreamy form fit well with the unexpected character of Shkodra, which is both Catholic and Muslim. But under Albanian Communism, Shkodra and its spiritual heritage were objects of deep suspicion by the country's evil rulers. The city was fiercely anti-Communist and hewed defiantly to its own local literary tradition. Finally, all its churches, mosques, and many Sufi *teqes* were ordered closed by the dictator Enver Hoxha, and the delightful Bahçallëku Bridge was destroyed as an alleged symbol of pre-Communist "backwardness." The Communist commissar who ordered this act of vandalism was Mehmet Shehu, number two in the Albanian state and, disgracefully, the son of an Islamic shaykh. The bridge was replaced by an ugly minimal steel span.

I have visited Shkodra often and frequently remembered the story of the Bahçallëku Bridge and its destruction. But I did not see the place where it had stood until 2006, when I toured Albanian Sufi tombs and *teqes* in Montenegro, Kosovo, western Macedonia, and the northern and central areas of Albania. Going to the river, I watched the rainswollen stream glide past, between overgrown banks of vegetation. The sky was overcast. A small café, really just some benches, had been erected at the edge of the water by an elderly Albanian who had lived in America. When I described my journey, he told me of a small *teqe* different from any other of which I had ever heard. Nearby, he said, was a hidden underground *teqe* maintained by a community limited to women, with a female shaykh. The *teqe*, he said, was open only in the evenings.

I was reminded of Hojja Yasawi's tomb and subterranean chamber, but the image from Bembaša in Sarajevo seemed to reappear—a Sufi site by a river where women might mysteriously come forth and where young couples sought enchantment. This, I thought, must be a central point of Sufism—its connection with nature and with physical love. I had come to Sufism in search of inner tranquility but had instead become involved in interreligious strife, conflict within Islam, and the war against terror. Where was true serenity to be found? When I returned to the riverbank at the end of the afternoon, I went down a small set of steps to a belowground door, knocked, and was met by Shaykha Myzejen Shehu, a small older woman in a traditional head covering. The *teqe* is Halveti and includes the tombs of its founder, Shaykh Qazim-Ali Sultan, and his son, who died five centuries ago. Women meet there for *dhikr* without a set date, sometimes daily.

The maintenance of the Halveti *teqe* at the former Bahçallëku Bridge has been paid for by Albanian Americans. Miraculously, the Halvetis of Shkodra and many other Sufis in Albania survived the antireligious devastation of the Communist era.

*Rifa'is:* Voluntary shedding of the Sufis' own blood became a habit among the Rifa'is, an order formed by an Iraqi, Sayyid Ahmad Rifa'i (d. 1182). Many Rifa'is are famous for their practices of body piercing, or the illusion of it, with large needles, spikes, or other metal tools, cutting their flesh with blades, swallowing hot coals, and handling snakes as proof of faith. More than 150 years after Sayyid Rifa'i's death, these customs were borrowed from Mongolian shamans who practiced their rituals during the invasion of Iraq, before the Mongol rulers of Baghdad became Muslim. Probably because of their Mongolian origin, the Rifa'is were especially hated by Ibn Taymiyyah. There are many Rifa'is in the Albanian lands. *Zaynis* are a *tariqa* originating with the Rifa'is.

Sunni Muslims disapprove of the piercing of the skin and flow of blood in spiritual ceremonies such as those of the Rifa'is, and a *fatwa* against the opening of veins and related practices by Shia Muslims during commemorations of the death of Imam Husayn was issued in the aftermath of the Islamic Revolution in Iran. Since then, such spectacular behavior has become rare among Shias. While the piercing and other rituals of the Rifa'i are deeply impressive to outsiders, they are viewed with disdain by other Sufis.

Two notable and powerful *tariqas* that may be considered offshoots of the Rifa'is are the *Shazalis* and *Badawis*. Shazalism influenced the origins of the Arabian and Southeast Asian Ba'Alawis, but the Shazalis and Badawis are dominant in North Africa. The Shazalis associate themselves with the "sober" tradition of Junayd Al-Baghdadi; yet the Shazalis originated with the followers of a Spanish-born Muslim, Abu Madyan (1126–1198), who lived in Morocco and traveled to Iraq, where he met Sayyid Rifa'i. Abu Madyan was persecuted by the Almohads (*Muwahhidun*), a Berber dynasty that seized control of Muslim Spain and temporarily implanted a fundamentalist regime. His later successor, Abu Hasan Ali ash-Shazali, for whom the order is named, also began as a Rifa'i disciple.

The antecedent of the *Badawis*, Ahmed Al-Badawi, was born in Fez, Morocco, a center of Jewish as well as Muslim learning in the classical Islamic age. He visited the tombs of Hallaj and other Sufis and also frequented Sayyid Rifa'i, then moved to Egypt, where this order remains extremely influential, with Badawi a popular saint. Thousands visit his mausoleum in the town of Tanta.

Baba Rexheb relates that in his youth Ahmed Al-Badawi was fond of horsemanship but suddenly turned toward religion and undertook withdrawal from daily affairs, adopting continuous prayer, meditation, and extended fasting. Like the Rifa'is, the Shazali and Badawi orders are often associated with extremes of mystical behavior, regardless of the claim of alignment with the "sober" Junayd Al-Baghdadi. Morocco is one of the greatest centers of Islamic metaphysics, especially distinguished by achievement of mystical ecstasy through performance of exquisite music as well as chanting of God's names.

*Naqshbandis:* Much has already been said in this chronicle about the Naqshbandis, their conflicted history, their political ambitions, and their devotion to *Shariah*. But Islamic mysticism, even in its most inert forms, is full of surprises. The Naqshbandis began in "ecstatic" Khorasan and became fanatically "sober"; the Nimatullahi order emerged from the Sunni Naqshbandis and surprisingly adopted Shiism. The Naqshbandi milieu has always been diverse, if not contradictory. Muslim Sufis often belong to more than one order; Shaykh Abd al-Aziz Bukhari, an Uzbek Sufi who lives in East Jerusalem, told me in an interview that he is affiliated with the Naqshbandis, Qadiris, and Mawlawis. A direct descendant of Imam ul-Bukhari, the great scholar of *hadith*, Shaykh Bukhari is a peace activist[3] who expresses pride in his extensive relations with Israeli intellectuals (he speaks Hebrew and English along with Uzbek and Arabic).

Naqshbandism has millions of adherents in both West and East, and many are fine individuals and good teachers. In one of the least-known and most curious interfaith intersections of mysticism, the Naqshbandi Imam Shamyl, the jihad leader of the Caucasus, is venerated by mystical Jews—indeed, by the Lubavitcher Chasidim, the most spiritually intoxicated, it seems, of all the descendants of Abraham, Isaac, and Jacob. Shamyl was not Jewish—he was a Muslim from the small nation of Avars in Daghestan—but the Lubavitchers, in the company of their *rebbe* (i.e., their equivalent of a shaykh), Menachem Schneerson, enthusiastically sang, even cried out, "Shamyl's Song," a wordless melody. The lament by the mystical Jews so strongly resembles a Naqshbandi *dhikr* that one need only replace the Lubavitch repetition, *"ay ay ay ay ay ay ay,"* with *"la il-laha il-Allah"*—Arabic for "there is only one God," and it becomes the commonest of all meditative chants in Sufism. It is said that the Chasids, imprisoned by the Russians, learned "Shamyl's Song" from Sufi political prisoners. Schneerson's father lies buried in Turkestan, where he was sent as a political exile by Stalin.

*Tijanis:* These comprise a remarkable order; while their greatest influence is felt in their place of origin, Morocco, they spread across sub-Saharan Africa and throughout the world, including the Balkans, Western Europe, and the United States. Their history begins with Ahmad Al-Tijani, who was born in 1737 in Algeria and retreated into the Maghrib desert before returning to the settled part of Morocco. His tomb, in Fez, is a place of constant pilgrimage by Sufis. He was influenced by the Halvetis and Shazalis, but his teaching somewhat resembles that of the Naqshbandis in that, under the influence of Wahhabism, his disciples asserted their adherence to a narrow interpretation of religious practice, apart from their Sufism. Nevertheless, he was known for his kindness and respect for all human beings and taught, "God also loves unbelievers." The Islamic Studies and Research Association (ISRA), mainly comprising Tijani and located in Georgia, is one of the most dedicated institutions of Islamic metaphysics in America.

The Tijanis spread especially deep into West Africa. In Mali, a Tijani shaykh of great wisdom appeared early in the twentieth century, Tierno Bakar Salif Tall, the "sage of Bandiagara," born in 1875. The Tijanis had conquered the local African territories for Islam in the generation before Tierno Bakar's birth. A grandson of a Qadiri Sufi who had turned Tijani, Tierno Bakar had a gift for religious teaching and was deeply committed to Islamic studies, including the works of Al-Ghazali and Ibn Arabi. As it does today, West Africa then suffered from the campaigns of competing warlords. Furthermore, in 1885 the population was called on to fight French invaders. Tierno Bakar was shocked by the constant outbreak of new conflicts. But he turned his teaching center into a house of love and charity in one of the most ravaged areas in Africa.

In a concise statement of Sufi wisdom and Sufi disregard for the pretensions of pious exhibitionism, Tierno Bakar answered a student who asked him what behavior he most hated. The Sufi replied, "The conduct of which I most disapprove and for which I have the most pity is that of the ridiculous hypocrite. Such are those individuals who, with turbans carefully wound eight times around their heads, and a [Sufi rosary or *tesbih*] of heavy beads around their necks, walk with unnecessary dependence on the shoulder of a disciple and wave a cane that appears more like a fetish than a pilgrim's staff. Such a person pronounces the declaration of faith with more noise than fervor, and preaches with an ardor motivated by nothing so much as immediate attention. Such an individual corrupts the spirit and perverts the heart. He is a thousand times worse than the murderer who only kills the body."

*Chishtis:* The Indian shrine of this order's most famous saint, the twelfth-century mystic Moinuddin Chishti, was bombed, presumably by Wahhabi or other Muslim fundamentalists, on October 11, 2007, with two people killed and almost a score injured. The Chishti order played an important role in bringing Islam to India; they and the adherents of Suhrawardi were the main initiators of Sufism in the subcontinent. The peaceable introduction of Islam to the peoples of India, who like the Turks and later the Southeast Asians were called to the faith of Muhammad by articulate preaching and examples of saintly living, is typically contrasted by traditional Muslims with the conquest of non-Muslim territories through jihad.

Indian Sufism has also produced some of the least known and most fascinating phenomena in Islam. The country is a hive of religious teachers. A unique product of Indian Sufism is the school of Tibetan Sufism, practiced by the small Muslim community of a few thousand living in the Himalayas. Tibetan Muslims are known as *Kha-che,* after Kashmir. They speak and write Tibetan and have integrated into the majority Buddhist culture to such an extent that a Sufi text, *Kha-che Phalu-i rNamthar,* or *Kha-che Phalu's Counsels,* has entered the Tibetan classic canon. Its authorship is controversial, with some Buddhists claiming it for one of their lamas.

Tibetan Muslims allege that the name Kha-che Phalu is translated "the Kashmiri Fazurallah." A Tibetan academic in India, Dawa Norbu, finds the origin of *Kha-che Phalu's Counsels* in the works of the Iranian poet Muslihud'din Sa'adi Shirazi (1208–1292), who was influenced by Suhrawardi. The *Gulistan* (*Rose Garden*) and *Bostan* (*The Orchard*) of Sa'adi are justifiably considered among the finest works of world literature—the American author Ralph Waldo Emerson honored Sa'adi, as did, on yet another side of the planet, Bosnian Jews—and both of Sa'adi's books were an important element in schools attended by young Tibetan Muslims before the coming of Chinese Communism.

*Kha-che Phalu's Counsels* includes the following:

*All the sides of life are full*
*Of slopes and precipices;*
*It is easy to slip and fall down.*
*Be careful along such a path.*
*Sounds of life are like nomads playing dice . . .*
*When you don't know the measure*
*Of loss and gain,*
*It's better to stay out of the game.*
*I, Kha-che Phalu the limitless,*
*Have gone beyond the limit;*
*Precious words have fallen on this paper.*
*When you estimate the cost,*
*Don't make mistakes.*
*I have won high stakes, my son.*

Tibetan Sufism seems rooted in this world, but at an altitude as high as the Himalayas and as obscure as Tibet itself. Thus the metaphysics of Islam has influenced spirituality in all of the major religions.

Two other, mysterious variants of Sufism have existed and may always exist: first, the *Malamis,* who gave no external sign of their commitment, including no practice of *dhikr.* Do they exist today? Of course. Can they be easily identified? Of course not. Similarly, *Uwaysi* Sufis do not study with shaykhs but are believed to derive guidance directly from the great teachers of the past.

Returning to Naim Frashëri, the great Bektashi poet, we read:

*The power of the divine*
*Appears wherever it wants,*
*For the spirit of all things*
*Is the same.*
*It is there in all that exists*
*It is in all places,*
*It appears at every point,*
*In the body and the mind.*
*It is visible in the heavens,*
*In the rain and in the clouds,*
*In the moon and between suns*
*And even on earth.*
*But the heart is where to find it*
*Since it has it for its throne,*
*Can you hear its voice?*
*Is your heart unheard?*[4]

I have left for last the *Sa'adi-Jibawis,* who were among the "recognized" orders in the Ottoman system. They originated with the fourteenth-century teacher Sa'ad'ud'din Jibawi, born in Palestine and buried in Damascus, and are widely represented in the Muslim world. They also relate their *silsila* to Junayd Al-Baghdadi.

I feel close to the Sa'adi-Jibawi Sufis because of several incidents during the Kosovo war of 1998–99 and my own experience in the aftermath of that atrocious conflict. I refer in particular to the martyrdom of the Albanian Sa'adi-Jibawi shaykh Zejnelabedin Dervishdana at the hands of Serbian terrorists. These events revealed a war against the Sufis hidden, like that in Iraq, from the world.

The involvement of Albanian Sufis in the Kosovo struggle provides the ultimate proof of Bernard Lewis's observation that Sufis are peaceful but not always pacifist. The most climactic episode of ground fighting in the 1998–99 war included a Serb massacre in a Sufi *teqe*. On July 19, 1998, the first pitched battle between Serb forces and the Kosovo Liberation Army occurred in the town of Rahovec. Open fighting in the streets culminated in a Serb assault on the Halveti-Karabashi Sufi complex in the town, known as the Shaykh Myhedini *Teqe*, in which hundreds of frightened residents had gathered, believing it a sanctuary. The elderly leader of the *teqe*, Shaykh Myhedin Shehu, was killed by the Serbs, along with up to 150 other people. His sons, Hilmi Shehu and Jahja Shehu, continue his work today. The Myhedin Shehu *Teqe* in Rahovec, which I have visited many times, is another focus of mystical force for me in the world; I often imagine Shaykh Myhedin in the green lands of Kosovo, in the company of "the green man," Al-Khidr.

After the slayings in the *teqe* at Rahovec, within two days the Serbs had buried the victims in two mass graves in the southern Kosovo center of Prizren. Prizren is also the headquarters of a coordinating body of non-Bektashi Albanian Sufis on the territories of former Yugoslavia, the community of Aliite Dervishes. I was told by Shaykh Adrihysen Shehu of the Prizren office and *teqe* (maintained by the Rifa'i Sufis) that in the 1998–99 conflict Rifa'i *teqes* in the city of Peja and in the industrial town of Mitrovica were wrecked by the Serbs. The late father of Shaykh Adrihysen, Shaykh Xhemajl Shehu Rifa'i, temporarily left Kosovo for America during the conflict.

Shaykh Adrihysen further reported that a major Halveti *teqe* in the mountains of Junik, a historic combat zone near the Kosovo city of Gjakova, had been devastated. Shaykh Xhafer Shehu of the Junik Halvetis lost his library to the Serb troops and terrorists, who destroyed hundreds of Islamic manuscripts. Some 1,300 rare books belonging to Shaykh Xhafer were reduced to ashes, including the oldest known manuscript written by the poet Hafiz Ali Riza Ulqinaku: the text of an Albanian-language *mawlid* recitation in praise of Muhammad. In 2006 the Junik *teqe* was being rebuilt by Shaykh Xhafer, and is intended to be the largest Sufi structure in the Balkans.

Baba Mumin Lama, the chief Bektashi cleric in Kosovo, recounted to me in 1999 how Serbs devastated his *teqe* in Gjakova, along with its library of 2,000 rare books and 250 manuscripts. These included a twelfth-century manuscript in Persian and a thousand-page work describing the pilgrimage to India and back, on foot, of another Bektashi divine who was curious about Buddhism. Baba Mumin's educational work had included the printing in 1997, in Gjakova just before the Kosovo conflict began, of the *Hadikat es-Sauda* or *Garden of Pleasures* by the Azeri Turkish Sufi Fuzuli (1483–1556), which had been rendered into Albanian by Baba Rexheb. Bektashis from Gjakova who became prominent in the Kosovo struggle include the martyr Luan Haradinaj, who was killed by the Serbs on the Albanian-Kosovo border in 1997. His brother Ramush Haradinaj, a leading Kosovar politician, has left an affecting memoir of rescuing his brother's body in extremely difficult circumstances.

When I met him, I appealed to Baba Mumin to sit down with representatives of the Serbian Orthodox Church in an interreligious dialogue. Baba Mumin told me then that it was too soon after the combat in Kosovo, although he agreed in principle with such a proposal. In 2007, however, Baba Mumin told me quietly that the right moment had finally arrived for such colloquies to be held, and that he had attended a large interfaith gathering with the main Serb Orthodox clerics in the territory. There, he noted, he had urged that all present remember first that they were people of religion and that all believers should put peace before politics.

But I return, in an enduring memory, to the Serb murders in the Gjakova *teqe* of another mystic, Shaykh Dervishdana of the Sa'adi-Jibawi Sufis. The Dervishdana incident figured in the indictment of Slobodan Milošević at the International Criminal Tribunal for Former Yugoslavia (ICTY) in The Hague. Shaykh Zejnelabedin Dervishdana was killed by masked Serbian paramilitaries (*četniks*) on March 26, 1999, two days after the NATO bombing of Kosovo began. The shaykh was slain along with two sons, two neighbors, and a friend. The family of Shaykh Dervishdana maintains the *teqe*.

Eli Dervishdana, the daughter of the shaykh, said her family had included "seven generations of *hoxhas* [Islamic teachers], four of dervishes, and four successive generations of Kosovar *shehids* [martyrs for Islam], with all the main male line now dead." Her young brother Nesemi, then seventeen, was killed at a demonstration for Kosovo autonomy under Yugoslavia, in 1981.

She described to me the night in 1999 when Serbian terrorists "in black masks came to the door. I only saw three of them, but there were at least fifteen." Shaykh Zejnelabedin, age fifty-nine, along with his two sons, Fahri, thirty-seven, and Emin, thirty-two, two close friends, Arif Bytyci, seventy-three, and his son Urim, thirty-eight, and a neighbor, Sylejman Begolli, forty-eight, were slain.

Three of the victims were executed in the house, but Shaykh Zejnelabedin and two others were taken into the *teqe,* and in the presence of the sacred objects of the dervishes and a portrait of Imam Husayn, the Shia martyr, they were done to death.

The bloodstains remain today on the floor, under the carpets.

Shaykh Zejnelabedin's deputy, Shaykh Rama, was killed in another and even worse Serb massacre in the nearby village of Korenica in April 1999, a month later. On August 9, 2006, a Kosovar Albanian Catholic woman, Lizane Malaj, appeared as a witness before the ICTY at The Hague, in the trial of a group of six Serbian nationalist and Yugoslav leaders, Milan Milutinović, Nikola Sainović, Nebojša Pavković, Sreten Lukić, Dragoljub Ojdanić, and Vladimir Lazarević. Aside from Milošević, the six were the highest officials of the Belgrade regime involved in the assault on Kosovo in 1998–99. The case was known as *Milutinović et al.*

The testimony of Lizane Malaj recalled her presence in Korenica on April 27, 1999. That day, she suffered the deaths of her husband, son, brother, and nephew in an hours-long eruption into the community by Serbian police, paramilitaries, and soldiers of the Yugoslav army. As Mrs. Malaj stated in her testimony, "Korenica is neither big nor small, I would say. It has about seventy houses . . . We are all Albanian. We are Catholics and some Muslims." No more than 15 percent of Kosovo is Catholic, but the vicinity of Korenica is overwhelmingly Catholic, and Gjakova itself has one of Kosovo's largest and most respected Catholic communities. Gjakova has a special history of Albanian patriotism, and in the Kosovo war Gjakova suffered the worst Serb violence of all the territory's cities.

Serb paramilitaries arrived in Korenica on April 27, 1999, in buses, with red bandanas tied on their heads or as armbands, as described by a local resident, Tom Dedaj. When the Serbs had completed their raid on Korenica, as many as 377 people were dead, all unarmed, including women and children. One survivor said every man in the village over age sixteen had been killed. The ratio of victims was approximately the same as that of the living: 90 percent Catholic, 10 percent Muslim.

The inhabitants of Korenica then stayed away from the town for some weeks, but returned in June 1999. They found mass graves filled with bones and hair, although many of the dismembered corpses lay where they had fallen. In a burned house, limbs and other parts of men's bodies lay on the top floor.

On the day of the crime, survivors had rushed to the Catholic church at Gjakova—its bell towers visible from the village—and a courageous Franciscan priest, Pater Ambroz Ukaj, went to a Serb army commander and demanded to know what had happened. Pater Ambroz was interrogated as to how he knew anything had happened at all, and he replied that women in the village reported the mass arrest of all males. "I was told to shut up," Pater Ambroz recalled when I interviewed him in 1999. "Then I said that there were injured people in my church. Thank God I had already sent them to a hospital, because the Serb officer was prepared to take them away."

This massacre of Albanians almost a decade ago, in which Catholics were slain along with Muslim fellow Albanians, expresses the unity of the Kosovo Albanians regardless of religion and their common suffering at the hands of the Serbs. It also provides an example of how Sufis can perform acts of charity in the contemporary world.

At a 2006 meeting in London, I was informed of an effort to reinforce Albanian interfaith links in the rural area of Korenica, where such terrible events transpired. Franciscans in Austria have donated funds for the reconstruction of the houses in Korenica. In Guska, a small village nearby, a primary school is being rebuilt through private donations. The school is named for Pjetër Muqaj, an Albanian Catholic killed at eighteen in 1943 while fighting the Nazis.

During the period of Serb oppression from 1987 to 1999, hundreds of thousands of Kosovar Albanians were expelled from the educational and health systems, as well as from ordinary employment. Albanians of all faiths (and some of no faith) organized a parallel school and health system that educated children, mainly in homes, with teachers paid by parents or in food and other in-kind income. Serb police and soldiers repeatedly harassed the students and staff at the Guska school.

After the NATO occupation of Kosovo, it became clear that the creation of a new and adequate school system was low, if not nonexistent, on the agenda of the international community governing the territory. Albanian parents who wanted to transform the parallel system into a legitimate educational system were rebuffed. Teachers are among the lowest-paid employees in Kosovo.

The Guska school serves mainly Catholic but also Muslim children. The building is dilapidated; it has no indoor sanitation; water is taken from a well, and the only heating is provided by small woodstoves. Like the rest of Kosovo, the school undergoes frequent electrical power cuts. Furniture and textbooks are old. Three computers were donated to the school in Guska, but without a proper facility for them they must be brought to the school one day per week for use by older pupils. New texts and notebooks are provided by parents and teachers. Bread is served to the students twice daily—once in the morning and once at the end of instruction. The school has no medical service for the children, who in 2006 numbered 136, ages six to fifteen.

Of the pupils who attended school at Guska in the 2005–6 term, twenty-five lost their fathers in Serbian massacres and twelve more are orphans. In addition, of the school's twelve teachers—ten males and two females—one instructor lost all the males from her family.

Since I worked in Kosovo in 1999–2000 and made repeated later visits, I have frequently criticized the foreign occupation authorities for their neglect of educational improvement. I believe the school at Guska must be rebuilt. But more important, the habit of educating Catholic and Muslim children together is an old one in the Balkans, and especially among Albanians. The maintenance of this custom will, I think, do much to benefit coexistence between the two faiths. Sufis have contributed some thousands of dollars to the Guska school.

I have included this digression on the afflicted Sufis in Kosovo in recollection of a fortuitous visit to the tomb of Baba Dan, founder of a Sa'adi *teqe* in Korenica, with a mausoleum that contained the body of Shaykh Rama, the Sa'adi-Jibawi Sufi from Gjakova, as well as those of several children, slaughtered in the Serbian pogrom of 1999. I received a blessing at the Baba Dan *turbe* within months of the end of the war that year. Later, as night fell, I visited the Korenica graveyard, where many markers showed no names or otherwise indicated that the victim could not be identified. The horror I have described among the Sufis of Kosovo occurred in Europe, and in a place to which one may fly in little more than two hours from Vienna. It must not be forgotten.

# 5

## Sufis in the Crisis States

### *Iraq, Saudi Arabia, Iran, and Israel*

IRAQ WAS A BIRTHPLACE of Islamic metaphysics, and, as described throughout this narrative, has always been a center of Sufism. Including in Kurdistan, Iraqi Sufis had maintained a wide network of *zawiyas* (the Arabic-language equivalent of *tekke*) at tombs of Muslim saints. *Mawlid* for the Prophet's birthday was celebrated by large crowds each year. The Qadiris, Rifa'is, and Naqshbandis have been the most consistently influential Sufi orders among Iraqi Arabs and Kurds. The indefatigable historian of heterodox Islam H. T. Norris, however, recently exposed to Western scholars the traces of a twentieth-century Bektashi Sufi tradition in Iraq. This seems natural considering the Shia disposition of the Bektashis and their love for the martyred Imam Ali and Imam Husayn.

Bektashi *tekkes,* which kept their Turkish name, were established in both the Shia holy city of Karbala and the Shia theological center of Najaf, as well as in Kurdish and other towns. This is a significant item in Sufi history—the Bektashis, with all their nonconformist habits, were sheltered in the most sacred Shia precincts, aside from Mecca and

Medina. Further, the Bektashis in the Albanian lands maintained an intellectual link with Iraq and Iran, and at least one Bektashi center in Greece was administered by Arab *babas*. An Iraqi-born professor of comparative religion, Muhammad Sa'id Al-Turayhi, published an account of Bektashism in Baghdad in a periodical oriented toward the Iraqi Turkmen minority in 2003. Al-Turayhi described Bektashi devotion to the Hurufi spiritual numerology similar to that found in the Jewish Kabbalah, and their casual attitude toward prayer, charity, fasting at Ramadan, and the *hajj* pilgrimage—practices considered "pillars of Islam." Norris paraphrases Al-Turayhi, writing that all these elements of observant Islam "concern the 'beginner' in the [metaphysical] path but have no meaning for him or her who has attained the spiritual state when such have no relevance whatsoever." The Iraqi Bektashi Sufis also shared with the Shias the view of Imam Ali as a "human ideal" and the belief in the return of the hidden Twelfth Imam, or Shia *mahdi*.[1]

Karbala, the most important Shia sanctuary, has its Bektashi *tekke* in the courtyard of Imam Husayn, although in the twentieth century its keepers had become ordinary Shia Muslims. In Najaf, the theological center of Iraqi Shia religious education, even after the war that began in 2003, the Bektashi *tekke* remained located inside the shrine of Imam Ali. Hajji Bektash himself is reputed to have gone there. Similar structures were located in Baghdad, with one in the city of Kirkuk and another nearby, along with at least one more in Iraqi Kurdistan. Prior to the First World War a major Iraqi Bektashi property, the *tekke* in Karbala, was usurped by the Naqshbandis, thanks to support from the Ottoman authorities. With the breakup of the Turkish empire and rupture of the ancient commerce between Anatolia and Iraq, unfortunately, Bektashis ceased going to Mesopotamia.

It is easy to see why Iraqi Sufis, with such memories of a libertarian Islam in their historical consciousness, would like Shias have come under attack in the Wahhabi terror waged by Saudi proxies in Mesopotamia during the U.S.-led intervention. But in reporting on "Sunni" terrorism, especially against Sufis, much was ignored by international media; the heritage of Sufism in Iraq was among many significant but unreported stories during the Iraq war.

In Kurdistan and elsewhere in Iraq, far from being a simple response to the U.S.-led intervention, "Sunni" terrorism had the same ideology and history as that visible elsewhere in the Muslim world for 250 years. The correct name for the main influence inciting Sunni Muslim Iraqis to attack Coalition forces, Kurds, other Sufis, and Shias is, to repeat yet again, Saudi Wahhabism.

Kurdish Sufis in Iraq had been persecuted by Saudi-Wahhabi agents allied with Al-Qaida even before the fall of the Saddam regime. Sufis from the Iraqi Kurdish elite, many of them Naqshbandis, were famously prominent in fighting Saddam and actively promoted an alliance of the new Iraq with the United States. But from the beginning of the Iraq intervention, Kurdish Sunnis expressed fear of Wahhabi incursions. Iraqi Kurdistan reported continued Wahhabi desecration of cemeteries—always an early sign of the Saudi-backed efforts that have been going on since the early 1990s, from the Balkans to China.

Saudi-Wahhabi religious organizations had been introduced into Kurdistan before the 2003 war, but with the beginning of the intervention, the Wahhabi militia Ansar Al-Islam (Volunteers of Islam), which had previously intruded in Kurdistan, was reactivated. Attacked and scattered by U.S. forces during the main offensive in April 2003, Ansar Al-Islam reconstituted itself and struck in the towns of Halabja, Biahrah, and Dohuk, according to a Kurdish leader. The car bomb was Ansar's weapon of choice.

Saudi individuals played a major role in Ansar Al-Islam, which continued attacking Iraqi Kurds until the organization was destroyed by Coalition and Kurdish forces. Propaganda in its favor appeared in the Saudi media, and the commander of Arab anti-Coalition volunteers in northern Iraq was Yassin al-Sihli, a Saudi citizen from the city of Dammam in the kingdom, killed by Kurdish troops.

First in Iraqi Kurdistan and then elsewhere in Iraq, including in Baghdad, Ansar Al-Islam operated under the long-distance command of an individual born Najmuddin Faraj Ahmad and calling himself Mullah Krekar. As the "religious guide" of Ansar Al-Islam, the mullah kept himself in a place of safety, having gained political asylum in Norway in 1991. Mullah Krekar had trained in Afghanistan with Osama bin Laden and was a disciple of bin Laden's mentor, the jihadist organizer Abdullah Azzam, who was killed in Pakistan in 1989. The mullah had gone to Iraqi Kurdistan as an armed Wahhabi missionary. From the beginning of the Wahhabi movement's introduction into Kurdistan the Muslim world was shocked by reports of beheadings ordered by "freelance" *Shariah* courts, the slaying of Sufis, the targeting of non-Wahhabi Kurdish leaders—many with long careers as patriotic fighters and tragic family losses at the hands of Saddam—as well as the destruction of graves and other depredations.

When the Coalition invaded Iraq in 2003, Krekar's followers again unleashed terror. On March 23, 2003, they carried out a bombing in Iraqi Kurdistan in which an Australian journalist, Paul Moran, was killed and eight other people were injured. Krekar's disciple in that case was another Saudi citizen, Abd al-Aziz al-Gharbi. Ansar Al-Islam acknowledged responsibility for the bombing from inside Saudi territory.

Mullah Krekar declared, in a television debate with me produced by the Lebanese Broadcasting Corporation, that he was proud to be described as a disciple of Ibn Abd Al-Wahhab, founder of the eponymous movement. From his Scandinavian sanctuary, the flamboyant mullah had long sent others to kill and die in Kurdistan. But early in 2004 a Norwegian court ordered Mullah Krekar held in prison while an investigation of his links to terror activities continued. Yet, did it matter whether the Norwegians investigated Krekar? Charges against him were dismissed and he continued controlling terror in Iraq while hiding behind the skirts of Norwegian women.

Unlike the effete Norwegians, the Kurds were anything but helpless in the face of Mullah Krekar's threats. In October 2006, eleven of his followers were executed in Iraqi Kurdistan. Meanwhile, the U.S. government accused him of slipping in and out of Iraq to coordinate terrorist attacks. Norwegian media then alleged that the U.S. Central Intelligence Agency had planned to kidnap Mullah Krekar from Norway. The new government of Iraq wanted him for trial, and even the Norwegians had pronounced him a terrorist. But he remained safe in his far, far northern hideaway.

The Iraq conflict, paradoxically, also provided the Wahhabis opportunities for another familiar pretext for their infiltration—humanitarian aid. Despite all the worldwide exposure of the misuse of Islamic charities to promote terrorism, the same official Saudi relief organizations that came under investigation after the atrocities of September 11, 2001, entered Iraq. The Saudi-based International Islamic Relief Organization (IIRO), for example, investigated by U.S. and other governments for involvement in the funding of terrorism across the globe, was lauded in the Saudi daily *Al-Watan* (*The Nation*) for its "relief work" in Sunni districts of Iraq.

The Wahhabi-Saudi religious bureaucracy made clear that it would seek to dominate the religious life of Sunnis in a new Iraq. Anti-Wahhabi Muslims warned that the Saudis would worm their way into the U.S.-directed rebuilding of Iraq with the intention of "Talibanizing" Iraq's Sunnis. True to form, the Saudis announced another of their notorious telethons to raise money for the relief of Iraq, which—as in the Palestinian Authority—would doubtless be spent mainly on Wahhabi colonization and the fomenting of "martyrdom."

Indications of stepped-up Wahhabi activity in Iraq should have raised red flags among Coalition leaders—for they conformed to a pattern already familiar from Afghanistan, central Asia, Bosnia-Herzegovina, Kosovo, and Chechnya. The Wahhabi strategy in pursuit of the extremists' mad dream of imposing their "pure" Islam on all Muslims, then launching a jihad against the world, begins with indoctrination. Food, clothing, tents, and other relief supplies are distributed to those willing to take instruction in Wahhabi doctrine. Preachers are sent from the Gulf states with the mission of Wahhabizing local Muslims by opposing the "unbelief" alleged to be rife in local Islam, especially in Sufism and Shiism. And according to the Wahhabis, forms of "unbelief" may also include friendship with Jews and Christians and acceptance of women driving, going out without extreme body covering, or attending school, as well as the traditional customs Wahhabis condemn such as visiting graves and attending *mawlid* events.

The next step is the establishment of training centers and camps where unemployed youths are taught to fight and lead irregular combat operations, especially suicide attacks. These centers are often directly linked to relief distribution points. Incitement of "martyrdom" includes a typical offer of stipends for recruits' families if they perish in suicide operations, which Saddam and the Saudis used to send to Palestinian families and which rich Saudi and other Wahhabi fanatics now pay to families whose children have died as terrorists in the jihad in Iraq.

Then, crucially, Wahhabi agitators seek to eliminate opposition from local religious leaders. New mosques and *medresas* are built with Saudi subsidies and staffed exclusively by Wahhabi imams and teachers. The system of *medresas* is expanded, where possible becoming an independent extremist educational system on the Pakistani model, setting neighbor against neighbor and son against father. Where necessary, established imams are paid cash to "convert" to Wahhabism. Uncooperative imams are boycotted and loudly labeled unbelievers or government spies. Imams who actively oppose the extremists risk their lives—witness the murder of traditional Sunni clerics in Iraq, Afghanistan, Chechnya, Daghestan, Pakistan, Uzbekistan, Algeria, Egypt, Morocco, and other countries.

IN THEIR HATRED of Sufi and Shia practices, Wahhabi agents insistently vandalize and bomb local graveyards, historic mosques, and the tombs of Muslim saints. In Iraq, several Sufi leaders had expressed alarm at Wahhabi intentions and were prepared to sit down with the American authorities from the beginning of the intervention. All of them were in the sights of the terrorists and needed immediate protection.

When Americans were murdered and Coalition troops came under fire in places like Fallujah, it could not be assumed that local insurgency was the essential explanation. The scheme to defeat the American intervention mainly originated in Saudi Arabia. It could be thwarted, with the help of Iraqi Sunni leaders. But first the Coalition authorities had to take a closer look at their enemies.

Iraqi Muslims generally expressed loathing for Wahhabis. Shia Muslims were particularly known for this attitude, rooted in the memory of Wahhabi attacks on Karbala beginning two centuries past. "We believe every recent bombing at a Shia shrine or mosque in Iraq can be traced to the Wahhabis," said an Iraqi Shia leader in New York. But numerous Sunni Muslims, as well as Sufis, also expressed disdain for Wahhabis. "When we were growing up in Iraq, to call someone a Wahhabi was a serious insult," a leading Iraq-born Sunni religious figure told me. "They were held in contempt because of their ban on praying in mosques that had graveyards or saintly tombs on their grounds"—once again, the familiar Wahhabi complaint against Sufis.

Through much of the Saddam era, the Ba'athist regime, showing its secular and modernist face and inspired by the dictator's resentment of the Saudis, repressed the Wahhabis. But in the final stages of the dictatorship, Saddam welcomed the Wahhabis into Iraq out of frustration at his inability to organize Ba'ath support in Sufi-dominated Kurdistan, which bitterly hated the Ba'ath because of its history of local atrocities. The Wahhabis built mosques with Saudi money, recruited followers, and obtained arms and military training. For Iraqis there was no surprise in the decision of post-intervention "Sunni insurgents" to, at least at first, submit to the leadership of Al-Qaida.

While Western media and politicians, in the aftermath of Iraq's liberation, focused on Syria and Iran as destabilizers in Iraq, more attention should have been paid to Saudi Arabia. Throughout the U.S.-led military campaign, Riyadh publicly sought to maintain its alliance with the United States without effectively reining in the venomous rhetoric of its religious bureaucracy in opposing Western influence in the Islamic countries and inciting jihadist terror.

Complacency on the part of U.S. diplomats benefited the Wahhabi cause. In a 2003 incident, the U.S. ambassador to Saudi Arabia Robert Jordan gave an interview to the *Future of Islam,* a monthly publication of the Riyadh-based World Assembly of Muslim Youth (WAMY), which was involved in the financing of Al-Qaida and the dissemination of extremist literature in the United States and throughout the Muslim world. Ambassador Jordan, however, had declined to meet with Saudi democratic activists.

In the same April issue, the *Future of Islam* published a cover interview with the Saudi cleric Ayed al-Qarni, an adviser to prince Abd al-Aziz bin Fahd, youngest son of the visibly dying King Fahd. Al-Qarni was also the author of a poem repeatedly broadcast on Saudi-subsidized television and radio during the Iraq intervention, which said in part: "Slaughter the enemy infidels and say there is but one God." In the *Future of Islam*, al-Qarni stated that he prayed for the destruction of America, the main source of global suffering, several times a day. He also urged Saudis to go fight in Iraq and contribute money to help defend Saddam.

Al-Qarni was not alone in his call to arms. In the first week of April 2003, a notorious Saudi Wahhabi cleric, Naser Al-Omar, preached in favor of suicide attacks on Coalition forces in Iraq. At the beginning of the Iraq operation, he was among the signers of a *fatwa*, distributed in Saudi government offices and hospitals, calling for the defense of Saddam's Iraq. The incitement to terrorist "martyrdom" did not go unheeded. Saudis joined hundreds of "volunteers" who went to Iraq to confront the Coalition, and a number were killed, with their photographs printed in Saudi media. Iraqis, as well as Coalition commanders on the ground, were quick to disclose this fact, which military and political planners in Washington, ever concerned not to offend the Saudis, sought to evade.

Fallujah, in the western, Sunni-dominated part of Iraq, became a front-line area for open war between Iraqis and the U.S.-led Coalition. But why Fallujah? Why should this relatively obscure Iraqi city of half a million have become a crucible of horror? Some analysts said Fallujah was a stronghold of Ba'athist sympathy. The reality was rather different. The Al-Jumaili clan, which is a leading force in the area, had produced two pre-Saddam presidents of Iraq, the brothers Abd As-Salaam Arif, who ruled from 1963 to 1966, and Abd Ar-Rahman Arif, whose tenure lasted from 1966 to 1969. The first died in a suspicious aerial accident, and the second was driven from power, and then from Iraq, by the Ba'athists under Saddam. The Al-Jumailis have a long memory, and the downfall of the Arif brothers fostered a blood feud between the powerful tribal shaykhs and Saddam, so that when Coalition troops appeared in Iraq the Al-Jumaili shaykhs ordered their followers not to interfere with them. That, at least, was the version told by an Al-Jumaili representative in the United States.

But the Al-Jumailis claimed that tensions with the Coalition began with U.S. military raids on their strongholds soon after Saddam's fall. The *San Francisco Chronicle* reported in late 2003 that Shaykh Mishkhen Al-Jumaili denounced U.S.-inflicted fatalities in his area. The reporter Anna Badkhen added, "Important members of the community, like al-Jumaili, went from being supportive of the U.S.-led alliance to being openly anti-American."

A more significant ingredient in the stewpot of Fallujah's discontent, however, was Wahhabi interference. Here and there, Western journalists alluded to this in a distorted fashion. An Associated Press report noted questionably that of the residents of Fallujah, "many adhere to Sunni Islam's austere Wahhabi sect." Wahhabi militants in Kuwait and other nearby states had begun collecting money, blood, and supplies to sustain the combat at Fallujah. Even in the United States, some leaders of the "Wahhabi lobby" that dominates American Islam declared their solidarity with the "resistance" in Fallujah.

"The Fallujah region is filling up with Wahhabis," a tribal representative from the district had warned in a late-2003 discussion in Washington. He had come to the capital in hopes of brokering a new agreement between his people and American troops following disorders in the town. "They are streaming in, exploiting the confusion and misunderstandings between the local residents and the U.S. forces." According to Iraqi sources inside the country, Wahhabi imams in the Fallujah mosques, backed by dozens of preachers from Saudi Arabia, had begun yet more aggressive incitement of suicide bombings against Coalition forces.

Fallujah gained world attention, although little was said in the West, immediately, about the Saudi involvement there. By mid-2003, international media had already reported continuing attacks on U.S. troops in Fallujah. On June 1, 2003, the Saudi Wahhabi website Alsaha.com proudly reported the combat deaths in Fallujah of two Saudi subjects, Faisal Sultan Al-Rougi Al-Otabi and Tahir Ash-Shoumani. The writer, Nassim Al-Islam (doubtless a pseudonym—it means "wind of Islam"), adopted a tone of adulation: "Congratulations, Faisal, the color is that of blood and the scent that of musk. I wish I were with you to win great honor as a martyr."

On the ground in Iraq, the *Newsweek* reporter Scott Johnson also picked up signs of Saudi involvement. In a story in the magazine's issue of June 16, 2003, Johnson quoted a U.S. intelligence officer in Baghdad who said that, increasingly, Iraqi sources were identifying the armed men organizing to fight the Coalition as Wahhabis. Johnson explained the term as "Muslims akin to the extremist sect that inspired Al Qaeda." Said the U.S. intelligence officer, "Now, all of a sudden, these Wahhabi guys have been appearing. We're hearing that word a lot more: Wahhabi."

Spurious claims by Western experts that Saddam's Ba'athist state was so secular as to be anathema to Osama bin Laden, Al-Qaida's Saudi backers, and other Wahhabis were never taken seriously in the Islamic world. Among Muslims, the Wahhabis were understood to be natural allies of the Butcher of Baghdad in his campaign against Kurdish Sufis as well as Arab Shias. Furthermore, in the long decay of Saddam's regime, the Iraqi Ba'athists repeatedly tried to salvage their image by claiming an Islamic mantle, with such efforts as the inscription of the Islamic cry *"Allahu akbar"* (God is great!) on the national flag in Saddam's handwriting (since refashioned in traditional script). In turn, the Saudis valued Saddam as a bulwark against Iran.

AT THE END OF 2003, a report from Iraq by Vernon Loeb in the *Washington Post* included the following significant comments: "Division commanders also said they now have solid evidence that Ba'athists loyal to Hussein are cooperating with Iraqi Islamic radicals whom the military refers to as Wahhabis, a particularly puritanical sect of Muslims dominant in Saudi Arabia. 'The Wahhabis love Osama bin Laden, the former regime loyalists love Saddam, they both hate us, and the enemy of my enemy is my friend,' said one officer. 'They are in cahoots 100 percent.' "

Yet, as noted, Saudi names had already begun appearing among those of "martyrs" publicized as killed in Iraq. The Saudi opposition website Arabianews.org, which had chronicled the deaths of various Saudi jihad fighters in Iraq, reported the demise of Adel Al-Naser from Riyadh. Al-Naser was killed in November 2003 in Baqubah near Baghdad. The website observed that "the number of Saudis fighting [in Iraq] has been rising over the past few months." Furthermore, Saudi guards on the Iraqi border told the website's writers, "Saudi fighters are still heading to Iraq, with little scrutiny by Saudi authorities." A guard commander in Rafha, a border outpost southwest of the Iraqi line, complained that he had asked for more equipment and personnel to monitor the area but never received them. The guards merely fired warning shots when they observed people crossing the border illegally. Another guard, quoted in the same account, said, "The infiltrators are highly skilled at crossing the borders."

In a related report on the same website, a Saudi border guard noted, "We used to have problems with Iraqis fleeing into Saudi territories, but now the problem is with hundreds of Saudis crossing into Iraq." And Saudi jihadists did not need to go to Syria or sojourn in Afghanistan or Chechnya for training on the way to Iraq. In 2004 the Associated Press reported the Saudi government's recognition, as if it were a sudden discovery, that Al-Qaida had desert training camps near Saudi cities.

The jihadists were concerned from early on that Iraqi Sunnis might turn against them. Some Wahhabis were bold in rhetoric but faint of heart about involvement in a zone of operations, watched by the world, where most of the victims of their violence would be Muslims. But the main terror command—Al-Qaida—valued the Iraqi theater as a diversion from events in Saudi Arabia. At the end of 2003, an Al-Qaida website, Qoqaz.net, which became well known for its propaganda focusing on Chechnya, posted an audio interview with Shaykh Abu Omar Al-Seif, a leading Saudi figure in Wahhabi mischief in the Caucasus. As translated by the Middle East Media Research Institute (MEMRI), Al-Seif told the interviewer, "It is essential that the Jihad groups [in Iraq] unite and not separate, and that they have the political dimension to assemble the Sunnis, including the Kurds, the Arabs, and the Turkmens. All must be united under the same political power. Similarly, there must be an information and a religious preaching arm . . . I recommend to the Mujahideen that instead of engaging in clashes and warfare against the Saudi government, it is better to go to Iraq."

He emphasized the last point by repeating it: "Turn to Iraq instead of confronting the Saudi government." The Saudis had a substantial history of using foreign jihad campaigns to divert attention from crises at home and to reinforce the hold of Wahhabism over their own subjects. In Iraq, they returned to one of their original fields of bloodshed, which Wahhabi troops attacked two hundred years ago. In the early nineteenth century, a British writer traveling in the region, Thomas Hope, recorded rumors that "in the very midst of Baghdad, in the broad face of day, Wahhabis had been seen—scarcely disguised—taking note of the individuals and marking the houses, which their vengeance or avarice had devoted to destruction."

Rahul Mahajan, publisher of an anti-American weblog titled Empire Notes, admitted the Wahhabi connection to Fallujah on April 7, 2004, politely denoting the fanatics by the camouflage term they prefer, "Salafis." Mahajan wrote, "Many inhabitants were Salafists (Wahhabism is a subset of Salafism), a group singled out for political persecution by Saddam."

And where Wahhabis go, Saudis are never far behind. At the beginning of April 2004, as reported by Arabianews.com, the Supreme Mufti of Saudi Arabia, Shaykh Abd Al-Aziz Bin Abd-Allah Aal Ash-Shaikh, a descendant of Ibn Abd Al-Wahhab, publicly called on the kingdom's Muslims to "send hundreds of fighters to participate in the ongoing battle in Fallujah." Even the controlled media of the Saudi government encouraged the kingdom's subjects to hurry across the border. The official newspaper *Al-Riyadh* used its front page to praise the terrorists in Fallujah, describing them as "creating an epic chapter of combat against the American military invaders."

The consequences? On April 12, 2004, a Riyadh resident, Fahed Al-Razni Al-Shimmeri, reported that his son Majed, age twenty-five and a student, had become "a martyr . . . in resisting the American forces' aggression in Fallujah," according to the website Middle East Online. The son was said to have left for jihad in Iraq just a month after the overthrow of Saddam.

Wahhabi aggression against the Coalition in Iraq was not limited to the Sunni-dominated western hinterlands. A Wahhabi presence became obvious in Baghdad itself when a major mosque in the capital was renamed for Ibn Taymiyyah. In Iraq, efforts were consistently made to bluff Americans, and the world, into seeing an incipient civil war between Sunni and Shia political constituencies, or a "resistance" to Western incursion, rather than the reality of the situation: intervention by Al-Qaida, supported by the Wahhabi hardliners in Saudi Arabia, who loathed the Iraqi Sufi heritage no less than the idea of a Shia-led democracy in Iraq. But the evidence often seemed scarce, and official opacity was maintained in the West. In mainstream media and government statements, the jihadist killers were rarely identified with accuracy beyond noting that they were "foreign fighters."

In 2005 superior information emerged and the verdict predictably pointed south of the Iraqi border. The Global Research in International Affairs Center in Israel, a highly reputable and reliable think tank, published a paper titled "Arab Volunteers Killed in Iraq: An Analysis." Written by Dr. Reuven Paz, the paper analyzed the origins of 154 Arab jihadists killed in Iraq during six months in 2004–5, whose names were posted on Islamist websites.

The sample did not account for all jihadists in Iraq, but it provided a useful and eye-opening profile of some of them. Saudi Arabia accounted for 94 jihadists, or 61 percent of the sample, followed by Syria with 16 (10 percent), Iraq itself with only 13 (8 percent), and Kuwait with 11 (7 percent.) The rest included small numbers from Jordan, Lebanon, Libya, Algeria, Morocco (of which one was a resident of Spain), Yemen, Tunisia, the Palestinian territories (only one), Dubai, and Sudan. The Sudanese was living in Saudi Arabia before he went to die in Iraq.

Of the 94 Saudis, 61 originated in the region of Najd, birthplace of

Wahhabism. The total of 154 included 33 suicide terrorists, of whom 23 were Saudis (with 10 from Najd). Given that Najdis make up 43.5 percent of Saudi suicide bombers in Iraq and 65 percent of all Saudi jihadists on the list, Paz concluded that the "Wahhabi doctrines of Najd—the heart of Wahhabism—remain highly effective."

Paz emphasized that "the support for violent Jihad in Iraq against the Americans was encouraged by the Saudi Islamic establishment." But he also offered some interesting observations:

- "Jihadi volunteers constitute a significant portion of the Sunni insurgents," suggesting that referring to the terrorists as if they represented Iraqi Sunnis in general, or were merely local guerrilla fighters opposed to a foreign invader, was inaccurate.
- "Another element to note is the relatively small number of Iraqis involved in the fighting on behalf of the Zarqawi group."
- "Particularly striking . . . is the absence of Egyptians among foreign Arab volunteers [in] Iraq, even though Egypt is the largest Arab country, with millions of sympathizers of Islamist groups." Paz noted that Egyptians were previously prominent as combatants in Afghanistan, Bosnia-Herzegovina, and Chechnya. He ascribed the failure of Egyptians to enlist in the Iraqi jihad to a combination of the decline of Islamist influence in Egypt, effective Egyptian government action against extremism, and orders from the Muslim Brotherhood in Egypt not to participate physically in the Iraqi jihad.

Still, few in the West seemed to notice in spring 2004 when two thousand people assembled in the city of Hilla, near Baghdad, to protest a car bombing that killed at least 125 people. The demonstrators chanted, "No to terrorism! No to Ba'athism and Wahhabism!"

Paz concluded his study with words difficult to surpass for their clarity and relevance: "The intensive involvement of Saudi volunteers for Jihad in Iraq is . . . the result of the Saudi government's double-speak, whereby it is willing to fight terrorism, but only if directly affected by it on its own soil. Saudi Arabia is either deliberately ignoring, or incapable and too weak, to engage in open and brave opposition to Jihadi terrorism outside of the Kingdom. Their blind eyes in the face of the Saudi Islamic establishment's support of the Jihad in Iraq may pose a greater threat in the future, as the hundreds of volunteers return home."

Only one thing needed to be added: It was long past time to close Saudi Arabia's northern border, silence the jihadist preachers, and cut off the official financing of international Wahhabism by the kingdom.

IN MID-2007, MORE than four years after the beginning of the U.S.-led intervention in Iraq, the American government and media admitted what every informed and honest Muslim in the world had known all along: Saudi Wahhabi clerics preached and recruited for terror in Iraq; Saudi money sustained it; the largest number of those who carried out suicide bombings north of the Saudi-Iraqi border had been Saudi citizens, that is, Wahhabi fanatics. Apparently it was now out in the open in the West. In addition, in a salutary development, the straight term "Wahhabi" began to replace the bogus title "Salafi" applied to fundamentalist Sunni terrorists in Western media.

On July 27, 2007, the *Washington Post* and the *New York Times* reported on the links between Saudi Arabia and the Wahhabi terror in Iraq, employing their usual cautious and polite language when dealing with the desert monarchy. The *Post* ran a Reuters rewrite of the *Times* reportage, casting the problem in terms of Saudi distrust for the Shia-led Iraqi administration of Prime Minister Nouri al-Maliki. Resulting difficulties faced Condoleezza Rice and Robert Gates as, just then, they went to visit the Saudis. Seven paragraphs down, Reuters quoted the *Times* about the real issue: "The Saudis had offered financial support to Sunni groups in Iraq and U.S. officials were increasingly concerned about its close Arab ally's 'counterproductive' role in Iraq."

"Counterproductive" was quite a euphemism for Saudi state subsidies to Wahhabi clerics who demanded the genocide of Sufi and Shia Muslims, urged young men to go north and sacrifice themselves to that end, and preached eulogies after their deaths. Others might call such behavior acts of war rather than merely "counterproductive."

The *Times* itself, in an article by Helene Cooper, said, "Of an estimated 60 to 80 foreign fighters who enter Iraq each month, American military and intelligence officials say that nearly half are coming from Saudi Arabia and that the Saudis have not done enough to stem the flow." Administration officials, the paper reported, "spoke on the condition of anonymity because they believed that openly criticizing Saudi Arabia would further alienate the Saudi royal family." Then came the bald truth: "The majority of suicide bombers in Iraq are from Saudi Arabia [and] about 40 percent of all foreign fighters are Saudi. Officials said that while most of the foreign fighters came to Iraq to become suicide bombers, others arrived as bomb makers, snipers, logisticians and financiers."

Meanwhile, the *Wall Street Journal* "revealed" information, most of which had been in print for several years, about the Al Rajhi Bank, one of the main Saudi financiers of Wahhabism. The *Journal* admitted that the Al Rajhi name appeared on a document many Westerners were loath to take seriously, the "Golden Chain" roster of Al-Qaida donors seized by Bosnian authorities in Sarajevo and handed over to the U.S. government in 2002. Yet even the *Journal* seemed not to have noticed that the Al Rajhi financial system's Suleiman Abdul Al-Aziz Al Rajhi also created the SAAR Foundation, an object of the U.S. federal raid known as GreenQuest, which struck a nest of Islamist entities in northern Virginia in 2002.

Why was there so little mainstream media interest in the role of Saudi money and influence in Iraq and elsewhere? The best explanation was media cooperation with the official U.S. preference for the "quiet, behind-the-scenes influence" to which one administration after another defaulted in dealing with Saudi problems, and which the Saudis exploited to continue their deceptive ways.

Saudis and Iraqis, even with their own imperfect media, were much better informed. Here is what they were reading when the *New York Times* and the *Wall Street Journal* made their "disclosures":

- On July 25, 2007, the Saudi newspaper *Al-Watan* reported on sixty-one Saudis held in Iraqi jails. The inferred charge was terrorism.
- The day before, *Al-Watan* described an uproar over Saudi clerics' advocating the destruction of Shia holy sites in Iraq. According to Iraqi sources, the Wahhabis specifically called for a new destruction of the shrines of Imam Husayn in Karbala and of Imam Ali in Najaf—to repeat, the two most sacred Shia sites except for Mecca and Medina. They had been among the earliest targets of raiding in Wahhabi history. As also reported in Iraqi media, students at the Muhammad Ibn Saud Islamic University, located in Riyadh and known as the "terrorist factory," had organized activist groups and sent

more Saudis north to join the onslaught on Iraqi Sufis and Shias.

- On July 17, 2007, the chief Saudi cleric Shaykh Aal Ash-Shaikh, in a vocabulary different from the one he had employed in 2003, cautioned Saudis not to go to Iraq to engage in terror and said, "Those who mislead young Muslims, calling them to jihad, refuse to send their own sons to participate in the same conflict."

- On July 16, the Saudi daily *Al-Sharq Al-Awsat* (*The Middle East*) quoted Prince Nayef, the Saudi interior minister who wriggles like an eel on this issue, claiming that Saudis lured to participate in the Iraq terror are "brainwashed teenagers." The same day, the Arab daily *Al-Hayat* (*Life*) interviewed the U.S. Treasury undersecretary Stuart Levey, who argued that financing terror in Iraq is no different from contributing to Al-Qaida elsewhere.

- And the day before that, on July 15, the Wahhabi website *Al-Sahat* (*The Battlefields*) posted a list of Saudi terrorists recently killed in Iraq, with their names, home addresses, and dates and places of their demise.

These were merely examples of a long inventory of such information reported in the Muslim world. Nobody could say the Saudis, Iraqis, and other Muslims did not know who organized and supported the Wahhabi terror against Sufis, Shias, and other Muslims, as well as non-Muslims, in Iraq. The parade of alleged "disclosures" about Saudi Arabia and the terror in Iraq continued, and on November 22, 2007, the *New York Times* published a new report, by Richard A. Oppel, Jr., describing a collection of seven hundred biographical sketches of jihadists in Iraq, which had been captured in a large documentary hoard, by U.S. soldiers in September 2007 at a camp near Sinjar in western Iraq. Of the biographies, 305, or 40 percent, were Saudi.

By "The Year of Rumi," 2007, Saudi Arabia itself had already seen a revival of Sufism, which emerged as a major force in the development of civil society. The Wahhabi monarchy of Ibn Sa'ud had been established in the 1920s, with a new conquest of Mecca and Medina. Before then, Sufism was well established in the Holy Cities. Each of the *tariqas* maintained a chain of hostelries across Arabia, for the use of pilgrims; each had a *tekke* or *ʒawiya* in the Holy Cities. Each prayed and recited *dhikr* as it saw fit. And the classic Sufi works were available for the benefit of all Islamic scholars.

All of that ended when the Saudi Wahhabis triumphed in Mecca and Medina in 1924–25. Sufism was forced underground, the inns and *tekkes* and shrines closed or were demolished, and the Sufi classics were barred from importation to the kingdom. But as the fortunes of the kingdom changed, so did those of the Sufis, especially in Hejaz, the territory of the Holy Cities themselves.

Four years before the death of Saudi Arabia's King Fahd in 2005, his regime was seriously tainted by the Al-Qaida attacks on America. As young Saudi subjects began to feel disillusion with the established order and repulsion for the jihadism of Osama bin Laden, Sufism became popular as an alternative culture. The commercial capital of the kingdom, Jidda, was nicknamed "the Saudi San Francisco" because of its intellectual independence and diversity. Sufism became prominent in Jidda; Sufi *dhikr* and lectures were held in private houses, without interference from the infamous religious militia, or *mutawwa*. After King Abdullah, the successor to Fahd, came to the throne, the *mu-*

*tawwa* kept their heads down in Jidda, and many women in the town refused to cover their faces.

Sayyid Muhammad ibn 'Alawi Al-Maliki, described in the previous chapter as the *qutb*, or pillar of the Alawi Sufis, died in 2004, in Mecca. He had succumbed to diabetes. At the end of 2003, he had appeared at a meeting of a "Convention for National Dialogue" sponsored by the Saudi authorities in Mecca. As reported in the *Dubai Gulf News*, another independent voice was heard at that convention: the architect and preservation expert Dr. Sami M. Angawi, who openly spoke the forbidden truth: "The root of the problem [in Saudi Arabia] lies in the single [i.e., Wahhabi] interpretation of religious matters . . . For a long time, we have only had a single opinion on religious matters, from a group of people who think along a single direction . . . That there is only one interpretation is wrong . . . My main objective is to allow a diversity of opinion on every level, and different schools of thought, starting from mosques, education, and the media," he said. "The two holy mosques in Mecca and Medina have always allowed diversity in opinion. For 1,400 years, we had a diversity of opinion and interpretation. This diversity started to slowly fade out about fifty years ago, until there was only one school of thought left." Angawi reminded his fellow Saudis, "The Prophet told us to follow our hearts after listening to a wide range of advice. When you have only one [source of] advice, you have no choice. Today the problem is that young people are not given a choice. They are taught one school of thought."

Descriptions of the burial of the Saudi Sufi Sayyid Al-Maliki were contradictory. I was informed that Wahhabi clerics refused to authorize a funeral for him, but his followers were allowed to organize a service in the Grand Mosque of Mecca. That a leading Hejazi imam could have a funeral in the Grand Mosque of Mecca was considered a kind of miracle, and it was described by one of my informants in the kingdom, who must still maintain anonymity, as "a very spiritual event."

Sayyid Muhammad ibn 'Alawi Al-Maliki struggled against fundamentalism as a defender of Islamic tradition by his example of patience and study, by the word and the pen. He did not bend and did not break. He was a true Muslim moderate. There are many more like him, waiting in Arabia for the end of Wahhabism. And neither corrupt rulers nor terrorist criminals, nor ranting ideologues, Muslim or otherwise, but men and women like him hold the destiny of the faith of Muhammad in their hands.

Irfan Al-Alawi, whose eulogy for Sayyid Al-Maliki was cited in the preceding chapter, wrote of him,

> Having succeeded his father in Mecca, he maintained the tradition of indefatigable teaching for over thirty years. Even when he was prevented from teaching in the Mosque by the Wahhabis, who had declared him an apostate, the school which he had started in his own house remained active.
>
> His debates with the Wahhabis are well known. Suffice it to say that they increased his popularity worldwide, for books were written in his defense by Moroccan, Yemeni, Emirates, and other scholars, in addition to countless magazine articles. He was a close friend of King Fahd, who . . . invited him to his palace in Mecca many times. Even after the late King had a heart attack the Shaykh would visit him and recite . . . Fahd made it clear that they were on good terms.
>
> In a conference about opposing extremism Sayyid Al-Maliki pointed out that twenty years before, in his famous book *Necessary Corrections of Certain Misconceptions,* he had suggested a meeting to resolve the differences between himself, some fac-

tions of *Ahl al-Sunna* [the Sunni majority], and the Wahhabis. Ten years after the conference he wrote a short treatise on extremism and *takfir* and warned of their dangers. He concluded by hoping that the Muslims had learnt their lesson and that school curricula in Saudi Arabia would be altered and the media used appropriately to reduce the likelihood of terrorism in the future.

He passed away on Friday, the 15th of Ramadan 1425 (2004) in a state of fasting at his house in Mecca, surrounded by his children, his brother Sayyid Abbas and other family members.

His *Janaza* funeral prayer was first offered at his residence, and attended by many prominent Shaykhs, Ministers and *murids* [Sufi disciples] from all over the world. His [coffin] was then taken to the Grand Mosque and placed near the *Ka'bah* to perform the final prayers. The imam was heard crying as he recited the funeral prayers; even the Wahhabi imams recognized that a great Islamic scholar was gone.

Much to the surprise of the assembled mourners, then Crown Prince Abdullah and Prince Sultan, the defense minister, appeared and praised Sayyid Al-Maliki. According to Al-Alawi, "The bier was then lifted to be taken towards Suk al-Layl which leads towards the famous cemetery Al Mu'al'a. The *Janaza* was followed by a procession of thousands which filled the streets of Mecca from the Grand Mosque to the graveyard. Five hundred soldiers had to be deployed at the cemetery to control the crowds."

Finally, as Al-Alawi recalled, "The Shaykh was laid to rest next to his father and grandfather, near the grave of his ancestor Sayyidah Khadijah," the wife of Muhammad. Nothing about Sayyid Al-Maliki or this event appeared in English-language Arab media.

. . .

SAYYID AL-MALIKI HAD DEFENDED Sufi and Islamic traditions in the form of architectural heritage no less than metaphysical learning. Among Sufis and other traditional Muslims in the Saudi kingdom, there is currently no more dramatic issue than that of Wahhabi disrespect for the holy sites, aggravated by Saudi royal machinations to transform Mecca from a Holy City into a modern urban center, with elaborate condominiums in a Las Vegas style overlooking the Grand Mosque in which the *Ka'bah* is located. Sayyid Al-Maliki, Sami Angawi, and Irfan Al-Alawi had been consistent opponents of this ravaging of culture. The "sober" and anti-Western Naqshbandi G. F. Haddad, writing about his *hajj* trip to the holy cities, described how the *mutawwa* or religious militia would beat pilgrims who went to the Prophet's Mosque in Medina, the Jannat al-Baqi cemetery of the Prophet's family and Companions (wrecked by the Wahhabis), and related sites. The offense of the visitors was to recite the opening *surah* or chapter of the *Qur'an, Al-Fatiha,* for the dead, an ordinary Islamic practice the Wahhabis violently condemn.

In 2007, the abuses of ordinary citizens by the Saudi *mutawwa* had become the major topic of public discussion in the country. In July, religious militia members were brought into Saudi courts for the first time, charged with arbitrarily killing people taken into custody for morals offenses (including possession of alcohol and an unchaperoned meeting between a man and an unrelated woman).

The misdeeds of the *mutawwa,* officially styled the Commission for the Promotion of Virtue and Prevention of Vice, had become so resented that some members of the royal family, as well as lower government agencies, had promised reform. On August 22, 2007, the daily *Al-Watan* announced that the Saudi Bureau of Investigation and Public Prosecution had turned over two members of the *mutawwa* to a higher court for trial in the May 2007 death of Salman Al-Huraisi. The victim had been swarmed by eighteen *mutawwa* in his family home on suspicion of keeping liquor, and died at their hands.

The only function of the *mutawwa* is to enforce the strict fundamentalist code of Wahhabism. Militia members patrol the shrine of Muhammad in Medina to assure that traditional Muslims do not "worship" him by praying directly to or touching the Prophet's tomb. They also walk the streets of the ancient city looking for anybody visibly diverging from Wahhabi doctrine in their physical actions or prayers, including Shia pilgrims to Mecca and Medina.

On August 10, 2007, according to Reuters, a group of eight Iraqi Shia men aged sixteen to twenty-six, holding American and British citizenship, accused the *mutawwa* of assaulting them in Mecca a week before. The eight Shias claimed they had been detained overnight and beaten by the religious militia for praying in the Shia manner, which differs slightly from Sunni prayer. A member of the Iraqi parliament said that two of the men were sons of Iraqi political figures. One of the pilgrims, Amir Taki, twenty-four, declared, "We were handcuffed and savagely beaten with chairs, bats, sticks, shoes, and police radio communication devices." They claimed to have been denied water, food, medicine, and toilet facilities and to have been subjected to threats of murder. They escaped because one used a hidden cell phone to contact U.S. and British diplomats.

Irfan al-Alawi, who is a British Sunni Muslim, had an experience similar to that of the Iraqi Shia pilgrims on August 12, 2007. He wrote,

> I went to the Prophet's Mosque to read my prayers. I moved
> close to the sacred chamber where the prophet is buried, which
> is made of a green colored metal grill and has a wooden wall

surrounding it. The *mutawwa* and police sit behind the wooden wall and stop people from looking inside, touching the grill for blessings and praying towards it.

As I took out a book consisting of salutations for the Prophet, one of the *mutawwa* had left to change duty. I was reading the salutations facing the sacred chamber when a police officer told me to move away. The *mutawwa* who had left to change his shift told me not to face the sacred chamber. I made a gesture indicating I needed only two more minutes to finish praying, but the *mutawwa* insisted that I leave the area immediately. I continued reading from my book while sitting for approximately five more minutes, and then got up to leave. As I walked around the sacred chamber towards the exit, another *mutawwa* grabbed me at the indication of the first one, and led me towards the first. The first asked me for my card, to which I replied, "Which card?" in English. He repeated, "Card, card." A well-dressed old Saudi man told the *mutawwa* to leave me alone, to which the *mutawwa* replied, "Mind your own business and don't interfere." He asked me my nationality and when I replied that I was British he smirked.

We then went to the head office of the *mutawwa*. The one who arrested me reported the incident and told his senior that I ignored his instructions three times against praying facing the sacred chamber. I waited for ten minutes before a Pakistani dressed in the blue uniform of the Saudi Bin Ladin Group came into the office and sat down next to me. He asked me in Urdu why I was there, and I described the incident, to which he replied, "Why were you facing the sacred chamber?" He then asked me which book I was reading. He looked through it and then asked me whether I was a Shia to which I replied that

I was not, but that I was a mainstream Sunni. He then said that the book I was reading was written by a Shia, which happens to be untrue.

I asked him to ask the senior *mutawwa* whether I could leave as I needed to be at the airport at 10:30 A.M. The *mutawwa* refused and said since I had broken their rules and regulations I had to wait for another *mutawwa* by the name of Shaykh Ibrahim to come and speak to me. The senior *mutawwa* took out a large book. [Before allowing me to leave] he asked me for my name and my father's name, wrote down an account of the incident, and took my thumb print. [Such prints are typically substituted for signatures in Saudi Arabia because so many people, even members of the royal family, are illiterate.]

Al-Alawi's experience—detention by the Saudi religious militia for facing the "wrong" direction while praying, not for any violation of civil or criminal law—was sadly typical of the abuses daily meted out to Saudi citizens. In one of the most shocking expressions of renewed Wahhabi militancy, women were being recruited to the *mutawwa* with the aim of patrolling the Grand Mosque in Mecca and the Prophet's Shrine in Medina. They were ordered to exclude pious women and girls, in the footsteps of the Sufi saint Rabiya Al-Adawiyya, from praying in the sight of the *Ka'bah*, a break with 1,400 years of Islamic life. Meanwhile, the Saudi media had become filled with continuous complaints about the allegedly humiliating difficulties encountered by the kingdom's subjects in getting student visas to the United States.

All these problems—homicidal adventurism in Iraq, abuses by the *mutawwa*, suspicion about issuing visas to Saudis in the aftermath of the atrocities of September 11, 2001—had a root cause: state-sponsored Wahhabism. There could be only one way for Saudi Arabia to change for the better: to disestablish Wahhabism as the state religion, to abolish its doctrinal monopoly, and to allow religious pluralism such as exists, at least on paper, in many Muslim countries.

*Al-Fatiha,* the opening of the *Qur'an,* reads:

*In the name of God, the compassionate and merciful*
*Praise be to God, Lord of the Universe,*
*The Compassionate, the Merciful,*
*Sovereign of the Day of Judgment!*
*You alone we worship, and to You alone we turn for help,*
*Guide us on the straight path.*
*The path of those whom you have favored,*
*Not of those who have incurred your wrath,*
*Nor of those who have gone astray.*[2]

*Al-Fatiha* is the basis of Muslim prayer, including those for the dead, but, once again, the Wahhabis ban prayer for the dead as they do the celebration of Muhammad's birthday. Repeating *Al-Fatiha* is a common custom among all traditional Muslims, but Sufis have been especially unflinching in continuing the practice while on *hajj* to Mecca and Medina, even though they are harassed, abused, arrested, and deported. The Wahhabis also forcibly censor the exclamation *"Ya Muhammad!"* (O Muhammad!) from Muslim speech, on the argument that it equates Muhammad with God and is therefore polytheistic. In this they have been noticeably more successful. According to G. F. Haddad, these vexations have been accompanied by constant propaganda directed to *hajj* pilgrims, condemnation of "illicit" Sufi practices, "disinformation" disseminated by word of mouth and in printed form during brief talks after prayer and discourses in the main mosques, via audiotapes, and in books, as well as on the local radio. This clamor has taken place in numerous languages.

But the demolition of sacred architecture remains the most inflammatory issue. Chief among the structures ruined by the Saudi-Wahhabi authorities is the birthplace of Muhammad. A Kuwaiti Rifa'i Sufi, Shaykh Yusuf ibn al-Sayyid Hashim Al-Rifa'i (b. 1932), wrote in 1999, *"Alas, woe and misery for a Sect that hates its Prophet, whether in word or in deed, holding him in contempt and trying to eradicate his traces!"* (emphasis in original).

Shaykh Al-Rifa'i wrote against the Wahhabis, "You tried and continue to try—as if it were your goal in life—to destroy the last remnant of the historical vestiges of the Messenger of Allah, namely the noble place where he was born. This house was razed, then changed into a cattle market, then some pious people transformed it into a library . . . You began to pry at that place with evil stares and vengeful threats, trying to entrap it with the official departments. You openly requested that it be destroyed."[3]

Shaykh Al-Rifa'i delivered the most eloquent modern condemnation of the Wahhabi clerics, accurately describing the shame they would inflict on Islam and the chaos they stir throughout the world:

You brain-washed gullible young men with your School and rigid opinions, such as Juhayman al-'Utaybi, executed for seizing the Grand Mosque in Mecca with his cohort [in 1979]. Your teacher was his teacher and spiritual master . . . They would roam under your sights, harassing the Muslims in Mecca and Medina, commanding and forbidding and strutting until their force increased, their claws grew long, and they did what they did, so they were surrounded and killed, or wounded and taken prisoner. Then you announced that you had nothing to do with them and were innocent of their misdeeds! But their books and the publications they left behind are the best witnesses to the facts. For they declared themselves fully in agreement with your extremist views and became completely intoxicated with them. Still you continue on your way, without the least shame—all in the name of *Qur'an* and the *Sunna*!

You built a university in Medina and named it the Islamic University, near the tomb of Muhammad, peace and greetings be upon him. People and scholars then flocked to it with their cherished children, rejoicing at the chance of drinking from this spring, thinking it would increase them in love and devotion to their beloved Prophet, peace and greetings be upon him, his dear Family, his Companions, and the Successors. But there you were teaching them how to deprecate him and all of them! You also had the students spy and eavesdrop on one another, reporting to you the names and activities of those you called grave-lovers. Namely, those who made frequent visits and salutations on the Prophet—so that you might wage war against them, ostracize them and expel them! You would only keep whoever became your client and obeyed you—for those alone are truthful and trusted according to you.

Whoever graduated successfully at your hands, having drunk in your assorted beliefs, you sent back to their countries as your representatives to sound your warnings and announce your glad tidings that their misguided fathers and wayward nations must renew their Islam. Such graduates you pampered with lavish salaries, opening offices for them and providing them with every conceivable opportunity. As a result, dissension and enmity flared up between them and the clerics and pious Muslims of the generations of their fathers and past Shaykhs. Such graduates resemble time bombs you manufactured and filled with all kinds of bad opinions of others and deep-seated contempt. This has transformed Muslim countries, especially in Africa and Asia, into battlefields of perpetual dissension among Muslims. This condition has even spread to the Muslim countries that gained their independence from Russia only recently, all the way to Muslim minorities and communities in Europe, America, Australia and elsewhere!

Yet you gave full license to repeat and shout at the top of their lungs, in Medina right next to the Prophet's body, *"The father and mother of the Prophet, peace and greetings be upon him, are in hellfire! The father and mother of the Prophet, peace and greetings be upon him, are in hellfire!"*

Wahhabis insult Muhammad's parents because they died before the revelation of Islam and did not become Muslim. The individual most infamous for this behavior was a certain Abubakr Jabir, who had deserted from the Algeria revolutionary struggle of the 1950s–60s to Saudi territory. The path from these insults in Medina to the bloodshed in nearby Iraq is a short one.

In refuting the Wahhabis, Haddad cited a companion of the Prophet's, Umar Ibn Abd Al-Aziz, whose comment may be paraphrased and updated, for simplicity, as follows: The differences among the Muslims are good, because they offer space in which to develop. This is a powerful statement in favor of pluralism in Islam. Even Ibn Taymiyyah, the ideal of the Wahhabis, agreed that pluralism in religious opinion, as in the difference between the Sufis and the official Saudi clerics, is a mercy and blessing, because it allows the believer and the scholar freedom to think. Comparisons between the ideological configuration of Saudi Wahhabism and Western totalitarianism are rejected by many Western academics as well as fundamentalist Muslims, but as a great poet once said, tyranny is tyranny. It cannot be disguised, and its characteristics are more often similar than different.

Haddad further offers a Quranic reference to nighttime as a mercy for humanity; it does not follow, argued one of the greatest of the mainstream Sunni scholars, Al-Nawawi (1233–1278), that daytime is a punishment. Fundamentalism inhabits a dualistic world in which all is always in conflict—a heresy in Islam. Islamic metaphysics, by contrast, evokes *wahdat ul-wujud*, the unity of creation. Night is a mercy, but day is not a punishment, we may repeat, and add the following: Islam is good, but the other religions are not bad; Sunnism is good, but Shiism is not bad; ordinary religious observance is good, but metaphysics is not bad; defending Muslims against oppression is good, but doing so by peaceful and respectful means, in Muslim and non-Muslim lands, is not bad. Night and day, so utterly different from one another, do not make war between each other. This unity is implicit in political democracy, based on a pluralism intrinsic to the traditional Islamic soul, for which so many people claim there is a battle.

Here, then, is a "sober" Sufi path to the liberation of Islam from the prison in which it has been confined. Works such as those of Sayyid Al-Maliki, Shaykh Al-Rifa'i, Irfan Al-Alawi, and G. F. Haddad, directed against the spiritual corruption of the Saudi kingdom, are of the highest significance: they form a multichapter religious manifesto for pluralism. And in the new history of Islam, like so many dissident documents produced during the crisis of Soviet Communism, they may go unread or misunderstood in the West.

. . .

THE SUFI ROLE in the struggle for change in Saudi Arabia matches a similar public profile in Iran, where protests by Sufis against clerical suppression broke out in 2006. Iranian Sufism is so deeply embedded in that country's culture that it seems natural for it to become a prominent civic force, representing an alternative to the Khomeinist state. Shia dissidents, many of them traditionalists who never intellectually accepted Khomeini's scheme for clerical rule, could overshadow Sufi teachers in dismantling the present Tehran regime. This is especially possible if the new government in Iraq succeeds in embodying a Shia alternative to Khomeinism, which most close readers of Iraqi Shiism expect. In turn, by osmosis thanks to the constant stream of Iranian pilgrims to Karbala since 2003, discontent will increase with the regime in Iran. A democratic, Shia-majority Iraq would affect clericalist Iran as Poland and its Solidarity movement did the Soviet Union.

The Nimatullahi *tariqa* is the main Sufi order in Iran, but it has become riven with discord as the Islamic Republic begins to fracture. Although the Nimatullahis are strict in their adherence to *Shariah*, some clerics have issued anti-Sufi *fatwas*. The Shia clerics are divided, with many favoring acceptance of Sufism as a living reality, as well as an established part of the Iranian intellectual landscape. But three figures, Ayatollahs Husayn Nuri Hamadani, Makarem Shirazi, and Fazel Lankarani, have agitated against Sufism and even against the poetic legacy of Shah Nimatullah, who they claim was a concealed Sunni, making his followers equally guilty of hidden Sunnism. Lankarani has issued repeated attacks in the reactionary newspaper *Jomhouri Eslami* (*Islamic Republic*) against the Gonabadi branch of the Nimatullahis.

Threats against the Sufis are somewhat moderated by the official approval granted them by Ayatollah Khomeini, the Imam of the Islamic Revolution. Although Khomeini admired the Sufis, however, he was unwilling to defend them and alienate other clerics. Today, because the slow disintegration of the clerical state leaves nearly all Iranians discontented, abuses by reactionary clerics have an inflammatory nature.

Early in 2006, global media reported that the religious city of Qom, center of Iranian Shia theological training, was rocked by the arrest of as many as two thousand people after a private home used as a Nimatullahi-Gonabadi meeting place (a *husayniya,* or Shia prayer hall, rather than a *tekke*) was closed. Police shot tear gas into crowds of Sufis and their supporters, leaving more than three hundred injured. The *husayniya* was then demolished, along with the homes of two active Sufis. Predictably, local officials alleged that the Sufis were participants in a foreign conspiracy. But the confrontation followed a denunciation of the Sufis by Ayatollah Nuri Hamadani, who assailed them as a threat to Islam. Residents of Qom said the clash had been precipitated by clerical resentment over the growth of Sufi activity as well as by a continuing stream of Iranian and foreign visitors, including Sufis, academic experts, and simple tourists.

In the aftermath of the Qom uproar, fifty-two Sufis involved in the events, including their lawyer, were sentenced to imprisonment and flogging. In October 2006 Nur Ali Tabanda, leader of the Gonabadis, was ordered to stay away from his home in Gonabad (he also resides in Tehran). But Iranians began to stay away from mosques, and they filled the Sufi meeting places. Sufis were dismissed from work and otherwise subjected to discrimination, their literature and events suppressed.

A new clash with the Gonabadis occurred in the town of Borujerd in western Iran in November 2007. A mob led by police, in which the Basij, or revolutionary militia, also participated, demolished a Sufi meeting place after allegations, later printed in *Jomhuri Eslami,* that the spiritualists had committed vandalism at a Shia mosque. Eighty people were injured, 180 arrested, and in a detail revealing the modernization of the Sufi spirit, twenty-five motorcycles belonging to the Sufis were reported wrecked.

But Iranian Sufism cannot be destroyed; its roots are too deep in the spiritual soil of their country. The Iranian Sufis potentially represent a powerful challenge to the clerical regime.

AMID WARS AND RUMORS of wars we come to the surprising story, for some, of Sufism in Israel. During my first trip to the Jewish state, in 2006, I visited Safed (*Tsfat* in Hebrew). Safed is small, and it is the holy city of the Lurianic Kabbalah, a Jewish mystical movement that began in the sixteenth century under the charismatic guidance of a Jerusalem-born rabbi, Yitzhak Luria. This was a profound development in Judaism, having almost nothing in common with today's Kabbalah fad—though I condemn nobody who sincerely seeks after the divine.

I close my eyes and savor Safed as I first observed it so recently, in the sunlight of peace. My memory moves back to the year 1979 and my first trip to Paris. I knew little of Kabbalah then—hardly anything more than fragments. I was thirty-one. It was November, cold, and I sheltered in an American tourist trap, the Shakespeare & Co. bookshop on the Left Bank of the Seine. I was invited into the inner sanctum upstairs (and did not realize until later that it was infested with fleas). There was a red-bound volume on a crowded shelf: *The Zohar in Moslem and Christian Spain,* by Ariel Bension "Manastirli," the sole twentieth-century Jewish Sufi of significance, born in Jerusalem and a rabbi in the Balkans.

*The Zohar* (*Splendor*) is the greatest work of Kabbalah, and I had read at it for years. Eyes closed, I watch my hand reach for the Bension book as I ask if it is for sale; it was, and it was my door to Jewish spirituality and to the relationship of Kabbalah to Sufism. It was my first introduction to the lore of Safed. I followed the path laid out in *Rav Bension's* book through Spain to the former territories of the Ottoman Empire, entered Sufism and Islam, took my own side trip to Turkestan, and finally landed in Safed. My hand touching the red spine of the book in Paris marks the biggest turning point in my life.

In 2006 I visited synagogues in Safed named for Luria, for the Kabbalist rabbis Moshe Kordovero and Shlomo Alkabetz, and for an outstanding lawgiver, Rabbi Yosef Karo, who based his famous compendium of Jewish law, *Shulkhan Aruch* (*The Set Table*) on *Shariah*. I sat in a café and looked through the window at a hill where the fabled second-century Jewish mystic and leader of an anti-Roman rebellion, Shimon Bar Yochai, is reputedly buried. It is said the Kabbalists came to Safed because Bar Yochai's remains rest there.

Safed is green, a welcome relief after the dry stone of much of Israel; it lies in hills reminiscent of California. But only weeks later, I was told, Safed was empty, with the beginning of the 2006 Hezbollah war, and the town's population in shelters, under rocket attack from Lebanon.

It was for so long my dream to see Safed, and I could not imagine that I would come to it so close to the explosion of bombs in its ancient streets. I observed there that a historic Arab mosque had been transformed into an art gallery and imagined that the mosque could be reconsecrated. The mosque had been empty, I was told, since 1948. I am committed to preservation of mosques and Sufi shrines in Saudi Arabia, Bosnia-Herzegovina, Kosovo, Kazakhstan, and elsewhere. But for the moment, nothing seemed to me more appropriate than the rehabilitation of the Safed mosque as an Islamic institution—a center for the study of Sufism and Kabbalah that would welcome experts and adepts from both religions, in both mystical disciplines, as well as Christian and other scholars, for a fruitful dialogue at the highest level in green Safed. Such a center could help free Sufism and Kabbalah in Safed from New Age accretions as well as from hostility between Israelis and Arabs.

Beyond such intoxicated visions, I spent a good deal of time talking about and with Sufis in Israel. My first contact was with an Orthodox rabbi, Dov Maimon, who is well informed on the school of Jewish Sufism created in Egypt by the son and other descendants of Maimonides. Rabbi Maimon is profoundly dedicated to religious pluralism and is also associated, in the interfaith group known as Jerusalem Peacemakers, with a Sufi from East Jerusalem I had previously met, Shaykh Abd al-Aziz Bukhari. An ancestor of Shaykh Bukhari's was sent to Jerusalem from central Asia in 1616 to found a *khaniqa,* or Sufi lodging house for pilgrims of the Naqshbandi order. Shaykh Bukhari has honored his heritage by his interfaith work and by serving as head of the Uzbek Muslim community in Israel and Palestine, which counts some 1,300 members. But in 2008 Sunni fundamentalists occupied the historic mosque in his home.

Shaykh Bukhari has said of his work as a member of the Jerusalem Peacemakers: "At least I tried; I am not just waiting for change." He was criticized by some Muslims in the Old City of Jerusalem for welcoming non-Muslims to his *dhikr,* and was accused of being a Baha'i, a Freemason (the focus of much paranoia in the Muslim world), and an adherent of a "false belief that all religions are one." The latter is a common reproach hurled at Sufis, yet Shaykh Bukhari answers serenely, "We are all born with no distinct religion, and it is the decision of the Creator how people will come to religion." But the shaykh could not yet make the *hajj* to Mecca because he does not hold a Jordanian passport—when I interviewed him only Israeli Muslims who could show pre-1948 residence papers, which he lacks, were allowed into the Saudi kingdom for *hajj*.

He spoke fondly of Avraham Elqayam, a controversial scholar at Israel's Bar-Ilan University who has written extensively on Sufism and its relationship to Jewish mysticism, and of the Sufi Center of Nazareth, headed by Shaykh Abd al-Salaam Manasra. But these points of Sufi light are by no means isolated in the Land of Israel. I received a blessing in the Mosque of Umar, near the Dome of the Rock, and throughout my visit to Jerusalem was inspired by the unique manner in which the Jewish and Muslim elements of the city—notwithstanding their friction—embody universal and intertwined customs. On the way to Umar Ibn Ul-Khattab Square in the Muslim Quarter, I could hear ululations, typically associated in the West with Muslim women, rise from the nearby Western Wall, where Moroccan and other Jewish women of Arab culture thus express their joy in the holiness of the site. A procession of Bukharan Jews approached the Wall in commemoration of a bar mitzvah with the blowing of the same long brass trumpets one hears throughout central Asia, among Tibetans, and even, in times past, in Beijing.

I proceeded then to Safed and, afterward, to the old Crusader and Ottoman city of Akko (*Acre*), where I met the elderly but sparkling-eyed Qadiri shaykh known as Abu Filistin. I found him at the historic Al-Jazar Mosque, immediately recognizable by its slender minaret as an Ottoman creation and described as the second-largest mosque in Israel. The shaykh's name—"Father of Palestine"—is derived from his own pre-1948 life in Akko. Shaykh Abu Filistin and I joined in the evening prayer in the Sinan Basha Mosque, a smaller Ottoman landmark, and then startled the rest of the party with which I traveled (made up of secular and religious Jews and Muslims) with our lively discussion of Ibn Arabi.

I next journeyed to Baqa Al-Garbya, just inside the Green Line separating Israel from the West Bank, where I was introduced to the shaykhs and imams of the Qasemi-Halveti Sufi order, which maintains one of the most remarkable and inspiring establishments in Israel: the Al-Qasemi Academy. The academy is a college devoted to the Sufi teaching of Islam, as well as to excellence in all areas of contemporary education, ranging from proficiency in English (which I have long supported as a means for the reform of radicalized Muslim *medresas*) to the inculcation of respect for other faiths and, of course, metaphysics. The Al-Qasemi Academy has "one of the most inclusive academic libraries in the Arab sector in Israel. It contains 50,000 entries in Arabic, Hebrew, and English in all subjects: educational, literary, theological, scientific, and others," according to material distributed by the school. Al-Qasemi is linked to Texas A&M University and the University of British Columbia. It is also supported by the American Jewish Committee, by the state of Israel, and, like the Pjetër Muqaj School in Guska, Kosovo, by foreign Sufis. As previously described, the Al-Qasemi School sent a delegation to the "Year of Rumi" event in Bosnia-Herzegovina in March 2007.

The Al-Qasemi Academy, which has numerous women students, represents the most relevant aspect of Sufism at present—its role as the vanguard of an Islamic renaissance in which Muslims will embrace a modern and global identity, with the assistance of Jews and Christians.

But even as I visited Safed, and Akko, and Baqa al-Garbya, war was approaching. Within a few weeks the disastrous conflict between Israel and Hezbollah had exploded, and Safed was bombarded with missiles.

Wahhabi fanatics destroyed the birthplace of Muhammad; rockets from Lebanon scarred the Kabbalistic city of Safed. Libraries and *teqes* were burned by the Serbs in Bosnia-Herzegovina and Kosovo. What may be said of Sufism in a world wracked by war, terror, and destruction? Is it good to pray at *turbes* and recite *dhikr* but better to preserve books in which the thoughts of the dead mystics are reported and make them available to new readers? Is it good to rehabilitate *tekkes* and other historic sites but better to build schools? It is unquestionably good to study Islam but undeniably better for Muslim and non-Muslim children to study together. America can assist moderate Muslim networks, in the phrase of the 2007 RAND Corporation report, but much will have to be done by Sufis and other moderate Muslims themselves. Non-Muslims can help. But, to reiterate, Sufism cannot be a policy tool. It can be only what it is: the path to God.

# 6

## Sufism in Transition

*The West, Central Asia, Indonesia, and the World*

SUFISM FIRST CAME TO the West through medieval Spain and the impact of Islam there on Jewish and Christian mystics. Renaissance European travelers to Turkey and Persia wrote about Sufism. Sufism attracted new attention in Europe in the nineteenth century: the German philosopher G. W. F. Hegel drew on Rumi. But Sufism came across the Atlantic not long after, through its influence on American classic authors including Ralph Waldo Emerson, Henry David Thoreau, and Walt Whitman.

Emerson and Thoreau were prominent in transcendentalism, an intellectual and spiritual movement, and an important early New Age chapter in American culture. The transcendentalists sought to experience the unity of being through nature and intuition, interests that made their attraction to Sufism easy to understand.

Emerson became America's first enthusiast of Sufi poetry, anticipating the acclaim for Rumi 150 years later. After reading translations into English and German of the Persian masters, Emerson embraced Muslihud'din Sa'adi Shirazi, author of the *Gulistan* and *Bostan*. Emerson wrote of Sa'adi that he, "like Homer, Shakespeare, Cervantes, and Montaigne, is perpetually modern."

Sa'adi also impressed Thoreau, the author of *Walden*. Thoreau observed in 1852, "A single thought of a certain elevation makes all men of one religion[;] I know, for instance, that Sadi entertained once identically the same thought that I do, and therefore I can find no essential difference between Sadi and myself. He is not Persian, he is not ancient, he is not strange to me. By the identity of his thought with mine he still survives." In this, Thoreau showed an inclination toward Sufi doctrines about the universe and the nature of the soul.

Walt Whitman was similarly affected. He began his poem "A Persian Lesson,"

> *For his o'erarching and last lesson the greybeard sufi,*
> *In the fresh scent of the morning in the open air*
> *On the slope of a teeming Persian rose-garden . . .*

With the arrival of other New Age movements in America at the end of the nineteenth century, such as theosophy, interest in Sufism increased. All the New Age movements turned to the East, but unlike Hindu and Buddhist threads introduced by spiritualism and then by the Beat poets of the 1950s, Islam remained more than exotic to Americans. It was considered an Oriental and distant "other," complicated and difficult to penetrate, with which Americans had little contact.

Western Sufis, that is, metaphysical students who had not made the Muslim profession of faith, began to appear in organized groups in America in the 1950s. At the same time, fleeing the dictatorship of Communism in the Balkans, the earliest significant American community of authentic Muslim Sufis, affiliated with the Albanian Bektashi order, settled in the Detroit area. Their guide was the saintly Baba

Rexheb Beqiri; in 1954 he established the First Bektashi *Teqe* in America, in Taylor, Michigan, and thirty years later he published a rare but important book in English, *The Mysticism of Islam and Bektashism*. With the founding of the *teqe* in Taylor, he tried to explain Sufism to Americans in an idiom never previously articulated on these shores. Launching a small Albanian- and English-language periodical that saw only four issues, *Zëri Bektashizmes* (*Voice of Bektashism*), he wrote in a Shia vein about the martyrdom of Imam Husayn. Baba Rexheb declared that the grandson of Muhammad was persecuted and slain because he defended a constitutional attitude toward religious rule, liberty, and the welfare of the people. Imam Husayn, according to Baba Rexheb, "kept alive the flag of liberty, the prestige of religious democracy." The people rebelled against the injustices of their rulers and Imam Husayn joined them in their protest, but the evil usurpers of authority replied with "terroristic actions."

This anticipation by an Albanian Bektashi exile in America of the key questions in the relations between Islam and the West a half-century afterward is more than remarkable. The principle of "religious democracy"—meaning democracy *within* religion, not a democracy ruled by religion—is a great challenge to *Shariah*-driven conformity in Islam, and the description of Muslim tyrants maintaining their position by terror could be taken from the pages of any newspaper in the world as this book was written. But because his activity was mainly limited to the Albanian-speaking community in America, Baba Rexheb remains almost unknown to the world today.

By contrast, the Western Sufi current became associated in the 1960s with the New Age revival, which was followed by the growth of Sufi groups claiming an Islamic character. Charles Upton, translator of Rabiya, came to Sufism from the Beat writers' milieu in San Francisco, as did the poet Daniel Abdal-Hayy Moore—the first of the Bay Area authors, aside from some African Americans, to publicly become Muslim. The award of the Nobel Prize for Literature to the eighty-seven-year-old British writer Doris Lessing in 2007 may represent the pinnacle of intellectual influence reached by the Western Sufis. But the Sufism of Doris Lessing is profoundly different from that of contemporary Islamic mystics whose endeavors, often tragic, in the Balkans, Iraq, and Saudi Arabia I have narrated here. Lessing's involvement with Sufism has always been controversial among scholars of Islamic metaphysics, because she drew her Sufi inspiration from a curious person of Afghan origin who called himself Idries Shah and wrote many books on mysticism. Very little of Idries Shah's work is well founded, aside from a sole insight: that a great shamanic cultural system extended from central Asia across the Arctic to the heart of indigenous America. I encountered this hypothesis in the American West forty years ago and, after much reflection, reading, travel, and empirical observation, made it my own. Still, while he has been taken up by certain Naqshbandi Sufis, Idries Shah is generally viewed as a charlatan.

I began this book praising Doris Lessing as a sharer in the Secret of Secrets, but this illumination is visible less in her imaginative novels, which have veered into science fiction, than in her original classic, *The Golden Notebook* (1962). That volume, which inspired a generation of feminists, also told the story of the author's break with the self-repression of Stalinist Communism in a world beset by an unresolved war in Korea, anti-Western strife in Africa, brutal purges in the then Soviet zone of Eastern Europe, and, everywhere a sensitive personality looked, crass ideological manipulation. After more than a half-century, it might appear that titles and flags have changed but nothing else—a long resistance to tyranny over thought continues, within the individual and in the public space. The Secret of Secrets is, I believe, revealed equally in the struggle of twentieth-century Western intellectuals to escape Communist illusions and the combat of nonconformist Muslim mystics such as the Turkish and Kurdish Alevis and the Bektashi Sufis against fundamentalist Islam. That is, humanity cannot survive without spiritual freedom—paired in Sufism with humility before God. Sufism is not, as it is often portrayed, a means of escape from a world of injustice, the rule of violence, and the crisis of Islam and the West. Rather, it entails a more profound knowledge and experience of, and confrontation with, the capacity of humans to do wrong to one another.

The journey of Doris Lessing from Marxism to metaphysics may herald the most powerful challenge of the twenty-first century: to redeem a liberating faith in God as a means to global harmony, in response to the inhuman fantasies of statists, nationalists, and theocrats, as well as the heartless, empty universe of the militant atheists. There could, I believe, be a hidden Sufi *silsila,* beginning with Rabiya Al-Adawiyya in Iraq 1,300 years ago and leading to the Sufi women of Shkodra in Albania as well as to Doris Lessing. A book similar to *The Golden Notebook* but describing the evolution of a Muslim woman away from Wahhabi fundamentalism and written with the talent of Lessing would be worth a thousand times more than the mass of critical literature on Islam that has appeared in the West since September 11, 2001. God willing, such a work is being written as you read these lines—probably in Saudi Arabia!

IT MAY HAVE BEEN coincidence that the 2007 Nobel Prize in Literature for Lessing came a year after the same honor was granted to the Turkish writer Orhan Pamuk. In both cases, one may discern a desire in the Swedish Academy, which selects the literature laureates, to initiate a European dialogue with the Muslim world. Pamuk had been unfairly sanctioned by ultranationalist Turkish officials for writing on the mass murder of Armenians in the declining era of Ottoman rule. The persecution of Pamuk, although it was not to be pursued, was an act of intellectual reprisal that may also have motivated the Scandinavians to make their award a protest against arbitrary habits by the Turkish state. Yet Pamuk, viewed by Turkish critics as an imitator of the "magical realist" school of Latin American fiction, also gratuitously sought to amuse himself and his readers by trivializing the terrible history of the Albanian Bektashis in the late twentieth century. In his novel *The Black Book*, eliding the significant distinctions between the latter and the Turkish Alevis—although both share devotion to Hajji Bektash—Pamuk invented a scenario in which the Albanian Bektashis had merged with the Stalinist Communists of the Hoxha regime to propagate Bektashism in Marxist-Leninist camouflage. This unfortunate conceit demonstrated utter ignorance on the part of the acclaimed Turkish author about the martyrdom suffered by the Albanian Bektashis, whose *babas* were murdered and the ranks of devotees driven deep underground by Hoxha. An equally offhand and improbable reference to "conversations about the Macedonian Bektashis" taking place in Bosnia-Herzegovina during the 1992–95 war appears like an ostentatiously dropped name in the otherwise excellent prose narrative *State of Siege* by the Spanish author Juan Goytisolo. But Bektashism is absent or a cause for hostility in Sunni Sarajevo.

Pamuk, as a writer from a Muslim country, and the Spanish Goytisolo are not alone, viewed globally, in treating Sufism as little more than a diverting literary device. Esther Freud, great-granddaughter of the father of psychoanalysis, published a fictionalized autobiography, *Hideous Kinky*, in which she described an English New Age seeker of the 1960s, a generation after Lessing, who with her daughters attempts to redefine herself in the complex Moroccan Sufi milieu. The book, with its peculiar title, was made into a film with Kate Winslet. A similar New Age perspective on Sufism appeared in a memoir titled *I, Wabenzi,* by Rafi Zabor, which retells encounters with a Turk, Bulent Rauf, who attracted many Western students.

The writer Pico Iyer described the environment of Western Sufism more elaborately in his 2002 novel *Abandon,* coming to the topic after a series of books that seemed unlikely preparation. His *Video Night in Kathmandu, Falling Off the Map,* and *The Global Soul* glittered with the bright lights and media insights predictable in a homogenized, post-postmodern world. He produced a novel, *Cuba and the Night,* which showed a desperate need to find a place—even if it happened to be a brutal Communist dictatorship—unsullied by commercialization, uniformity, and standardization.

In *Abandon,* Iyer turned inward, ostensibly to an exploration of Sufism in search of an alternative to a globalized world. But the location for his inward search was late—too late—Californian. One would like to explain this away as a deep Sufi parable, but, a travel writer, Iyer took an approach to Sufism that remained that of a tourist among tourists. His Sufism is a marketable mysticism reduced to small bites of tranquility and enlightenment. He could have sojourned in Mali or Indonesia to describe living Sufism but chose the Pacific coast of the United States as an environment where he could invent it for himself.

The novel's protagonist, John Macmillan, is an English graduate student of unreported age and appearance. He meets with professors, attends seminars, and encounters a troubled woman, Camilla—a name Latin in origin, but a homonym of the Arabic name *Kamila,* meaning "perfect," a marvelous Sufi name, which is not mentioned in the narrative. Macmillan is shown obscure manuscripts (of which we learn almost nothing) by some Los Angeles Iranians and a Muslim in India. Finally, he obtains a collection of verse that, somewhat inexplicably given the limp lines cited from it, excites him. Interspersed with these episodes and the enervated consequences that flow from them are trips to places such as Damascus, Sevilla, and the cities of Iran that should be but somehow are not vivid, to meet individuals who should be but somehow are not filled with wisdom.

Macmillan also drives around California in a kind of Raymond Chandler reverie, but without gangsters, detectives, or blood. Bloodlessness is, indeed, the operating description of Iyer's *Abandon*: an empty landscape of happenings where nothing happens. Aside from Macmillan's dully enigmatic and petulant mentor, who is called Sefhadi, the book's experts talk about research without describing it, express an overdramatized self-importance, and lecture in New Age generalities. Macmillan's affair with Camilla is formalized and barely complicated.

In the pages of *Abandon* there are no real Sufis, only academic experts or weekend Sufis. For instance, *dhikr* is never mentioned and neither are the names of the Sufi orders. Everything in the novel seems pale and tired, and there is no self-awareness that would lift such unappetizing porridge to the level one might expect from a novel touching, even marginally, on the controversy with which, for instance, contemporary Iran is associated. One would never imagine, reading Iyer's book, that authentic Muslim Sufis, although few in numbers, are surprisingly easy to find in the United States.

Spiritual journeys do, in fact, beckon us today. But to embark upon them requires something more than lackluster campus colloquia about Rumi. All this makes a difference, because unlike the Sufis in Iyer's *Abandon*, real Islamic mystics today do not troll exotic locations for rare manuscripts to "liberate." Rather, they restore stolen manuscripts to their rightful owners and rebuild vandalized libraries, as in Kosovo. In Iraq, they also defend themselves against Saudi-incited terrorists. They advocate for the restoration of Islamic pluralism in Mecca and

Medina. They carry out charitable works in Turkey and Egypt. They work to reestablish Islamic customs in central Asia. They labor for reconciliation between Muslims, Christians, and animists in Sudan. They contribute to the highest levels of Islamic culture in West Africa, Morocco, Pakistan, and elsewhere. I have described many such Sufis in this narrative.

America has also encouraged some outstanding academic scholars of Sufism, such as the late Annemarie Schimmel, as well as William C. Chittick of the State University of New York at Stony Brook and Michael Sells of the University of Chicago, both of whom have commented brilliantly on Ibn Arabi. Iyer's protagonist, John Macmillan, goes to California to study Sufism. But leaving "California Sufism" is the first thing a serious student of Islamic spirituality should do.

American Islam began to take shape as a significant religious community in the 1980s, and from then until now it has been dominated by Sunni fundamentalists. Muslim Sufism remains weak in America, no matter how many copies of Rumi are sold. The lack of standing of Sufism in the broader American Muslim community reflects control of observant American Muslims and even of many professed Sufis by the Saudi-financed "Wahhabi lobby"—groups such as the Council on American-Islamic Relations (CAIR) and the Islamic Society of North America (ISNA). But American Islam in general is spiritually, intellectually, and organizationally stagnant in a way never before seen in a religion with a new and growing presence in the United States, or in the history of Islam in its spread across the world. American Islam produces no fresh leaders of substance, and none who effectively question why radicalism was promoted in American mosques for years, and even after September 11; it cannot change its idiom except to adopt perfunctory denunciations of terrorism.

As American Islam has so far failed to enter into the broader

American religious compact that would give it common standing with other religious minorities in the country, including Jews and Buddhists, so has American Sufism failed to establish a significant place for itself in the Western dialogue on Islam. But American Islam, if it is to survive, must soon begin a transition to standing as an American religious community alongside all the others, and in that process Muslim Sufism will likely play a central role. In other transitional societies described in this book, including Saudi Arabia, Sufism is already assuming such a place. Sufism itself is in transition, as it has become a factor in the revival of Islam in countries that suffered the nightmare of Communism and other forms of antireligious persecution. I have found the most attractive forms of Sufism emanating from the Balkans, Turkey, and central Asia, where Islam seeks spiritual rebirth after decades in which religion was suppressed.

LET US THUS RETURN near to the eastern end of that highway between the Balkans and Turkestan, in a most difficult place for today's Sufis: a Muslim city that boasts one modern achievement—a metro transit system built as a feature of Muscovite Communism—but which also suffers under a brutal dictatorship. Tashkent, the largest city in ex-Soviet central Asia, is the seat of Uzbekistan's ruler, a former Communist official named Islam Karimov.

Uzbekistan includes the wonder city of Samarkand, as well as its beautiful sister, Bukhara, but Tashkent was leveled by an earthquake in 1966 and rebuilt in an uninspired, shoddy Soviet style. So Tashkent is drab and poor. Yet it also shelters an organization, In the World of Sufism, that is an exhilarating element in the landscape of central Asian and post-Soviet Islam as a center for new generations of Yasawi mystics. In the World of Sufism maintains several branches in Uzbekistan, where its acolytes hold lectures and conferences, organize visits to sacred sites (most of them locations unknown to non-Muslim foreigners, including Russians), and propagate Sufi methods of healing, gymnastics, dancing, martial arts, and natural nutritional and cosmetic practices, through videos, CDs, and books. I was taken to its headquarters by an Uzbek sympathizer of the revitalized *tariqa*. A folder advertised that it is open to everybody interested in Sufism, regardless of religion, ethnicity, gender, or age.

Women, without head or face coverings, function in the new Yasawi centers in Uzbekistan, reflecting the role of Hojja Yasawi and his successors as active proponents of gender equality in Islam. It is said that when conservative Muslim clerics grew alarmed at reports that men and women met together for *dhikr* under the instruction of Hojja Yasawi, he sent the clerics a sealed inkstand in which they found a fire and some cotton—but the flame did not consume the fiber, and the substance did not suffocate the blaze. The scholars recognized the lesson of the fire and the cotton: that men and women could join in *dhikr* and prayer without committing sin. The same principle is sustained today by the Bektashi Sufis and the Turkish and Kurdish Alevis. In both groups women possess spiritual equality with men, and in neither are head or face coverings required.

One item distributed in the Tashkent center is a two-disc CD of Islamic recitation and chanting, as Sufism adopts modern methods of outreach. Titled *Seek Healing in Sufism,* the CD set consists of *dhikr* and Islamic prayers in Arabic, Uzbek, Russian, and English. Assembled by the Sufi teacher and healer Saparbai Kushkarov, the texts are addressed to God and praise the Creator as the master of all existing things, of mercy and compassion, of a universal light; they are accompanied by traditional stringed instruments in electronic arrangements. Yet their content is quite distinct from that found in many Western spiritual offerings, and their style is different from that of New Age meditation music. *Seek Healing in Sufism* includes the Muslim call to prayer, as well as *Al-Fatiha,* along with praise of God and his Prophets and of great Sufis of the Yasawi heritage.

Kushkarov writes,

> *Sufism is a mystical tradition aimed at spiritual awakening and perfection . . . Being a Sufi means to be in the world, but not of the world. Outwardly the Sufi goes among the people, aspiring to serve them and do good to them, while internally abiding as a friend of the Beloved—with God. Sufism reminds the human being of his true nature. The basic Sufi vision of the world is the principle of Unity of Being. As human beings are prone to forgetting, and an individual's worldly self is apt to be a distraction from reality, Sufis practice constant internal Remembrance of God, the* dhikr. *With each breath and with prayer they focus themselves on God, thus sustaining a state of spiritual wakefulness and sense of the Presence of the Most High.*

Kushkarov, following Yasawi methods, emphasizes synchronizing one's breathing with prayer and recitation as a meditative discipline.

Uzbekistan remains, at the time of this writing, authoritarian in politics, and it is in all such places that Sufism projects hope against oppression. The central Asian ex-Soviet republics have a long border with Chinese Turkestan; one may hike to the summits of the mountains near Almaty and look over into China, or drive past a road junction not far from Tashkent where a right turn would lead, in only two days' drive, to Kashgar, a historic Muslim city inside Chinese territory.

In 2004, partisans of democracy in China commemorated the fifteenth anniversary of the Tiananmen Square massacre of June 3–4,

1989—one of the events of a remarkable year that dramatized the accuracy of Ronald Reagan's description of Communism as evil. An observance of the Tiananmen anniversary in Washington over Memorial Day 2004 brought new lessons about China. The event was held at the fourth national convention of the Uighur American Association (UAA).

The Uighurs are indigenous Turkic inhabitants of Xinjiang, as the Chinese label Eastern Turkestan. They made up the first of the Turkic empires, producing valuable written literature and pictorial art. They are linked to Tiananmen in the person of Wu'er Kaixi, a prominent figure in the 1989 democracy movement and a Uighur, who spoke at the 2004 convention. Numbering at least nine million, Uighurs are overwhelmingly Muslims, of the Sufi variety. They know nothing of differences between Sunnis and Shias and nothing of *Shariah,* but they know they are Sufis—without large, organized Sufi orders. In this way, the Uighurs, in the cradle of central Asian mysticism, have become an example, if an extreme one, of Muslims among whom Sufism is a diffused but defining element.

The primary message the 2004 conference sought to convey to Americans was simple. As Wu'er Kaixi put it, "Beijing will never accept political or ethnic pluralism without significant pressure from other countries. Nationalism is the basis of the Communist Party's continued domination of China." As evidence, he cited Beijing's unsympathetic attitude toward Taiwan, Hong Kong, Tibet, and other properties it considers its own, as well as the Communist authorities' intention, noted in official Chinese media and Western news reports, to impose unification with these external territories by 2008.

Only a thousand or so Uighurs live in America, but we are likely to hear more from them as their aggrieved community inside China resists the intensifying nationalism sponsored by Beijing. "We are in the same position as the Tibetans," said Erkin Alptekin, president of the

World Uighur Congress in Munich, a former Uighur-language broadcaster for the U.S.-financed Radio Liberty, and a leading figure at the UAA convention. "The Chinese want to replace us with their own people as colonists and assimilate those of us who remain, wiping out our culture." Alim Seytoff, UAA president, pointed out that Uighur-language education is now limited in China and university courses must be taught in Chinese. There are no independent media in the Uighur tongue, and Radio Liberty discontinued its Uighur-language service in 1979 as a favor to the Chinese.

At the same time, the Uighurs have a curious bit part in the bloody history of recent Islamic extremism. There were reportedly twenty-two Uighurs among the terror suspects interned at Guantánamo. Some Uighurs were trained by the Chinese alongside Islamist Pakistanis to fight the Russians in Afghanistan. But Chinese repression also drove other Uighurs to flee into Afghanistan (which has a short border with China)—such people were natural targets for Al-Qaida and Taliban recruitment. Still more were Uighur children sent by their parents to Pakistan to escape Communist indoctrination, only to be trained in jihad and shipped off to fight in Kashmir, then to defend the Taliban.

A Uighur organization, the East Turkestan Islamic Movement (ETIM), was declared a terrorist group by the U.S. State Department in 2002 at the insistence of the Chinese, who alleged it had ties to Al-Qaida. However, information about the ETIM is hard to come by, and according to Erkin Alptekin, before September 11 the Chinese Communist Party secretary in Xinjiang, Wang Lequan, denied there was terrorism in his bailiwick. The global war on terror has been "hijacked by Beijing," Alptekin said, as an excuse to brand all Uighurs as radical Muslims. In 2006, five Uighurs were released from Guantánamo and accepted for resettlement in Albania.

Alptekin insisted, however, that he and his World Uighur Congress have made nonviolence a basic principle of their activities. Armed resistance to the Chinese would only lead to more victimization, he told me. Few Uighurs seek their own state, Islamic or otherwise. According to Wu'er Kaixi, "We don't ask for independence, but for respect, and an end to forced assimilation."

Chinese respect for minority rights will doubtless be a long time coming, and in the meantime foreign Islamists will exploit local grievances for their own benefit. Central Asian experts have long warned that the vast tracts where the Uighurs and other Chinese Muslims live have been infiltrated by Saudi-Wahhabi agents. Simultaneous with their September 11 attack on the United States, these agitators dreamed of seizing the oil-rich and nuclear-technology-littered states of former Soviet central Asia and joining them to Taliban-ruled Afghanistan. Grabbing a slice of Eastern Turkestan from the Chinese was considered a secondary but important goal of Al-Qaida.

China may have more Muslims living as a minority than any other country (India does not count, since in its democratic system Muslims are well represented and share power). In addition to the Uighurs, the country has a Chinese-speaking Muslim community of up to 20 million called the Hui, also living in the northwest. The Hui have been the object of extensive evangelism, going back a century, by Wahhabi fundamentalists from Arabia, assisted by Hui returning from the *hajj* in Mecca. As presented by Dru C. Gladney of the University of Hawaii, a leading Western expert on Chinese Islam, Wahhabism in Chinese dress enjoys the backing of the Communist authorities. In 1999, Gladney described how Beijing has supported an explicit Wahhabi trend in Chinese Islam through a movement called the *Yihewani*. This group takes its name from the extremist *Ikhwan*, or brotherhoods, that helped found the Saudi state in the 1920s and then emerged, in a somewhat different form, as the radical Muslim Brotherhood in Egypt.

According to Gladney, Chinese Wahhabism has millions of devotees, who show all the characteristics of the creed's Saudi inventors, beginning with hatred of Sufism. With the founding of the People's Republic of China, the state quickly suppressed all Sufi orders and endorsed the Chinese Wahhabis, financing an official "China Islamic Association" under their influence (much like the puppet "Chinese Patriotic Catholic Association" and similar phony Christian bodies). Beijing renewed state patronage of the *Yihewani* after Mao Zedong's so-called Cultural Revolution, which featured widescale depredations against all religious groups.

And thus, while ethnic suppression may have driven some Uighurs toward Al-Qaida, official Chinese Islam promotes the Wahhabi ideology from which Al-Qaida sprang. Either way, ordinary Chinese Muslims, whose total numbers are unknown, are being shoved in the wrong directions. The lesson here was well articulated by Erkin Alptekin: "The United States should raise the problem of the Uighurs to the same level as that of the Tibetans and pressure China to open dialogue with all its minorities," even if the Chinese government resents it. The alternative: more rather than fewer recruits for Islamist terrorism, drawn from the turbulence of the Chinese "continent."

Uighurs, although uneducated in it today, were historic followers of the Hanafi school of *Shariah*. Hanafi *Shariah* is the oldest and most open variant of Islamic jurisprudence and the most widespread of the four Sunni legal schools. A standard manual of Hanafi law compiled by the eighteenth-century Indian Muslim jurist Qazi Thanaa Ullah states, *"The spiritual light [of the Prophet Muhammad] should be sought in the hearts of the Sufis so that light might be kindled in your own heart. When this happens you will be able to recognize, through your own faculties of discernment, all good and evil. A true Sufi is a person who, following* Qur'an, *obeys God."* A Sufi master is described as *"one in whose company you are moved to Remembrance of God* [dhikrullah] . . . *In such company, your love for this world will decrease, while your love for God and the rewards of the next world will increase."* When you sit with a Sufi teacher, Hanafi law commands, your heart must be moved, and if it is not, you should depart that presence. We cannot predict but can only hope that Islam under the Chinese in Eastern Turkestan can restore and refine this spirit.

FINALLY, WE MUST PROCEED farthest east, to other great examples of "mass Sufism." These varieties are found in Indonesia. The Hotel Dharmawangsa, in the teeming, steaming capital of Jakarta, is an old Javanese palace that has been turned into a luxury resort. Fortunately for tourists if not for the Indonesians themselves, when I visited in 2005 the country's inflationary crisis reduced the hotel's rates to a little more than a hundred U.S. dollars a night. In the room, I immediately found an artifact of Indonesian religious pluralism: a small card stating, "We are pleased to present you with a copy of the Koran or the Bible should you require any during your stay." Contrary to what a non-Muslim might suspect, the offering of the Islamic holy book was not intended for *da'wa,* or Muslim missionizing, but as a customary courtesy in hostelries, comparable to the Gideon editions of the Christian gospels; when I asked for a *Qur'an,* I was told it was only available in Indonesian, which I do not read.

The year I went to Indonesia marked the sixtieth anniversary of national independence (in 1945) and the fortieth since the near civil war provoked by Indonesian Communists in 1965, which resulted in the deaths of hundreds of thousands of ordinary people. Indonesia has had serious problems with terrorism along with its economic woes; the Dharmawangsa hotel had armed guards posted at its doors, and they checked the undercarriage of arriving cars for bombs. Although it is a petroleum-producing country, Indonesia imports oil to meet its needs. Jakarta has the chaotic feel of any big, tropical Asian city, but the country's varied and pluralistic imagination is equally exceptional—and under attack.

For example, when I arrived, the Sunday *Jakarta Post* included the headline "Drinking wine: New, popular trend for Indonesian yuppies"—something that would be rare in media even in such European Muslim territories as Kosovo. Coca-Cola is widely consumed, with the word "*halal*"—that is, religiously permitted—on its bottle caps. But radical ideologues are fighting to impose a narrow interpretation of Islam on Indonesia. At the beginning of August 2005, the country's official body of Muslim clerics, the Indonesian Ulema Council (Majelis Ulama Indonesia or MUI), issued eleven *fatwas,* including condemnations of religious pluralism, against an organization called the Liberal Islam Network (LIN), and against the Muhammadiyah, a 20-million-member movement. I had some indication that the attack on pluralism was partly directed against none other than myself, since I had received e-mail from Jakarta asking if I considered Islamic pluralism to be the same as religious relativism. (I do not.) In addition, the LIN has discussed my book *The Two Faces of Islam,*[1] and I had been invited to meet with the Muhammadiyah. But the atmosphere in Jakarta, although challenging, did not feel tense.

The Jakarta media reported that the *fatwa* against liberalism, pluralism, and secularism was "unpopular" with ordinary Indonesians, many of whom consider MUI an accomplice of the former dictatorship of General Suharto, who ruled from 1965 to 1998. Peter G. Riddell, an expert on radical Islam in Indonesia, has described MUI, in a book to which I contributed, *Radical Islam's Rules,* as a group that after September 11 "increasingly began to embrace the rhetoric of

Islamic radicalism," calling for global Muslim unity in jihad against the U.S.-led Coalition's combat in Afghanistan. Reassuringly, the *fatwa* stated that the MUI favored no more than debate with the Liberal Islam and Muhammadiyah trends it condemned, rather than physical attacks.

Nevertheless, to cite another local headline, a "struggle for the nation's soul" is clearly taking place. Then recent events included the closure of dozens of Christian churches in West Java in 2004—and the government of president Susilo Bambang Yudhoyono refused to restrain such actions, on the argument that the Christian communities shut down were "illegal congregations." In a speech I attended, Yudhoyono declared his commitment to the struggle against extremism, saying, "We know that the terrorist cells are still active. They are still hiding, recruiting, networking, trying to find new funding . . . and even planning." But Yudhoyono also said that an amnesty for Abubakr Baasyir, the Al-Qaida ally who inspired the Bali bombings of 2002 and 2005, the Jakarta terrorist atrocity of 2004, and other recent crimes, would be unavoidable under the constitution. Baasyir was indeed released in 2006.

The Aceh region, long troubled by separatist violence and then still recovering from the tsunami of 2004—with considerable help from U.S. relief agencies—was the sole Indonesian province in which radical *Shariah* had been imposed. At the end of August 2005, an Islamic court in Aceh ordered the caning of two unmarried couples for consumption of alcohol and spending time together after nightfall in a private place. "The women fainted after being beaten forty times . . . outside a mosque," according to witnesses. A local human rights group, Elsham, denounced the punishment as "insane" and called for its review by the national supreme court. But the blows had already been inflicted.

Indonesian Muslims are subtle in their thinking, which cuts in multiple ways. For many of them, Wahhabism was a reform movement aimed at the purification of Islam. Thus, although they will disclaim any support for Wahhabi violence, some will defend the sect's original goals. The Liberal Islam Network, condemned in the above-mentioned *fatwa*, held an event in 2003, stating that in "emphasizing the importance of [the model of] Islam in the first two centuries after the life of Mohammed, prior to the emergence of differing interpretations, the Wahhabis have the same positions as the Liberal Islam movement." Indonesian Islam has assumed a complicated and dialectical cast that is unpredictable and that will, one hopes, fortify debate and acceptance of differences . . . even if its "liberals" defend what they see in Wahhabism.

Indeed, Wahhabi-style Islam has an old history in Indonesia, even though in a country with 235 million people—the largest Muslim country in the world—imposition of any single interpretation is probably doomed. In 2004, a local Islamic academic, Azyumardi Azra, recalled, "In the late eighteenth and early nineteenth centur[ies], the Padri—a Wahhabi-like movement in West Sumatra—attempted to force other Muslims in the area to subscribe to its literal understanding of Islam. This violent movement aimed at spreading what they believed was a pure and pristine Islam . . . but it failed to gain support from a majority of Muslims, and it was the only example of Muslim radicalism in Southeast Asia."

IN A VISIT to the Jakarta headquarters of the Muhammadiyah movement, which has a moderate reputation, I was struck by its novel rhetoric: a colorful booklet proclaims, "Welcoming Globalization." Muhammadiyah maintains an extensive social welfare and educational network, including thousands of preschools, elementary/primary schools, junior high schools, senior high schools, hundreds of general hospitals, maternity hospitals, clinics, orphanages, family care centers, banks, microcredit, and even a life insurance company. Its organizational structure includes centers in the smallest villages.

Acceptance of globalization and modernization leads Muhammadiyah to argue that it "faces certain challenges, such as amending its messages, even its core Islamic doctrine, so it can be assimilated by the masses. Some Muhammadiyah figures have even begun to develop Islamic Sociology, Social Islamic Psychology . . . Others are shaping Islamic sciences and technologies . . . This frenetic rush is an effort to catch up where Islam was left behind."

I had been told in an e-mail by my Muhammadiyah contact, "Islamic fundamentalism is in vogue in recent years in Indonesia, including within the Muhammadiyah community, even though not in the mainstream. Some leaders of radical Islam have a Saudi academic background, and want to spread their understanding of Islam." A few young members of the movement with whom I met were influenced by the Wahhabi claim of reforming Islam, but one among them, Ahmad Najib Burhani, has published articles in *The Jakarta Post* opposing such acts of Islamic extremism as a 2004 attack on a community of Ahmadis. Ahmadis are a sect shunned by most Muslims because they claim that their founder, a late-nineteenth-century figure named Mirza Ghulam Ahmad, was a prophet and messenger of the Last Days, or *mahdi,* comparable to the Messiah of the Jews—but Islam recognizes no prophets after Muhammad. Burhani wrote of the assailants in the Ahmadiyya case, which caused considerable debate in Indonesia, "Imprisoned in authoritarianism, someone would speak, attack, and kill in God's name . . . authoritarianism is heresy, the highest sin in Islam."

Indonesia is home to an even larger, Sufi-oriented movement,

Nahdatul Ulama (NU), organized in the 1920s and today counting an amazing 40 million members. NU has more adherents than the population of most Muslim countries. It was mainly founded by Hasyim Asyari, a local preacher, in reaction to the suppression of Sufism by Mustafa Kemal in Turkey and the seizure of Mecca and Medina by the Wahhabis. NU played a major part in the Indonesian anticolonial revolution after the Second World War, an important but nearly forgotten episode of modern Islamic history. Asyari's grandson was Abdurrahman Wahid, the first democratically elected president of Indonesia from 1999 to 2001 and founder of the Wahid Institute, which has an American partner, the LibForAll Foundation. Gus Dur, as Wahid is known, was educated at the global center of Islamic studies, Al-Azhar University in Cairo, as well as at Baghdad University. One of his achievements as president of Indonesia was to get rid of laws discriminating against ethnic Chinese living in Indonesia, and he is a consistent advocate of Muslim respect for other faiths.

Wahid has praised the concept of Islamic pluralism, writing, "There are those in the world today whose limited understanding of Islam, and whose actions, feed the cycle of anger, hatred and violence that threaten all humanity. The Wahid Institute and LibForAll Foundation believe that Indonesia can serve as a model for what many refer to as 'the smiling face of Islam,' and thereby help to untangle the knot of conflict that grips so much of the world." He expresses "hope of a better future for Indonesia and the world, and the growth of a global civilization in which Muslims and non-Muslims alike respect one another, and come to a mature understanding and appreciation of Islam as a true blessing to nature and humanity."[2] Little can exceed this summary of the moderate Muslim message for our time.

The Indonesian MUI *fatwas* of 2005 turned out to be nothing to worry about. Leaving the sometimes confusing but stimulating atmosphere of Indonesia, I proceeded to Singapore, a place widely identified with a "benign" authoritarianism. I was greeted on my arrival by a headline in *The Strait Times*, the state-controlled daily in English, proclaiming, "Moderate Muslims thrive in Singapore," and describing Singapore Muslims as "conservative in beliefs and practices [but] against radicalism and terrorism." Many moderate Muslims I have encountered believe that conservatism and traditionalism, rather than reform and liberalism, represent an appropriate alternative to radical Islam.

In Singapore, the restrictive rules under which media function led to a series of speeches I gave being subject to a media blackout. But there, as in Indonesia, Muslims are engaged in a highly creative process of self-definition. For example, the Naqshbandi Sufis are anathema to the Saudi Wahhabis, and the Singapore Naqshbandis had held their spiritual services in the Kampung Siglap Mosque, which increasingly came under the Wahhabi influence. Eventually the mosque officials barred the Sufis from entering the structure. The Naqshbandis responded by holding their observances in the mosque entranceway, and after several such instances, the Wahhabis gave up. Today, the youthful Naqshbandis of Singapore recount with a laugh, "We meet in a Wahhabi mosque!" From every indication, Sufi-saturated Islam in central and Southeast Asia will continue to produce unexpected and, let us hope, positive developments.

DOES SUFISM REPRESENT a path to global harmony today? It would be unseemly to make exaggerated claims for a metaphysical tradition that so persistently calls for modesty in the life of believers. And given that this chronicle has included many incidents of brutality against Sufis, it cannot be said the Sufi way is an easy one. For readers accustomed to the transcendent image of the Sufi garden, lush with mystical pleasures, my account may seem dissonant and dismaying. The image of Hallaj—a martyr for the freedom of imagination—should remain alive in the heart of every Sufi. Currently, Sufism and moderate Islam in general appear as if hanged on an executioner's gibbet, awaiting further torture and final execution, scorned from all sides.

Sufis can help Islam and the world by tenaciously maintaining their attitudes of independence, pluralism, respect for other faiths, and preservation of ancient wisdom—which as every religious believer knows is everlasting, and therefore, in the accurate terms of Emerson, is also modern wisdom. Whether the Sufis may completely overcome the conformism of the Sunni majority in Islam is impossible to predict, but it is unlikely if Sufism remains, in its essential definition, a discipline requiring committed choice. A positive role for Sufism in Iran seems more probable, but evidence for it remains thin; yet the flower of Sufism has always grown from a slender stalk, as graceful as an Ottoman minaret.

But how may concerned Westerners help the Sufis? First, by individually and officially taking them seriously, freeing them from policy clichés about "folk Islam" and including them in the purview of Western diplomats and human rights monitors throughout the Muslim world. It is absurd and shameful that the life and example of a Sufi in Saudi Arabia such as Sayyid Al-Maliki should remain completely unknown outside the kingdom and that foreign advocates of religious freedom under Saudi rule effectively ignored him.

The Sufis will not serve as Western mercenaries, but they can promote intellectual diversity, a renaissance of Islamic thought, and an

Islam of liberty, along with genuine and transparent cooperation with Christians, Jews, and other believers.

In 1896, the Bektashi poet Naim Frashëri wrote a Sufi manifesto known as "The Bektashi Pages." He affirmed,

*Truth and justice, intelligence and wisdom, are supreme.*

*The faith of the Bektashi is a broad Path lighted by wisdom, brotherhood, friendship, love, humanity, and all the virtues.*

*On one side are the flowers of knowledge, and on the other the flowers of truth . . .*

*Who does good, finds good; who does evil, encounters evil. Who sins against humanity has joined the beasts . . .*

*Humanity is not bound, but free in all ways, and accountable for all actions . . .*

*But the human person has a mind which reasons, knowledge by which to make choices, a soul filled with recognition, a heart of discernment, and a conscience that weighs all deeds. This is all one needs—no other help is required. God has granted humanity everything . . .*

*The Bektashi Sufis take as the book of their religion the Universe, and especially humanity, because as Imam Ali said, "The human being is a speaking book, faith is speech, but the ignorant add to it. Faith is in hearts, not in books" . . .*

*They who enter the Path leave all vices behind and retain only virtue. With an unclean heart, an evil soul, or a bad conscience, nobody can enter the company of the saints who achieve intimacy with God.*

*Here one must know the self, for whoever knows the self, knows God . . .*

*Brotherhood, peace, love, closeness to God, friendship, good conscience, and other virtues light the Path.*
*Above all things, love is the beginning and guidance of the Path.*

It may be too early to write a new libertarian Sufi manifesto—but one may be needed. Islam would not have survived as a religion and produced a series of civilizations—six of the seven Islams enumerated in the Introduction to this book—had it not appealed to the heart as well as, through history, the rational, moderate, and extremist mind.

Sufism is, ultimately, an indispensable element in any real solution to confrontation between Islam and the West. Until the Sufis are recognized as an important component of global religious, social, and cultural life, the fearful conflict of religious traditions may continue.

But, with the passage of years after September 11, 2001, some positive signs of recovery from that human trauma are visible. Al-Qaida and other violent fundamentalists did not force the majority of the world's Muslims to join them. The ugly outburst of Islamophobia that seemed to dominate Euro-American discourse for several years has run its course. The vision of democratization in the Middle East, held in public disrepute while the war in Iraq seemed destined to fail, has been, at least partially, redeemed by moderate success in that country. Good triumphs over evil; it is God's world, not Satan's domain.

As 2007 ended, Bosnian Muslim scholars of an independent character held a second commemoration of the birth of Rumi, at the Faculty of Islamic Studies overlooking beautiful Sarajevo, mutilated by war but spiritually reborn. Conflict with Islamist-oriented clerics continued, and none of the high officials of the Islamic community deigned to attend the event, at which I was extremely privileged to present a paper on the relations between Sufism and Kabbalah, as represented by the blessed rabbi Ariel Bension. My friend and teacher

Rešid Hafizović provided me with a paper he had recently completed on the seventeenth-century Sufi known as al-Bosnawi, a Bosnian commentator on the *Fusus al-Hikam* of Ibn Arabi.[3] Resid wrote, "[Rumi and Ibn Arabi] are doing more for the idea of Islam [in the West] than the entire Muslim world, even at its best, can offer nowadays."

I believe the world needs Sufism. It is God's most deeply hidden treasure, another Islam, a miraculous sanctuary. One need not go all the way to Turkestan to find it, for it is present in the hearts of many who live throughout this world. Its gates are open; and in the words of Rumi it appeals to all believers: only come.

*Tetova-Washington*
*2006–08*

# ACKNOWLEDGMENTS

I acknowledge my gratitude, in the guidance that led to the writing of this book, to my inspirers, teachers, and companions on the Sufi Roads:

The Blessed Baba Rexheb Beqiri (may his mystery be sanctified), Baba Mumin Lama of Gjakova, the Blessed Baba Tahir Emini of Tetova (may his mystery be sanctified), his successor Baba Edmond Brahimaj, and Kryëgjysh Dedebaba Reshat Bardhi, along with their students Dervish Abdylmytalib Beqiri, Shpëtim Mahmudi, and Didar Doko, all of the Community of Bektashism;

Shaykh Adrihysen Shehu and Shaykh Sadik Pelinko Ulqinaku of the Rifa'i Sufis;

Syed Farid Alatas and Irfan Al-Alawi, disciples of Sayyid Muhammad Al-Maliki;

Professor Rešid Hafizović of the University of Sarajevo; *Moj jaran* Saeid Abedpour; Ali Sirin; Shaykh Muhammad Sadiq Muhammad Yusuf; Alcaly Lo;

Mark, Philip, Paul, Gjon, and Vlado;

And the great Jewish Sufi of recent times, R. Ariel Bension "Manastirli."

I also express my thanks to my editors at Doubleday, Adam Bellow and Daniel Feder.

# NOTES

## INTRODUCTION: SUFISM—ISLAMIC SPIRITUALITY IN A WORLD OF FEAR

1. C.E.: common era, based on the Western calendar. All dates in this book are C.E.
2. *Tekke* in Turkish, *tekija* in Bosnian, *teqe* in Albanian, as described in this narrative.
3. *Qur'an* 2:115.
4. An Islamic *fatwa* is merely a religio-juristic opinion. It is not exclusively a death sentence or other criminal law verdict. Sunnis consider *fatawa* (the Arabic plural) to be nonbinding advice, whereas Shia Muslims consider them as obligatory rulings.
5. The term *libertarian* is used in this book in its original meaning—that is, promoting intellectual and spiritual liberty—rather than in an economic or policy sense.

## 1. THE GREAT AGE OF EARLY SUFISM

1. Pronounced *Rejeb Becheeri*; the name will reappear many times in these pages.

2. As noted in the Introduction, Muslims honor Jesus as a prophet but do not believe God had a son or other "partners."

3. These Eastern Christians were known as Nestorians, and were predecessors of the Assyrian and Chaldean Christians in Iraq and elsewhere today.

4. See Introduction, note 5.

5. Adapted from the version of Herbert Mason.

6. These supplications are known in Islam as *duas*.

7. Repeated study of the entire *Beginning of Guidance* is strongly recommended by the author to anyone sincerely interested in Islamic worship.

8. "Glass pavement" refers to that of King Solomon's palace; see *Q.* 27:44.

## 2. TURKISH SUFISM
## AND INTERFAITH COEXISTENCE

1. Jamshid was a pre-Islamic Iranian ruler.

2. The Jewish patriarch Joseph is often evoked in Islam as a model of physical beauty.

3. This version of Hojja Yasawi by Gary Leiser and Robert Dankoff, in Köprülü (2006).

4. This version of Hojja Yasawi by Talat Sait Halman, adapted by Stephen Schwartz.

5. The relationship of Jewish Kabbalah to Hurufism is one of the great unexamined topics of both Jewish and Islamic studies today. Unfortunately, very few Muslim experts appear interested in or conversant with the large and valuable literature by Israeli and other Jewish scholars on Islamic spirituality, both in its influence on Kabbalah and as a phenomenon in itself.

6. Examples of libertarian-revolutionary religious movements in the Judeo-Christian world include the Franciscan followers of the twelfth-century visionary Gioacchino da Fiore; the comparable acolytes of Jean de Roquetaillade (fourteenth c.); the Hussites in Bohemia (fifteenth c.); German peasant insurrectionaries of the sixteenth c. such as Thomas Müntzer; the Levellers, Ranters, Fifth Monarchy Men, and similar groups in the English Revolution

(seventeenth c.); and the movement of the seventeenth c. Ottoman Jewish "false messiah," Sabbetai Zevi. With the arrival of the European Enlightenment, mass libertarian-religious movements disappeared from the West, but not from the Islamic world.

## 3. THE WARS AGAINST SUFISM

1. Another Islamic ideologist who sought to reconcile religion and science was Sayyid Qutb (1906–1966), a theoretician of the Egyptian Muslim Brotherhood, who wrote in the same manner but condemned Sufism.
2. The Prophet's birthdate falls in the month of Rabi ul-Awwal in the Islamic lunar or *hijra* calendar. The dates in the *hijra* calendar move in reverse through the solar years.
3. See discussion of Lewis, the Naqshbandis, and the Wahhabis in my book *The Two Faces of Islam* (2002).

## 4. SUFIS IN TODAY'S MUSLIM WORLD

1. The Syrian Alawites are an Arabic-speaking Shia sect of several million. They have a military history and are closely associated with the Ba'ath regime in Damascus. They are seen as extreme in their devotion to Imam Ali, treating him as a manifestation of God. They have no connection with Turkish and Kurdish Alevis.
2. The angel Gabriel (Jibril) delivered the *Qur'an* to Muhammad.
3. For Shaykh Bukhari's biography see www.jerusalempeacemakers.org.
4. Translation of Frashëri's poem by Agim Morina and Stephen Schwartz.

## 5. SUFIS IN THE CRISIS STATES: IRAQ, SAUDI ARABIA, IRAN, AND ISRAEL

1. Shia belief in the "hidden" Twelfth Imam, Muhammad ibn Hasan ibn Ali, who vanished from the earth as a child and is destined to return as an equitable ruler, has become important in world affairs because of its role in the ideolo-

gies of Iranian leaders such as Ayatollah Ruhollah Khomeini and Mahmoud Ahmadinejad. For the Iranian Islamic revolutionaries, the return of the hidden imam came to symbolize a compelling need to organize a theocratic order. Their predecessors among Iranian clerics saw the absence of the hidden imam as an argument for "quietism" or deliberate abstention from politics. Belief in the hidden imam or *mahdism,* that is, announcement of the appearance of an Islamic messiah, are not significant elements in Sufism except in Africa, where *mahdi* movements have flourished.

2. *Q:* 1.
3. This and following citations in English from the work of Shaykh Al-Rifa'i are based on excerpts kindly provided to the author by Irfan Al-Alawi.

## 6. SUFISM IN TRANSITION: THE WEST, CENTRAL ASIA, INDONESIA, AND THE WORLD

1. My book *The Two Faces of Islam* was published in Indonesian under the title *Dua Wajah Islam* in 2007.
2. Wahid's writing is from the introduction, cosigned with LibForAll's C. Holland Taylor, to the Indonesian edition of my *Two Faces of Islam.*
3. Al-Bosnawi's work was partially translated into English by Bulent Rauf and published under the title *The Kernel of the Kernel,* incorrectly ascribed to another Sufi, Hakki al-Bursevi (Oxford: Muhyid'din Ibn Arabi Society, 1986).

# WORKS CONSULTED OR RECOMMENDED

*The Koran*. Trans. with notes by N. J. Dawood. London: Penguin, 1990.

Abd el-Kader. *Écrits spirituels*. Trans. Michel Chodkiewicz. Paris: Éditions du Seuil, 1982.

Abu-Manneh, Boutros. *Studies on Islam and the Ottoman Empire in the Nineteenth Century, 1826–1876*. Istanbul: Isis Press, 2001.

Al-Alawi, Irfan, and Stephen Schwartz. "Bulldozing Islam." *Weekly Standard*, October 9, 2006.

Alemanya Alevi Birlikleri Federasyonu. "Kerbela'dan Sivas'a: Ağittan Amuda" [From Grief Toward Hope], Cologne, 2006.

Algar, Hamid. "Bektas, Haji." *Encyclopedia Iranica*, online edition. New York: Columbia University, 2006.

———. "A Brief History of the Naqshbandi Order," and "The Present State of Naqshbandi Studies," in Gaboriau, et al., *Naqshbandis*, q.v.

———. "Hadith in Sufism." *Encyclopedia Iranica*, op. cit.

Amadou Ampaté Bâ. *Vie et enseignement de Tierno Bokar*. Paris: Éditions du Seuil, 1980.

Amedroz, H. F. "Notes on Some Sufi Lives." *Journal of the Royal Asiatic Society*, July 1912.

Arberry, A. J. "Junayd." *Journal of the Royal Asiatic Society*, July 1935.

Asín Palacios, Miguel. *Dante y el Islam*. Madrid: Voluntad, 1927.

———. *El Islam Cristianizado*. Madrid: Plutarco, 1931.

———. *Saint John of the Cross and Islam*. Trans. Howard W. Yoder and Elmer H. Douglas. New York: Vantage Press, 1981.

Attar, Fariduddin. *Tadhkara-tul-Aulia, or Memoirs of Saints*. Delhi: Taj, 2002.

Al-Attas, Umar bin Abd Al-Rahman. *The Rare Gift and the Key to Opening the Door of Union*. Trans. Sayyid Muhammad Al-Attas. Singapore: Ba'Alawi Mosque, 1999.

Azra, Azyumardi. "Southeast Asian Islam in the Post-Bali Bombing" [sic]. In *Indonesia Today*, ed. Norbert Eschborn, Sabrina Hackel, and Joyce Holmes Richardson. Jakarta: Adenauer Stiftung, 2004.

Baruh, Kalmi. "Islame Burimet të *Komedisë Hujnore* të Dantes." Trans. Hatipi Tajar. Prishtina: Fjala, 1969.

Beckwith, Christopher L. *The Tibetan Empire in Central Asia*. Princeton, N.J.: Princeton University Press, 1987.

Benčić-Rimay, Tea, ed. *Vlado Gotovac*. Zagreb, Croatian Writers' Association, 2003, with verse trans. by Stephen Schwartz. [See commentaries on Hallaj and Rumi.]

Bension, Ariel. *The Zohar in Moslem and Christian Spain*. London: Routledge, 1932.

[Beqiri], Baba Rexheb. "Ashureja," *Zëri Bektashizmes* [Taylor, Michigan], number 1, n.d. [1954]. The text is unsigned.

———. *Mistiçizma Islame dhe Bektashizma*. Shtëpia Botuese "Urtësia," Tirana, 2006.

———. *The Mysticism of Islam and Bektashism*, vol. 1. Trans. Bardhyl Pogoni. Naples, Italy: Dragoti, 1984.

Birge, John K. *The Bektashi Order of Dervishes*. London: Luzac, 1937.

[Al-Bosnawi, Abdullah Efendija Bošnjak 'Abdi bin Muhammad]. *The Kernel of the Kernel.* Trans. Rauf Bulent and incorrectly ascribed to Hakki al-Bursevi. Oxford: Muhyid'din Ibn 'Arabi Society, 1986.

Bowering, Gerhard. "Erfan." *Encyclopedia Iranica,* op. cit.

Bushati, Hamdi. *Bushatllinjte.* Shkodër: Idromeno, 2003.

————. *Shkodra dhe Motet,* 2 vols. Shkodër: Idromeno, 1999–2005.

Central Intelligence Agency. *The World Fact Book,* at www.cia.gov/library/publications/the-world-factbook/.

Chittick, William C. *Ibn 'Arabi.* Oxford: One World, 2005.

Cooperson, Michael. *Al Ma'mun.* Oxford: One World, 2005.

Dankoff, Robert. *An Ottoman Mentality: The World of Evliya Çelebi.* Leiden: Brill, 2004.

Dankoff, Robert, and Robert Elsie. *Evliya Çelebi in Albania and Adjacent Regions.* Leiden: Brill, 2000.

DeWeese, Devin. "The Yasavi Order and Persian Hagiography." In *The Heritage of Sufism,* vol. 3, ed. Leonard Lewisohn and David Morgan. Oxford: One World, 1999.

Elazar, Samuel M. *Romancero Judeo-Español.* Sarajevo: Svjetlost, 1987.

Elmore, Gerald T. *Islamic Sainthood in the Fullness of Time: Ibn ul-'Arabi's* Book of the Fabulous Gryphon. Leiden: Brill, 1999.

Erbakan, Necmettin. "Antisemitism and the Turkish Islamist 'Milli Gorus' Movement." Turkish Flash TV interview. Middle East Media Research Institute (MEMRI), August 29, 2007.

Erguner, Kudsi, trans. *Le livre des derviches bektashi (Villayet name).* L'Isle-sur-la-Sorgue: Le Bois d'Orion, 1997. Translation of the *Vilayetname* of Ferdowsi.

Esfandiary, Golnaz. "Iran: Local Authorities Try to Evict Sufi Leader." Radio Free Europe/Radio Liberty, October 12, 2006.

————. "Qom Authorities Crack Down on Sufi Group." Radio Free Europe/Radio Liberty, February 16, 2006.

Farhadi, A. G. Ravan. *Abdullah Ansari of Herat.* London: Curzon, 1996.

Fenton, Paul B. "Abraham Maimonides (1186–1237): Founding a Mystical Dynasty." In Moshe Idel and Mortimer Ostow, ed., *Jewish Mystical Leaders and Leadership in the Thirteenth Century,* q.v.

Frashëri, Naim. *Bagëti e Bujqësia, Lulet e verës, Vjersha të tjera.* Tirana: Dituria, 2001. Includes the Sufi collection *Lulet e verës* (*Summer Flowers*), of which an English translation by Agim Morina and Stephen Schwartz is forthcoming.

———. "Bektashi Pages." In *Christianity and Islam Under the Sultans,* by F. W. Hasluck. Oxford: Oxford University Press, 1929. Translation adapted by Stephen Schwartz.

———. *Qerbelaja.* Bucharest: Dituria, 1898. Reprint, Tetova: Teqe Harabati Baba, 1996.

Freud, Esther. *Hideous Kinky.* New York: Harcourt Brace Jovanovich, 1992.

Fuster, Joan. "Contra els moros," "Divagació entorn del *Cant Espiritual* d'Ausiàs Marc," and "Els jueus i un messies," in *Obres Completes,* vol. 7. Barcelona: Edicions 62, 1994.

Fuzuli. *Hadikaja ose Kopshti i të Përsosurvet.* Trans. into Albanian by Baba Rexheb [Beqiri]. Gjakova: Teqeja Bektashiane e Gjakovës, 1997.

Gaboriau, Marc, Alexandre Popovic, and Thierry Zarcone. *Naqshbandis.* Istanbul-Paris: Editions Isis, 1990.

Al-Ghazali, Abu Hamid. *Al-Ghazzali on Disciplining the Self.* Trans. by Muhammad Nur Abdus Salam; intro. by Laleh Bakhtiar. Chicago: Kazi Publications, 2002.

———. *Al-Ghazzali on the Treatment of the Love of Power and Control.* Trans. by Muhammad Nur Abdus Salam; intro. by Laleh Bakhtiar. Chicago: Kazi Publications, 2002.

Gladney, Dru C. "The Salafiyya Movement in Northwest China: Islamic Fundamentalism Among the Muslim Chinese?" In *Muslim Diversity: Local Islam in Global Contexts,* ed. Leif Manger. London: Routledge, 1999.

Goudsouzian, Tanya. "Makkah conference 'long overdue.'" GulfNews.com [U.A.E.], December 30, 2003.

Goytisolo, Juan. *State of Siege.* Trans. by Helen Lane. San Francisco: City Lights Books, 2002. Originally published as *El sitio de los sitios* (Madrid, Alfaguara, 1995).

Grousset, René. *The Empire of the Steppes.* New Brunswick, N.J.: Rutgers University Press, 1970.

Haddad, Gibril Fouad. *Albani and His Friends.* [U.K., n.p.]: Aqsa Publications, 2004.

————. *From the Two Holy Sanctuaries: A Hajj Journal,* 2nd. edition. Bristol, England: Amal Press, 2006. First edition, Damascus, 1999.

Hafizović, Resid. "A Bosnian Commentator on *The Bezels of Wisdom:* Abdullah Bošnjak." English-language manuscript. Sarajevo, 2007.

————. *The Human Image in the Mirror of Sufism.* Sarajevo: Ibn Sina Institute, 2005.

————. "Rumi's Spiritual Quest." English-language manuscript. Sarajevo, 2007.

Halilović, Safwat. *Hifz: Memorization of the Qur'an.* Zenica: Islamic Pedagogical Academy, 2005.

Hamzaj, Bardh. *A Narrative About War and Freedom* (*Dialogue with Commander Ramush Haradinaj*). Prishtina: Zëri, 2000.

Haqqani, Husain. Interview/discussion of Sufism with author. Washington, D.C., 2003.

Harvey, L. P. *Islamic Spain 1250 to 1500.* Chicago: University of Chicago Press, 1960.

Haxhi, Bektash Veli. *Makalat.* Tirana: Dajti, 2005.

Ibn 'Abd al Wahhab, Shaykh Muhammad. *Kitab al Tawhid.* Trans. into English by Ismail Raji al-Faruqi. Riyadh: International Islamic Publishing House, 1991.

Ibn Al-Jawzee [Abu Al-Faraj]. *The Devil's Deception.* Trans. by Abu Ameenah Bilal Philips. Birmingham, U.K.: Al-Hidaayah Publishing and Distribution, 1996.

Ibn Arabi, Muhyiddin. *The Seals of Wisdom.* Trans. by Aisha 'Abd-al-Rahman at-Tarjuman. Capetown: Madina Press, 2005.

————. *Sufis of Andalusia.* Trans. by R. W. J. Austin. Sherborne, U.K.: Beshara, 1988.

————. *The Tarjuman al-Ashwaq.* Trans. by R. A. Nicholson. London: Theosophical Publishing House, 1978.

[Ibn 'Ata'Allah Al-Iskandari, Abu al-Fadl. "Debate with Ibn Taymiyya."] English version included in *Islamic Beliefs and Doctrine According to Ahl al-Sunna*, by Shaykh Muhammad Hisham Kabbani. Chicago: Kazi Publications, 1996.

Ibn Khaldun. *The Muqaddima*. Trans. by Franz Rosenthal. Princeton, N.J.: Princeton University Press, 2005.

Ibn Pakuda, Bahya ben Joseph. *The Book of Direction to the Duties of the Heart*. Trans. and ed. by Menahem Mansoor. London: Routledge and Kegan Paul, 1973.

[Ibn Taymiyyah, Taqi Al-Din, Comments on *Mawlid*.] Cited in *The Prophet*, vol. 3 of *Encyclopedia of Islamic Doctrine*, by Shaykh Muhammad Hisham Kabbani. Chicago: Kazi Publications, 1998.

Ibrohimov, N., et al. *Uzbekistan: Islam Obidalari*. Tashkent: "Uzbekistan" [pub.], 2002.

Idel, Moshe, ed. *Mystical Union in Judaism, Christianity and Islam: An Ecumenical Dialogue*. Harrisburg, Pa.: Continuum, 1996.

————. *Studies in Ecstatic Kabbalah*. Albany: State University of New York Press, 1988.

Idel, Moshe, and Mortimer Ostow, eds. *Jewish Mystical Leaders and Leadership in the Thirteenth Century*. Jerusalem: Aronson, 1988.

Iqbal, Muhammad. *The Development of Metaphysics in Persia*. London: Luzac, 1908, and Sarajevo: Connectum, 2005.

Islomov, Z., ed. "Our Great Ancestors." Tashkent: Tashkent Islamic University, 2002.

Iyer, Pico. *Abandon*. New York: Knopf, 2003.

Jahanpour, Farhang. "Western Encounters with Persian Sufi Literature." In *The Heritage of Sufism*, vol. 3, ed. Leonard Lewisohn and David Morgan. Oxford: One World, 1999.

Jalimam, Dr. Salih, and Senad Mičijević. *Stolac od Najstarijih Vremena*. Mostar: Slovo, 2005.

Kaplan, Ismail. *Das Alevitentum*. Cologne: Alemanya Alevi Birlikleri Federasyonu, 2004.

Kara, Mustafa. *Metinlerle Osmanlilarda Tasavvuf ve Tarikatlar*. Istanbul: Sir Yayincilik, 2004.

Karamustafa, Ahmet T. *God's Unruly Friends*. Oxford: One World, 2006.

Katroshi, Pëllumb. *Gurgullima Shpirti: Këngë Bektashiane*. Tirana: albPAPER, 2006.

Köprülü, Mehmet Fuat. *Early Mystics in Turkish Literature*. New York: Routledge, 2006.

————. *Islam in Anatolia After the Turkish Invasion*. Salt Lake City: University of Utah Press, 1993.

Küçük, Hülya. *The Role of the Bektashis in Turkey's National Struggle*. Leiden: Brill, 2002.

Kushkarov, Saparbai. *Seek Healing in Sufism*. Tashkent, K'ok Masjit, n.d. sufimc@globalnet.uz. CD set.

Lambert, MAJ Stephen P., USAF. *The Sources of Islamic Revolutionary Conduct*. Washington, D.C.: Joint Military Intelligence College, 2005.

Lessing, Doris. *The Golden Notebook*. New York: Simon & Schuster, 1962.

Lewis, Bernard. *The Middle East*. New York: Touchstone, 1995.

Lichtenberg, G. C. *Aphorismes*. Trans. by Marthe Robert. Paris: Club français du livre, 1947.

Llull, Ramon. *The Book of the Lover and the Beloved*. Ed. by Mark D. Johnston. Warminster, U.K.: Aris & Phillips Ltd., 1995.

Loeb, Vernon. "Instead of Force, Friendly Persuasion." *Washington Post*, November 5, 2003.

Maimonides, Obadia [Obadyah] and David. *Deux Traités de Mystique Juive*. Trans. from Judeo-Arabic by Paul B. Fenton. Lagrasse, France: Verdier, 1987.

Maimonides, Obadyah. *The Treatise of the Pool (Al-Maqala al-Hawdiyya)*. Trans. by Paul Fenton. London: Octagon Press, 1981.

Al-Maliki, Muhammad ibn 'Alawi. *Celebrating the Birth of the Noble Prophet Muhammad*. Trans. by Khadijah Husein Alkaff. Singapore: HARTE, 2003.

————. *The Prophet's Isra' and Mi'raj [The Resplendent Lights of the Night-Journey and Ascension of the Best of Creation]*. Trans. by G. F. Haddad. Singapore: Warid Press, 2004.

March, Ausias. *Selected Poems*. Trans. by Arthur Terry. Edinburgh: Edinburgh University Press, 1976.

Marshall, Paul, ed. *Radical Islam's Rules: The Worldwide Spread of Extreme Shari'a Law*. Lanham, Md.: Rowman and Littlefield, 2005.

Massignon, Louis. *Hallaj: Mystic and Martyr*. Princeton, N.J.: Princeton University Press, 1994.

Mélikoff, Irène. *Hadji Bektach: un mythe et ses avatars*. Leiden: Brill, 1998.

Mičijević, Senad. *Blagaj*. Mostar: Slovo, 2004.

————. *Počitelj*. Mostar: Slovo, 2004.

————. *Tekija u Živčićima*. Mostar: published by the author, n.d.

Mojaddedi, Jawid A. *The Biographical Tradition in Sufism*. Richmond, Va.: Surrey, Curzon Press, 2001.

Murvar, Vatro. *Nation and Religion in Central Europe and the Western Balkans*. Brookfield: University of Wisconsin, 1989.

Nahon, Gérard. *La Terre Sainte au temps des Kabbalistes*. Paris: Albin Michel, 1997.

Nametak, Fehim. *Pojmovnik Divanske i Tesavvufske Književnosti*. Sarajevo: Orijentalni Institut, 2007.

Nurud'din Nimatullah Veli. *50 Poems*. Trans. unidentified. Posted at www.erfangonabadi.com/.

Norris, H. T. *Islam in the Balkans*. London: Hurst and Co., 1993.

————. *Popular Sufism in Eastern Europe*. London: Routledge, 2007.

Oppel, Richard A., Jr. "Foreign Fighters in Iraq Are Tied to Allies of U.S." *New York Times*, November 22, 2007.

Ortayli, İlber. "The Policy of the Sublime Porte Towards Naqshbandis and Other *Tariqas* in the Tanzimat Period." In ed. by Elisabeth Özdalga. Istanbul: Swedish Research Institute, 1999.

Özal, Korkut. "Twenty Years with Mehmed Zahid Kotku: A Personal Story." In Elisabeth Özdalga, ed. *Naqshbandis in Western and Central Asia*. Istanbul: Swedish Research Institute, 1999.

Özdalga, Elisabeth, ed. *Naqshbandis in Western and Central Asia*. Istanbul: Swedish Research Institute, 1999.

Pamuk, Orhan. *The Black Book*. New York: Random House, 2006.

Peuch, Jean-Christophe. "Turkey: Religious Orders Still Key Element in Secular Life." Prague: Radio Free Europe/Radio Liberty, February 15, 2001.

Phalu, Khache. *Khache Phalu's Advice on the Art of Living*, 2nd ed. Trans. by Dawa Norbu. Dharamsala: Library of Tibetan Works and Archives, 1993.

Platonov, Andrei. "Dzhan." In *The Fierce and Beautiful World*, trans. by Tatyana Tolstaya. New York: New York Review Books, 2000.

Popova, Tahir Efendi. *Mevlud*. Prishtina, reprint of 1965 edition.

Popovic, Alexandre, and Gilles Veinstein, eds. "Bektachiyya." *Revue des Études Islamiques* [Paris], 1992.

[Qazi Thanaa Ullah]. *The Essential Hanafi Handbook of Fiqh*. New Delhi: Kitab Bhavan, 1992.

Rabasa, Angel, et al. *Building Moderate Muslim Networks*. Santa Monica, Calif.: RAND Corporation, 2007.

Radtke, Bernd, John O'Kane, Knut S. Vikør, and R. S. O'Fahey. *The Exoteric Ahmad Ibn Idris*. Leiden: Brill, 2000.

Rentz, George S. *The Birth of the Islamic Reform Movement in Saudi Arabia*. London: Arabian Publishing, 2004.

Rexhepagiqi, Jashar. *Dervishet dhe Teqetë në Kosovë, në Sanxhak, dhe në Rajonet Tjera Përreth*. 2nd., expanded ed. Peja: Dukagjini, 2003.

Riddell, Peter G. "Islamization, Creeping *Shari'a*, and Varied Responses in Indonesia," in Paul Marshall, ed., *Radical Islam's Rules*, 2005.

[Al-Rifa'i, Sheikh Yusuf ibn al-Sayyid Hashim. *Nasiha li-Ikhwanina 'Ulama' Najd* (Advice to Our Brothers the Scholars of Najd). 1999.] Sections cited from *From the Two Holy Sanctuaries: A Hajj Journal*, 2nd ed., by Gibril Fouad Haddad (Bristol, England: Amal Press, 2006), or provided by Dr. Irfan Al-Alawi— the latter as indicated in note.

Rosenblatt, Samuel. *The High Ways to Perfection of Abraham Maimonides*. New York: Columbia University Press, 1927.

Rougemont, Denis de. *Love in the Western World*. Princeton, N.J.: Princeton University Press, 1983.

Rumi, Mevlana Celaleddin. *Divan-i Kebir*. English trans. by Nevit O. Ergin. Los

Angeles: Echo Publications / Republic of Turkey Ministry of Culture, 1995–. (Multiple volumes compiled according to the different rhymes and meters employed by Mevlana. The poems on Shemsud'din of Tabriz are found in meters 8a and 8b.)

Saadi Shirazi. *Gjylistani dhe Bostani.* Trans. by Vexhi Buharaja, Tirana, Onufri, n.d.

Said Nursi, Bediuzzaman. *Lights of Reality.* Trans. by Şükran Vahide. Istanbul: Sozler Nesriyat ve Sanayi A.S., 2006.

Samić, Jasna. "Oú sont les Bektachis de Bosnie?" In "Bektachiyya," ed. Alexandre Popovic and Gilles Veinstein. *Revue des Études Islamiques* [Paris], 1992.

Scholem, Gershom. *Kabbalah.* New York: Penguin, 1978.

———. *Major Trends in Jewish Mysticism.* New York: Schocken, 1941.

Schwartz, Stephen. "The Balkan Front." *Weekly Standard,* May 14, 2007.

———. "Bektashizm si model Universal." *Urtësia* [Tirana], April 2007.

———. "Beleaguered Uighurs." *Weekly Standard,* June 21, 2004.

———. "The Face of Iraqi Terrorism." *Weekly Standard,* March 4, 2005.

———. "I Am a Rose." *Journal of Croatian Studies* [New York], annual, 1990. (Also, "Yo soy una rosa." *Vuelta* [México], May 1994.)

———. "In the Shadow of a Fatwa." *Weekly Standard,* September 7, 2005.

———. "Jihadists in Iraq." *Weekly Standard,* February 2, 2004.

———. *Kosovo: Background to a War.* Preface by Christopher Hitchens. London: Anthem Press, 2000. (Albanian trans., *Kosova: Prejardhja e Nji Lufte.* Prishtina: Rrokullia, 2005. 2nd ed., 2006.)

———. "Letter from the Balkans." *Muslim Magazine,* Winter/Spring 2000.

———. "The Mysteries of Safed, the Banners of Haifa." Family Security Matters, www.familysecuritymatters.org, July 26, 2006.

———. "People on Our Side: Baba Edmond Brahimaj, a Balkan Sufi." Family Security Matters, www.familysecuritymatters.org, April 25, 2007.

———. *Sarajevo Rose: A Balkan Jewish Notebook.* London: Saqi in association with the Bosnian Institute, 2005. (Bosnian edition: *Sarajevska ruža.* Trans. by Enes Karić and Rešid Hafizović. Sarajevo: Tugra, 2006.)

———. "Saudi Arabia's Koran Kops." *Weekly Standard,* September 3, 2007.

———. "The Saudi Connection." *Weekly Standard,* July 30, 2007.

————. "A Sufi Poet Whose Time Has Come—Again." *San Francisco Chronicle*, October 25, 1998.

————. "Turkey Votes." *Daily Standard*, online edition, July 24, 2007.

————. "Two Books on Bektashi Islam in Albania." *Albanian Catholic Bulletin*, annual, 1991.

————. *The Two Faces of Islam*. New York: Doubleday, 2002. (Bosnian and Croatian eds.: *Dva Lica Islama*. Trans. by Enes Karić and Rešid Hafizović. Sarajevo: Tugra, 2006; Zagreb: Medžilis Islamske Zajednice [Assembly of the Islamic Community], 2006. Albanian ed.: *Dy Ftyrat e Islamit*. Trans. by Blendi Kraja. Shkodër: ars, 2005. Indonesian ed.: *Dua Wajah Islam*. Trans. Hodri Ariev. Jakarta: Wahid Institute and LibForAll Foundation, 2007.)

————. "What Defines Moderate Islam?" *TCSDaily*, November 15, 2004.

————. "With the Sufis of Israel." *Sephardic Heritage Update*. August 9, 2006.

"Scores Hurt as Iran Militia Clashes with Sufis: Report," Agence France-Presse, November 19, 2007.

Selimović, Meša, *Death and the Dervish*, Evanston, Ill.: Northwestern University Press, 1996.

————. *The Fortress*. Evanston, Ill.: Northwestern University Press, 1999.

Shah, Idries. *Oriental Magic*. New York: Philosophical Library, 1957.

Shahin, Badr, comp. *Abaz Aliu*. Tirana: Urtësia Bektashiane, 2006.

Shindeldecker, John. *Turkish Alevis Today*. Istanbul: Sahkulu Sultan Kulliyesi Vakfi, 1998.

Silay, Kemal, ed. *An Anthology of Turkish Literature*. Bloomington: Indiana University Turkish Studies, 1996.

Sirin, Ali. Interviews with author. Washington, D.C., and Duisburg, Germany, 2005–7.

"So'fylik olamida." In the Sufi World. Tashkent: n.d., www.sufism.uz.

*Statut i Komuniteti Alevian Islamik Të Shqiperisë*. Tirana, 2006.

"Taikazan." Almaty: Eurasia Media Forum, 2003.

Tolstoy, Lev. *Hadji Murat*. Trans. by Hugh Aplin. London, 2003.

Trimingham, J. Spencer. *The Sufi Orders in Islam*. Oxford: Oxford University Press, 1971.

Turabi Ali Dede. "Hyrje: Libra thelb i Qëllimit: Udha e Shpëtimit." Typescript, n.d.

Ulqinaku, Hafiz Ali Riza. *Mevludi Sherif.* N.p. [Shkodër?]: n.d.

Upton, Charles. *Doorkeeper of the Heart: Versions of Rabiya.* New York: Pir Press, 2003.

Veliu, Ilmi. *Mevludi.* Kërçovë [Macedonia], n.d.

Vishko, Ali. *Teqeja Harabati e Tetovës dhe Roli i Saj Historik e Kulturor në të Kaluarën.* Tetova: Komuna e Tetovës, 2006.

Watt, W. Montgomery, and Pierre Cachia, ed. and trans. *The Faith and Practice of Al-Ghazali.* London: George Allen and Unwin, 1953. (Includes *Deliverance from Error* and *The Beginning of Guidance.*)

————. *A History of Islamic Spain.* Edinburgh: Edinburgh University Press, 1965.

Website on Shaykh Abdul Qadri Jilani, http://www.al-baz.com/shaikhabdal qadir/.

Weismann, Itzchak. *The Naqshbandiyya.* London: Routledge, 2007.

————. *Taste of Modernity: Sufism, Salafiyya, and Arabism in Late Ottoman Damascus.* Leiden: Brill, 2001.

Yavuz, Hakan. "The Matrix of Modern Turkish Islamic Movements: The Naqshbandi Sufi Order." In *Naqshbandis in Western and Central Asia,* ed. by Elizabeth Özdalga. Istanbul: Swedish Research Institute, 1999.

Yavuz, Hakan, and John L. Esposito, eds. *Turkish Islam and the Secular State: The Gülen Movement.* Syracuse, N.Y.: Syracuse University Press, 2003.

Yeniterzi, Emine. *Jalal al-Din al-Rumi.* Trans. by A. Bulent Baloglu. Ankara: Türkiye Diyanet Vakfi, 2000.

Yeszhanov, Djuelkan, and Mukhtar Kozhaev. *Arystanbab.* Almaty: Demeu, 1992.

Zabor, Rafi. *I, Wabenzi.* New York: Farrar Straus & Giroux, 2005.

*Zani i Ashikëve të Ehlibejtit.* Prizren, n.d.

*Zani i Dervishve ose "Ilahi" prej Sheh Ahmed Shkodrës Kryëtar i Federatës Vllaznis Rrifai të Shqipnis.* Third printing by Mustafa Mehaj. New York: Waldon Press, 1980.

Zarifi, Baba Ahmed (Omer). *Pendname dhe Tesavvufname.* Rahovec: Teqeja e Halvetive, 2000.

The following periodicals were also consulted: *Alevilerin sesi, Die Stimme der Aleviten in Europa* (Köln); *Šebi Arus,* annual of the Tarikat Center of Sarajevo; and *Urtësia,* published by the Albanian Bektashi Community, Tirana.

# INDEX

Hui community of, 227
Tiananmen Square massacre in, 224–25
Uighur minority of, 47, 225–28
Wahhabism in, 227–28
China Islamic Association, 228
Chinese Patriotic Catholic Association, 228
Chinggis Khan, 75, 123–24
Chishti, Moinuddin, 2, 3, 7, 162
Chishti Sufis, 141, 162–63
Chittick, William C., 68, 221
Christian Democratic Party, German, 115
Christianity, Christians, 3, 4, 9, 15, 47, 51, 53–54, 80, 83, 90, 123, 130, 177
    Mongol invasion and, 123–24
    Muslim mysticism and, 65
    Sufism and, 23, 24–26
    Turkish Sufism and, 106–7, 108
*CIA World Fact Book, The*, 51
Committee for the Promotion of Virtue and the Prevention of Vice (*mutawwa*), 192–93, 196–99
Communist Party, Chinese, 225, 226
"Convention for National Dialogue," 193
Cooper, Helene, 189
Corbin, Henry, 68
Coşan, Mahmud Esad, 117–18, 122
Council on American-Islamic Relations (CAIR), 221
Croatia, 81
*Cuba and the Night* (Iyer), 219

**D**
Dairbek, Talgat, 98
Dan, Baba, 171
Dante Alighieri, 71–72
David, 14
Dawkins, Richard, 30–32
Dedaj, Tom, 169
Dede, Turabi Ali, 142
Defense Department, U.S., 28

*Deliverance from Error* (Al-Ghazali), 55, 58
Dervishdana, Eli, 167
Dervishdana, Nesemi, 167
Dervishdana, Zejnelabedin, 165, 167, 168
*Devil's Deception, The* (*Talbis Iblis*), (Al-Jawzi), 132
*dhikrullah* (remembrance of God), 10, 42, 63, 75, 102, 135, 146, 153, 160, 164, 192, 220, 223
Dhul-Khuwaisara at-Tamimi, 132
Dhul-Nun, 40–43, 60
*Divan-i Hikmat* (*Poems in Praise of Wisdom*) (Yasawi), 93, 102
*Divine Comedy* (Dante), 72
Diyanet, 75, 115
Doctors of the Church, 71
Dubai, 186
*Dubai Gulf News*, 193
Durán, Khalid, 40, 48
*Duties of the Heart* (Bahya ibn Pakuda), 57

**E**
East Turkestan Islamic Movement (ETIM), 226
Egypt, 7, 15, 19, 40–41, 113–14, 141, 159, 178, 187, 209, 221
Elijah, Prophet, 93
Elqayam, Avraham, 210
Elsham (human rights group), 231
Emerson, Ralph Waldo, 163, 213–14, 236
Empire Notes (weblog), 185
Emre, Yunus, 103
Erbakan, Necmettin, 121
Erdoğan, Recep Tayyip, 53, 113–14
Ergin, Nevit O., 76

**F**
Fahd, Abd Al-Aziz bin, 180
Fahd, King of Saudi Arabia, 180, 192, 194
*Falling off the Map* (Iyer), 219
Fenton, Paul B., 64–65